Behind the Dolphin Smile

BEHIND

THE

DOLPHIN

SMILE

BY RICHARD O'BARRY

Trainer of the Television Star "Flipper"

WITH KEITH COULBOURN

Algonquin Books of Chapel Hill 1988

published by
Algonquin Books of Chapel Hill
Post Office Box 2225
Chapel Hill, North Carolina 27515-2225

in association with
Taylor Publishing Company
1550 West Mockingbird Lane
Dallas, Texas 75235

"The Dolphin Song"
Words and music by Fred Neil.
Copyright © 1965 Coconut Grove Music.
Used by permission. All rights reserved.
"Long Time Gone"
Words and music by David Crosby.
Copyright © 1969 Guerilla Music, Inc.
Used by permission. All rights reserved.

Design by Molly Renda.

Library of Congress Cataloging-in-Publication Data
O'Barry, Richard, 1939–
Behind the dolphin smile / by Richard O'Barry,
with Keith Coulbourn.

p. cm.
ISBN 0-912697-79-2
1. Dolphins. 2. Animals, Treatment of. 3. Wild animals,
Captive. 4. Wild animal collecting. 5. Wild animals as pets.
6. Flipper (Dolphin) I. Coulbourn, Keith, 1928– . *II. Title.*
QL795.D7023 1988
636'.953—dc19   *87-30642*
CIP

Dedicated to the following dolphins, both the living and the dead—

ABACO

BEA-BEA

CLOWN

DEEDEE

FLORIDA

SQUIRT

KATHY

LIBERTY

MAWANA

SHARKY

SOAPY

CHA-CHA

JOE

ROSIE

MITZI

OPO

PEDRO

PATTY

SCOTTY

SUSIE

CHARLIE BROWN

CAROLINA SNOWBALL

SONNY BOY

SAMBA

RICOU

CAN-CAN

JOKER

GEORGIA

SUNSET SAM

And to HUGO THE KILLER WHALE

CONTENTS

LIST OF ILLUSTRATIONS

PREFACE

In being true to both the times and the reader, several questions of terminology and viewpoint should perhaps be clarified.

Flipper is a dolphin, a *Tursiops truncatus* or Atlantic bottlenose dolphin. Dolphins are members of the whale family, and thus, like all whales, they are mammals. Many people use the term "porpoise" instead of "dolphin." Porpoise, from the Latin word for "pig fish," was the term commonly used until recently, but now it more often refers to a small branch of whales. Unfortunately the name "dolphin" also refers to a popular game fish, *Coryphaena hippurus*. The important thing to remember is that when you order dolphin in a restaurant, you are served the fish, not the mammal.

Though Flipper in the movies and television series was a male dolphin, the role was always played by a female; in fact over the years it was played by several female dolphins. Ricou Browning, cocreator of "Flipper," and I always made that distinction, referring to Flipper as "she" and "her" if we meant the actual dolphin, but "he" and "him" when referring to the *role* of Flipper. Others always referred to Flipper, both the role and the dolphins that played the role, as "he."

Technically, the tails of dolphins and whales are "flukes," which distinguishes their up-and-down motion from the back-and-forth motion of a fish's tail. Sometimes that distinction is not important, though, and people who work with dolphins all the time, particularly those who also work with fish, will variously use the term "flukes," the more general term "tail," and sometimes "tail-flukes."

The names of a few people in the book have been changed because, it seems to me now, they were less bad than simply ignorant. Even my own name was changed, but for a very different reason. In the days of this book, my last name was O'Feldman. But when the "Flipper" series ended and I turned to other kinds of work in the movie industry, to acting and to stunt work, I discovered that I had been "typed." When directors thought of O'Feldman, they thought automatically of "the dolphin man," and if dolphins weren't involved in the script, nobody called. Rather than struggle with that stereotype all my life, I changed my name. It had been Richard Barry O'Feldman, I shortened it to Richard O'Barry. And the phones began ringing again.

As the reader will soon realize, my dolphin-consciousness began with the belief that dolphins should never be held captive. Hence my mission to Bimini in the opening chapter. Over the years, I have realized that such an extreme position won't work. If all dolphins were free, we would never get to know them. I call this Lilly's Paradox. Rather than be bogged down by logic, I've decided—like most other dolphin specialists—that keeping a few captive dolphins is all right if (1) they are treated as well as possible on their own terms and (2) they serve to acquaint us with their true nature in the wild.

I

Mission to Bimini

This world may never change the way it's been,
And all the ways of war can't change it back again.
And I've been searchin' for the dolphin in the sea,
Sometimes I wonder do you ever think of me.

—Fred Neil, *The Dolphin Song*

That morning in the spring of 1970, I flew into Bimini in the Bahamas to do something at last about the dolphins. Some people would say that it was foolish, a vainglorious gesture that would do no good and would soon be forgotten. For that reason, I told no one. Actually I wasn't clear myself about why I was doing it. The only thing I knew for sure was that I *had* to do something.

These were the days when bad laws were under siege, ordinary citizens challenging the law by breaking it and facing the consequences for the right to speak out against it.

The law I wanted to strike down was the one permitting the ownership of dolphins. I wanted people to realize that it was wrong to own dolphins, and even worse, if possible, to make them do those silly tricks. Owning dolphins is wrong because it goes against their nature. Dolphins are part of the sea and should remain there.

Because dolphins don't complain, at least not in the conventional sense, we assume they don't object to their captivity. For a long time I went along with that, a willing accomplice, lulling myself into acquiescence with an acquired taste for the good life. But now with the death of Kathy, the dolphin I most dearly loved, I flew to Bimini as if on a pilgrimage to try to undo at least in part the mess I had made of things.

*   *   *

Diving is my life; diving, living in the water, studying fish and dolphins. Because of the nature of my job, I've probably spent more time in the water with dolphins than anyone else in the world, and probably I've trained dolphins to do more tricks and stunts than anyone else in the world—if that's really what I was doing. Looking back on it, I'm not sure whether I was training the dolphins or they were training me. Anyway, I was the trainer of the dolphins for the TV series "Flipper," the lovable and resourceful sea mammal that a whole generation grew up with. The series ran four years originally, and is still shown in about thirty-six foreign countries. So the whole world to some extent has grown up with him. I grew to respect and love all five of the dolphins who played the part of Flipper, but especially Kathy. The most valuable and highly trained animal in the world, she played the role most of the time. Six days before my flight to Bimini, Kathy had died most horribly in my arms of a broken heart.

Bimini, a dot on the map, is about fifty miles east of Miami—just across the Gulf Stream. The commuter trip is made by Chalk's Flying Service. From its terminal on Watson Island between Miami and Miami Beach, Chalk's twelve-seater amphibian makes the round trip twice a day, early morning and late afternoon. I traveled light, my only luggage a diving bag and the tools I would need for the job.

The westernmost island of the far-flung Bahamas chain, Bimini is actually two islands, North Bimini and South Bimini, the bay between them serving as a harbor and a landing strip for seaplanes. The keys and cays of Florida and the Bahamas are pronounced "keys," going back to the Spanish "cayos," which means "small island," and to the Bahamian corruption of that: "cay." To the later settlers, all this sounded like "keys," and that's what they called them. These days the island is full of smugglers wearing lizard boots, Rolex watches, and thick gold chains around their necks. Many of them carry beepers and can be seen taking off at all hours in their ninety-mile-an-hour ocean racing boats.

Smuggling is not new in the Bahamas. The same sort of thing happened during Prohibition, the Bahamas serving then as a home port for bootleggers. Before the dope dealers took over, Bimini had been for years the way Hemingway celebrated it in his book *Islands in the Stream*. His metaphor for the relentless flow of time was the Gulf

Stream, the huge river in the Atlantic that sweeps up from the Gulf of Mexico between Florida and the Bahamas, then swings northeast and curls its soft, warm tongue of tropic water along the southwest coast of Ireland. The Gulf Stream also turns Bimini into a sportsman's paradise. Bill fishing is especially good: swordfish, marlin, sailfish. In the Hemingway period, sports fishing was king in Bimini. Hemingway's people drank lots of rum and beer, they smoked long Havana cigars and laughed like gods, they got wonderfully drunk and, late into the night, they talked of fish with brave hearts that would never be forgotten.

Some things change, some things don't. From the air the water was a vast emerald, flashing a thousand greens and blues. As we approached Bimini, I could see everything it had to offer. Brown's Marina. The End of the World Saloon. The Bahama Mama Hotel. The native settlement of Alicetowne. My eye went to where I was headed, to the Lerner Marine Lab and its dolphin pen protruding out into the harbor.

Meeting Charlie Brown

As the plane cocked itself on its port side to come in for a landing, I squinted down for a glimpse of Charlie Brown alone in his pen and remembered spending time with him on my last trip here a couple of months earlier. I was here then to get underwater photos of what some people have called the Ruins of Atlantis. In Bimini they're called the Bimini Road, which is northwest of Alicetowne. These "ruins" look like concrete slabs that have been measured and poured. At least it makes a good story, which is not exactly discouraged in a tourist resort, but it's probably about as real as the Bermuda Triangle. On that particular trip the water wasn't as clear as it should have been for underwater photography. To get the kind of shots I wanted, the water had to look like gin. But the weather was squally that week, with thunderstorms popping up all around and roiling the water into what Bahamians call a "raging sea." To help keep down expenses while I waited for the water to clear, I stayed with a couple I had known in Coconut Grove, aboard their thirty-two-foot sailboat, which they had run aground on a sandbank when they approached Bimini and which was in drydock at Alicetowne for repairs.

There wasn't much to do because of the weather, so I wandered down to the Lerner Marine Lab and out on the dock to the pen area. They have several pens in a row about thirty by twenty feet. The pens are made of galvanized chain-link fence—one for sharks and rays, another for sawfish, barracuda and other sea creatures, and one, on the end, for dolphins. The water in the pens is about eight feet deep and the fence is nailed to a four-by-eight-inch beam running between the pilings. The beam goes in and out of the water as the tide comes in and goes out, but the top of the chain-link fence extends several feet above the water even at high tide. In the last pen there lived a single dolphin. As I knelt down by him, the guard came up. He had bloodshot eyes and seemed to be suffering from a terrible hangover. He frowned and probably would have tried to run me off but he noticed that I was wearing a Miami Seaquarium T-shirt, which must have made me seem semiofficial to him because he hesitated, looking at me with indecision for a moment.

"I was interested in the dolphin," I explained. The dolphin had surfaced and was taking it all in. Dolphins have a sophisticated sense of hearing. Like bats, they are sonar creatures, sending out sounds and analyzing the echoes. They "see" with their echolocation system. They can tell how far away something in the water is, its speed and direction, its size, and even its density. I've done tests to show that they can even tell the difference between gold and silver—blindfolded. They live in a world so different from ours that it would seem impossible that the two should ever touch. And yet they do. All the time. Dolphins make a number of different kinds of sounds: clicks, grunts, whistles, and high-frequency pings like musical notes, some of the sounds going not only through the water but also into the air. The dolphin in the pen was making airborne sounds like that now as he reconnoitered things.

The guard, arms akimbo, nodded and shot me a hooded look.

"What's his name?" I asked.

He weighed whether to answer me or to run me off. "Charlie Brown," he said finally.

I nodded. "Are they doing experiments with him?"

"Experiments?" He shook his head. "No, mon. He's a pet."

Some pet, I thought. I had been watching for several days and no one had come near the pen. I'm sure they did come to the pen to feed him, but he was hardly a pet. "Seems lonely to me," I said, squinting at the guard and frowning.

The guard, a Conchy-Joe, the Bahamian term for mulatto, seemed to have a chip on his shoulder. "Oh, yeah?" He smirked. "Seems happy enough to me, mon." Charlie Brown had reared his head up to see better what was going on. "Look, mon," the guard said. "He's laughing." With that he grinned crookedly and turned on his heel.

"He's blind in one eye," I said. I had noticed almost immediately that the dolphin always kept me on one side of him. I thought he must be blind in the other eye and confirmed it by waving my hand on that side, which he didn't respond to. The guard kept walking.

"Did you know that?" I said sharply.

The guard acted as if he didn't hear me.

"Do you know which eye he's blind in?"

The guard stopped and turned around. He was scowling. "He's not blind in either eye, mon." Then he turned again and was walking away.

"His *right* eye! He's blind in his *right* eye!"

The guard snorted and walked off. I went down to the end of the dock in Charlie Brown's pen and kneeled. Charlie Brown came over, clicking. I rubbed his back. His back was cut here and there. Grooved with old scars. Male dolphins often get battle scars in play or in their quest for suitable mates. That's one reason we used females in the Flipper series: fewer scars. The other reason is that dolphins are an amorous breed and producers don't want an unscheduled erection to mess up a scene. Many adult dolphins in the wild have scars from shark bites, and for that reason we used young dolphins in the role. Charlie Brown kept me in range with his good eye.

Charlie Brown and I had met briefly some seven years before. I was on the Seaquarium Collecting Team and we rounded up four dolphins that day, including Charlie Brown. He was then a young, vigorous male, swimming free in Biscayne Bay off Miami. All four of the dolphins caught that day were traded to Lerner Lab in Bimini for a box of electronic equipment. But it was a stormy crossing and one of them died of seasickness.

Then it occurred to me: where were the other dolphins who were part of that trade? I glanced around but I knew where they were. They were dead. Charlie Brown smiled at me with his mouth and looked at me with his one good eye. He was being held prisoner here. Dolphins are gregarious creatures. Social animals. In the wild, dolphins swim together in family pods, groups of from three to ten individuals, pods upon pods or tribes of sometimes hundreds of dolphins, all swimming in a straight line mile after mile. The kind of life that had befallen Charlie Brown in this small, ugly and boring pen was worse than death for a dolphin.

"Sorry, Charlie Brown," I said, patting him on the head. He clicked and bobbed his head with that implacable dolphin smile and I realized that it was I who had betrayed him to this and that I did not deserve his forgiveness.

The Job at Hand

It was a bright, hazy day, with a light chop on the bay as the plane landed smoothly between the islands. The pilot gunned the motor and headed for the ramp, then gunned it again, and the big seaplane, its wheels now lowered, pulled itself up by its own power. The plane turned slightly and the motors died with a cough of white smoke. There were only three other passengers on board with me and we filed into the customs shack. There the agent performed a perfunctory examination of our luggage. "Anything to declare?" he asked me.

I told him no.

"What's in the bag?"

"Diving gear. I've got a diving job to do here."

"Would you open it, please."

I opened my diving bag and exposed my black fins, a black face plate, gloves, my black tank suit and a black sweat shirt, a wire cutter and a bolt cutter. The wire cutter and bolt cutter were new. I had just bought them.

He touched the bolt cutter and threw me a skeptical look. "You don't intend to sell these things here, do you?"

"No. I intend to use them."

He nodded, then noticed my green arm band. "What's that?" he asked casually.

"That's for Earth Day," I said. It meant nothing to him, I could tell. In fact it had meant nothing to me till just a week before I had come over here, when Joe Browder, president of the Coconut Grove branch of the Audubon Society and a friend of mine, explained it to me and gave me the arm band. I wore it because it tended to legitimize what I was about to do. I didn't realize it then but 20 million Americans were celebrating the day and the federal government would soon join the crusade with billions of dollars. "Earth Day," I explained, "that's when we celebrate the blessings of the earth and demonstrate some concern for our environment."

"Hmm." The customs agent smiled slightly. "When is it?"

"Tomorrow."

He nodded again and turned to the next passenger.

I grabbed up my stuff and took off. I had to check out a boat for the job and make sure that Charlie Brown was still being held captive; I hadn't been able to see him from the air. But except for that there was nothing to do till nightfall, which comes late in the subtropics. I checked in at the Bahama Mama, a native hotel a few blocks north along Queen's Highway from Chalk's ramp. Everything is nearby in Bimini. I tossed the diving bag into the room, closed the door behind me and looked at myself in the mirror. "Am I really doing this?" I asked myself.

Unsurprisingly, I looked just like I felt inside: scared.

I waited in the bar downstairs, one of the few dark and cool places to while away the time in Bimini, and drank beer, working up my nerve. Someone was playing "Long Time Gone," by Crosby, Stills, and Nash, on the jukebox, the words aimed at me:

> *Speak out, speak out against the madness,*
> *Speak your mind if you dare....*

Time dragged. I made circles of water on the bar with the bottom of the beer bottle. I peeled off the label. Someone had left a swizzle stick there and I twisted that all around. Who was it said something like, "Fear, thy name is too much thinking"? Or did I make that up? The beer tasted heavy. I kept thinking in a circle. First I asked whether this was really the *right* thing to do. That was easy. The answer was yes. But then came the real question, not whether it was the right thing to do but whether it was the *best* thing to do. And who could tell?

I finally finished the beer and walked down to Lerner Marine Lab. The same guard was there. He was not just the guard, he was also the utility man. He cut the grass, changed the light bulbs and, as I noticed now, fed the fish. Fed the fish? He was dumping food in. Big chunks of it. Charlie Brown alone was supposed to eat 15 to 20 pounds of fish a day, so the guard must have been dumping 80 to 100 pounds of fish in all the pens every day. I had fed the fish at the Seaquarium for years. Six days a week and five shows a day I had walked around on the bottom wearing a Miller-Dunn helmet. I know when someone feeding the fish doesn't give a damn about them. And the guard at Lerner Marine Lab didn't. If you care, you make eye contact with them. I used to make eye contact with each of the creatures I fed, with turtles, moray eels, sawfish, and sharks. Dolphins were not fed like that. They were kept hungry so they would do their tricks later in the Topside Show.

If I had any doubts about what I must do, they were gone now. I looked closely at the fence. It was thicker than I remembered. The wire cutter probably wouldn't work. I would have to use the bolt cutter. Even then it wouldn't be easy. I walked down to Brown's Marina and rented a thirteen-foot Boston Whaler. I looked at my watch. Good Lord! Ten o'clock. I had ten more hours to kill!

I thought about my mission once again. It was a simple job but also quite exacting. I would cut down the fence of Charlie Brown's pen and he would escape. That was the simple part. At this point, it was mere vandalism.

The part that was quite exacting required that I break only the law that I intended to challenge. No point in being arrested for the wrong crime. After I had freed Charlie Brown, I had two options, it seemed to me:

1. I could turn myself in, defend myself noisily and deal with the consequences, even if it meant incarceration in Nassau's notorious Fox Hill Prison.
2. Or, I could tie my green Earth Day arm band where I had cut the fence, sneak away and free other dolphins in other pens. I could free dolphins everywhere, leaving my calling card of the green Earth Day arm band. My next target: the U.S. Navy Undersea Warfare School at Point Mugu in California, where dolphins were being trained to fight in the Vietnam War. I knew that was what they were doing there, because the CIA had tried to get me to help them.

The problem with making gestures in civil disobedience, whether political demonstrations or environmental statements, is that they depend on others for their meaning. You can make all the symbolic acts you can think of but if they're not interpreted the right way, there's no point to them. No matter which plan I followed, it was only a matter of time before I got caught, which was part of the plan. But the important thing was to get caught for the right reason. And that was the problem with Plan 2. If I had freed Charlie Brown, tied the green arm band on the cut fence and disappeared, then liberated the dolphins from the U.S. Navy Undersea Warfare School, chances are the Charlie Brown incident would be classed as vandalism and the other would have been lumped with the anti–Vietnam War demonstrations going on then.

Obviously, I must go with Plan 1.

A Moonless Night—Perfect!

I headed back to my hotel room. On the way I passed the bar, went in and sat down. Without a word, the bartender set me up with the kind of beer I had been drinking earlier. The jukebox kept telling me, "speak your mind if you dare." Halfway through the beer I realized I didn't want it. I put a dollar on the bar, went to my room, and looked at myself in the mirror again. No change. I closed the blinds, turned up the a/c, faked a yawn, and lay down on the bed. I took a deep breath, closed my eyes, and felt myself get very tense. I was now wondering if my plan, foolproof though it seemed to be, was the *smart* thing to do. Charlie Brown had crossed my path and look what had happened to him. Kathy had crossed my path and she now lay dead. How many dolphins had I done this to? I tried to count all the dolphins I had helped to catch. I marked them off, the living and the dead, and tried to recall where they all were now. These things were done and I couldn't undo them, but there were many other dolphin collectors still at work. Some of them harpooned dolphins, others tossed lassos around them, laid nets down, or shot huge metal pincers at them, called "tail grabbers." One collector chased dolphins down in his speed boat and leaped on them like he was bulldogging cattle. It was madness.

Lying down was a bad idea. I got up and went back downstairs to the bar and nursed another beer. Why hadn't I taken the second flight to Bimini instead of the first? I glanced at myself in the mirror. Face tense, mouth taut, eyes with a fanatical gleam. It was amazing that I hadn't been arrested for looking like this.

Like everything else in Bimini, nightfall takes an eternity, but evening finally came and began slipping into night. The last flight back to

Miami had left and I had drunk about all the beer I could hold, but once again I was full of doubt. This time I wondered if I was being professional about it. I was breaking all the rules. Rule No. 1 of the Diver's Code is: "Do not dive alone."

Especially at night.

And *never* just after drinking.

Even now I could back out. And that might be the smart thing to do, I thought. No one would ever know. Had I drunk too much beer? I was full of it but didn't feel it. I glanced at my watch. Eight-thirty. At last! I stood up and stretched. "Well," I said to the bartender, "guess I'll go on up and get some shut-eye." We hadn't said ten words all evening. He nodded. I went to my room and put on my black tank suit under my other clothes, put on a black sweat shirt, and got my diving bag with the tools, the fins and face plate. Then I headed for the boat at Brown's. I had paid for the room in advance as well as for the boat.

It was a dark night. No moon. Perfect.

I got into the boat, kicked it over and chugged slowly out to the dolphin pen. It was so dark I couldn't see the shore fifty feet away. At the pen, I put on the fins and face plate, got the wire cutter and, with a ripping belch that must have been heard in Alicetowne, I slipped over the side like a seal. In the water, I set the Danforth anchor by hand deep in the sandy bottom and away from the fence so that the Boston Whaler would look like one of the dinghies from the many boats at anchor there. I tried the new wire cutter first. It didn't make a dent in the chain-link fence, so I slipped it into the boat and got the bolt cutter. It wasn't easy but it worked. The first cut made a wonderful "pinging" sound underwater.

I can hold my breath about ninety seconds, two minutes if I have to. Even so, it was taking me more than one dive to cut each link of the fence. Working underwater is about a third as efficient as working in air, especially with a tide running. I would take a deep breath, go under and find the link I was working on by feel in the inky water, cut as long as I could and then come up, catch my breath as quietly as possible and go back down again. This took several hours, much longer than I thought it would take. And I was being much too noisy. Sounds, even the sound of breathing, carry amazing distances over water. That's why I had not brought a snorkel with me. When you clear the snorkel, you blow the water out and the noise seems to be magnified.

I hadn't given the job itself much thought because it seemed so simple: (1) cut the fence, which was nailed to the four-by-eight-inch beam, then (2) pull the nails loose holding the fence to the beam and let it fall.

When I cut the last of the links in the fence, I was flat on the bottom. I should have started at the bottom so that I would end up at the top. When I cut the last of the links, the nails holding the fence to the beam pulled loose and the fence fell silently through the water, pinning me to the bottom like a giant hand.

At first I couldn't figure out what had happened. Of all the rules in the Diver's Code, the most important one says: "Don't Panic."

No matter how long you live with that rule, there's a panicky moment when your stomach knots up and you have to think yourself out of it. "Easy," I said to myself. I was squashed down to the bottom, flat on my stomach. I couldn't move. What a dumb way to go, I thought.

It was a sandy bottom, or it once had been. Now it was littered with beer cans and broken bottles. Barnacles, which are as sharp as razor blades on top, had attached themselves to the bottom of the fence. When I tried to twist to get away from whatever had caught me, the barnacles slashed my back, legs, and arms. I was hung up on something. I was also almost out of breath when the fence had come down on me. My head was pounding.

In situations like this I try to get a mental image of where I'm at. It's like seeing myself from the outside. The fence had snagged the back of my sweat shirt. I tried to rip the sweat shirt to get free. I couldn't. My head was throbbing. Whether I had thought this thing through or was just reacting, I don't know, but I twisted and pulled myself out of the sweat shirt and felt for the fence again. I let it push me back to the bottom—it must have weighed a ton—and then, my lungs bursting, I drew my feet up under me, and gave a karatelike push with everything I had. Back went the fence. I pushed off the bottom and popped to the surface, gasping for air. In my hand was the bolt cutter.

I've had worse tight squeezes in my diving career, but none quite so dumb. In spite of it all, though, I was free now. And so was Charlie

Brown. I was holding on to the gunwale on the port side of the boat outside the pen as I caught my breath. I thought, or I hoped, that Charlie Brown would go streaking past me and out to the open ocean and to freedom. That's how Flipper would have done it on TV. But Charlie Brown was not Flipper.

I looked around for him. "Hey, old buddy," I called softly. "You're free!" I listened. And there it was, the excited clicking, the popping and other sonar sounds. He was still in the pen. "Come on, Charlie Brown. You're free!"

Like all dolphins, he was curious and came over to the edge of the pen to "see" what was going on, but also he was cautious and held back. One of the most difficult things I ever tried to get dolphins to do in the Flipper series was to go under something like the four-by-eight-inch beam. There was no fence below the beam now—except perhaps in Charlie Brown's mind. I think the problem is that they don't see an inside-outside relationship as we do. To us, Charlie Brown was *inside* the pen and I was trying to get him to go *outside*. Indeed, I was trying to get him to go outside to freedom. But to him, it was something else. Perhaps he thought he was already outside and I was trying to get him to go inside something else. Or *through* something. Or maybe it was simply that, after seven years, Charlie Brown thought of this grubby hole as a sanctuary. I don't know what he was thinking.

Something had to be done. I clambered over the beam—it was a foot or so underwater—and got into the pen with him. If he wouldn't come to my urging, I would simply lead him out. Charlie Brown came over to me, clicking, snorting and whistling. "Okay," I told him, "now follow me." I dog-paddled over to the beam but Charlie Brown hung back. Dolphins are the most empathetic of creatures, at times their insight approaches genius. Some people say this is because their brains are larger than ours, which they are, and so they must be more intelligent. But there's a semantic problem here about the word "intelligence." I think it may boil down to the simple fact that they are as intelligent in their world as we are in ours.

They are also just as individualistic. Charlie Brown, for instance, was being contrary. For at least an hour I tried to get him out of the pen. I chased him, I grabbed his flukes and tried to drag him. I would get him to follow me around, luring him on, then I'd go underwater so that he would follow me. But always at the beam he stopped and turned back.

"Come on, Charlie Brown. We gotta get the hell outa here!" I said. I was getting tired of all this so I went back over the beam to the boat and had a brilliant idea. I got into the boat and pulled up the anchor, got back into the water and swam the boat over to the beam, which was about a foot underwater. If only I had brought a saw! I got out on the beam and pulled the Boston Whaler over it and into the pen with Charlie Brown.

"Now I'll *run* you out," I muttered, cranking the motor. I threw the motor in gear and around I went. I never really knew where Charlie Brown was, though. When I went left, he went right. Or down the middle. Or someplace. Dolphins can hold their breath for as long as five minutes. It was one of those thick, velvety tropic nights where you can feel the blackness. I got the feeling that he was toying with me. If so, I would never be able to free him.

O'Barry's Law

How long I chased him around the pen, I have no idea, but when I stopped in total frustration I sat stock still in the boat, exhausted. My whole body ached. The cut on my back had stopped bleeding but it still hurt. Somehow I had also mashed a finger and had an unusual throbbing at the back of my head. This whole thing had become a nightmare.

Then O'Barry's Law came into operation: Just when things are at their darkest, they get darker. The tide had dropped and now I couldn't get the boat out of the pen. I would not be able to get the boat out of the pen till the tide came in again—hours from now. If I had brought a saw—but of course I hadn't and there was no way to get one now. I could hear the lapping of the water on the hull of the boat and, at some distance, a drunk who, though I couldn't see him in the dark, had apparently wandered down the pier and was cheering me on in soft, melodic Bahamian tones: "Everyting okay, mon?"

I sat in the boat for a while, trying to figure out what I ought to be doing. But I had tried everything. When the drunk wandered off, I swam over to the dock and pulled myself up. What a fine mess I had gotten myself into. I was beginning to think I ought to cut my losses and get out while I could. The Bahamian government has a list of people who are persona non grata, unwelcome. It's called the Stop List and is made up of criminals and other shady types. As an underwater movie stuntman, diver, and trainer of dolphins, I worked a lot in Bahamian waters. If I was put on the list and denied a work permit, my income would drop to almost nothing. I wouldn't have minded making the list for civil disobedience. Moral convictions shouldn't come cheap. But for cutting a fence? For not returning a rented boat? No. To be put on the list for that would be ridiculous.

I went back to my hotel room. It was sometime in the early morning and I needed to figure this thing out. Exhausted, I lay down on the bed for a minute to think. It was fairly simple:

1. They'll find the boat in the dolphin pen.
2. They'll discover that the fence to the pen has been cut down.
3. Then they'll trace the boat to me, me to the fence, and suddenly I'll be in Fox Hill Prison charged with criminal vandalism or something.

How could I have been so stupid! Clearly the key to getting out of this mess was to finish what I had started, which was to liberate Charlie Brown. If Charlie Brown were freed, my civil disobedience would be intact and everything would work. I got up and marched back to the pen.

It was almost dawn, when things take on a ghostly glow. I stood there a moment on the dock till I had spotted the dolphin in the exact center of the pen. "Now or never, Charlie Brown," I said. He clicked and snorted. I eased into the water and dog-paddled over to him. "Please," I said. "I'm trying to *help* you." But he wanted no part of it. I hadn't slept a wink. I had forgotten to eat. I was sick to my stomach. And I was about to be in big trouble.

2

The Bimini Jail

One has to experience being caged if one is to appreciate freedom.

—Meher Baba, *Discourses*

When Earth Day dawned with an eye-splitting brilliance, I was perched on the dock like a horrible hangover. A small crowd of sports fishermen and yachtsmen began to form. They sauntered down the dock and eyed the Boston Whaler in the dolphin pen, then they stared at me, my head bowed, avoiding their looks. The tide was coming in now but it would be noon before the water was high enough to pull the boat back out.

Finally, I went back to the Bahama Mama and got my diving gear. I had no breakfast. I wasn't hungry. And at eight o'clock that morning I found myself at Chalk's ramp, ready to leave. The other passengers got their tickets and sat down; I waited. The pilot and his copilot got aboard and revved up the engines, passengers ambled up to the gate, the gate was lowered and they went aboard. The ticket seller looked at me but said nothing; and neither did I. The plane waddled down to the water like a duck, the engines came on full and the big plane lumbered through the water, picked up speed and finally got airborne, a straight shot for the mainland. I watched it leave. And there I still was with my diving gear, too hungry and sick to my stomach to eat, not knowing what to do about the Boston Whaler, about the dolphin pen I had virtually destroyed, or about Charlie Brown, who refused to be saved.

Maybe with the dawn, Charlie Brown had seen the light and had escaped. There was not much hope of that, though. It occurred to me that even if he had got outside his pen, it's quite possible that he might never find his way to the open sea. Because he pictures the world around him by his sonar waves, the clicks and pops and whistles he sends out and gets reflected back to him, he might have felt himself trapped forever in Bimini Harbour. Who knows? That was not the only dolphin mystery we needed to clear up. We needed to know what they're like in the wild, free swimming in the ocean, which is where they are most truly themselves. That was why I was trying to free Charlie Brown. I wanted to free him because he was one of the dolphins I regrettably had helped capture, but also it was my first step in trying to free all dolphins in captivity.

Having eaten too little, drunk too much and slept not at all, having escaped a watery grave and jeopardized my whole diving career in Bahamian waters, I felt ready for anything that morning. I walked over to the pen again. Nothing had changed: the thirteen-foot Boston Whaler floating in the dolphin pen, the ugly gap in the fence, Charlie Brown still a prisoner. And since I was already involved in this, I decided that I might as well do it right. I opened up my diving bag and got out the green arm band and put it on. Then I walked down Queen's Highway to the lab and Dr. Kingsley's house, where I knocked on the door. It was about eight-thirty, still quite early by Bimini standards. I knocked on the door again and Dr. Kingsley appeared, no shirt, a towel draped over one shoulder, and in his right hand a straight razor. His face was covered with shaving cream. He made a half-hearted attempt to smile and cocked his head inquisitively at me.

What Happened to the Others?

I introduced myself, he looked at my Seaquarium T-shirt and smiled. "Oh, yes, the trainer of Flipper." He was nodding genially. "Good show on TV. I've probably seen them all."

I told him that I had also been on the Collecting Team of the Seaquarium, that we had captured four dolphins and traded them for electronic gear seven years before, though one had died en route, and now I had been able to find only one of those dolphins. "What happened to the others?"

Dr. Kingsley was nodding his head, trying to pick up on the subject. "To the others?"

"Yes," I snapped, "the other dolphins."

"Oh, yes," he said, trying to remain agreeable. "They passed away."

"I thought so. Do you know that the one remaining dolphin down there is blind in one eye?"

"Charlie Brown? No, I don't think he's blind."

"I'm not asking you, Dr. Kingsley. I'm telling you. He *is* blind." I felt my face pinch with anger. "When was the last time you spent any time with him?"

Dr. Kingsley frowned. "Is there something you wanted?"

"Do you perform experiments on that dolphin?" I demanded.

"No," he said, shaking his head. "Charlie Brown is a pet."

"And you don't even know that he's blind?"

He wiped his hands on the towel over his shoulder. "What can I do for you?" he said evenly.

"I want you to know that I participated in the capture of Charlie Brown and the other three that you got from the Seaquarium. I helped capture the only albino dolphin known in the world and most of the Flipper dolphins, Patty, Scotty, Susie, Squirt, and Kathy, too, Dr. Kingsley—that I have taken them from the sea, their home, that I have exploited them like everyone else who has had anything to do with them, that I am dreadfully sorry about it and that if I could undo it I would. But I can't."

I looked at him helplessly for a moment. Dr. Kingsley's mouth was open and he was looking worried. He tried to ease the door closed but I put my foot in it.

"I feel responsible for what I have done. Do you know what I mean, Dr. Kingsley?"

He nodded.

"And when I see Charlie Brown being held like a common criminal—and for what? He's done nothing wrong. Why is he being treated this way?"

"Take your foot out of the door, please."

"Is it a crime, Dr. Kingsley, to have come in contact with human beings? Is it? They've done nothing wrong. Their only fault is that they have been thrust into our world to be exploited and made fools of and tricked and finally slain, Dr. Kingsley, usually by neglect. Like Charlie Brown!"

Dr. Kingsley was nodding assent as if to placate a raving maniac. Indeed, my voice had gained a cutting edge as I told him about the death of Kathy, that cleverest and brightest of all creatures, who, when there was no further use for her, had been put into a tank to die. And die she did, me weeping for my having done this horrible thing to her. I wiped away the tears running down my cheeks and said, "I spent all night cutting down the fence to Charlie Brown's pen and trying to get him out, but he—"

"You did what?"

"I spent all night trying to—"

By this time he had wiped the shaving cream off his face with the towel. He threw the towel on the ground, cursed, and brushed past me out the door, where he stood, arms akimbo, looking down at the dolphin pen 100 yards away.

"Damn it," he said. "You've really put your foot in it, haven't you?" He didn't seem to have heard a word I said. He went to the phone and made a call, then came running past me again while I tried to explain exactly why I did it. When I planned all this, I realized that this was the time to establish my motive as civil disobedience, that it was necessary to keep clearly in mind that I was protesting the law permitting ownership of dolphins. If the proper motive wasn't established at the beginning, the chance might never come again. I followed him down, explaining all this as we walked to the pen and while he struggled into his shirt.

Charlie Brown was still in the pen. And so was the Boston Whaler.

Down came the utility man/guard. He had a bucket of fish and was mad as hell. He tossed a fish in to Charlie Brown, which Charlie Brown ignored, and glared at me.

"No, don't feed him," Dr. Kingsley yelled. "Get the net." The guard put the bucket down and rushed past me to the utility shed up on the bank. He drew back as if to hit me as he rushed past me and I braced myself, but he held back.

I went over to the bucket of fish. Just as I thought! Large chunks of mullet. Cheap stuff. Dolphins in the wild eat live fish, a wide range of schooling fish like mackerel, snapper, grunt, seatrout, blue runner, small tuna and kingfish. Dolphins hunt them down easily, hunting in pods and rounding up their quarry as cowboys round up cattle, herding them onto the flats and shallows where they can be picked off easily. In captivity, when dolphins have learned to eat dead fish, they prefer Icelandic herring, Spanish mackerel, blue runners, capelin and smelt, which are oily and full of protein. One of the most important secrets of my training technique was the discovery that a bottlenose dolphin will do almost anything for an Icelandic herring, yet that delicacy is not in the dolphin's natural diet because herring come from waters too cold for dolphins. They cost more than mullet but they're worth it if you care at all about dolphins. I put my hand in the bucket. Frozen. I knew it!

The Arrival of Sgt. Pepper

The guard returned with the net and began putting it across the pen where I had cut down the fence. A few minutes later the constable, a spit-and-polish military type but also laid back in the Bahamian style, arrived in an electric golf cart wearing a royal blue bathrobe and sandals. He was followed on foot by two deputies in T-shirts with wide suspenders on their pants. The constable was a short, muscular man with big square hands, the upper-body strength of a bull and a mask of perpetual suspicion. I thought of him as the Beatles' Sergeant Pepper. He and Dr. Kingsley huddled together off to one side, the two deputies casually watching me. Dr. Kingsley explained what had happened, or his version of it, gesturing broadly with his arms and shaking his head, the constable nodding, his eyes burning more intensely the longer Dr. Kingsley spoke.

The Lerner Lab utility man who had been summoned by Dr. Kingsley was boiling with rage at me. It meant more work for him and he took it personally. When Dr. Kingsley and Sgt. Pepper finished their confab in total agreement about what kind of rock I must have slithered out from under, the constable confronted me with a scornful frown. "You come over here and try to steal dat fish, mon?"

"No, no, no," I said. I first corrected his notion that the dolphin is a fish—that too was important to my plan—and then I launched into my explanation about freeing dolphins, a speech I had prepared for this moment. It was the height of conceit, I told him, to assume that anyone had the right to own a dolphin. "Dolphins are like the ocean itself," I said, smiling to show how simple it was and trying to seem reasonable. "Does anyone own the ocean? And what about the sea water that Charlie Brown swims in?" I shrugged my shoulders and grinned. "It ought to be obvious that we have no more right to own a dolphin than to own the air itself!" I waved my arms to indicate the air around us that was free and to show how simple the idea was that I was propounding.

There was a long silence. He had muscles in his face that bunched together when he ground his teeth.

"At least that's the way I feel about it," I said lamely.

Nobody had said anything but I realized when they put the handcuffs on me that I was under arrest, that I was expected to go with them back to jail, and that they would enjoy nothing more than the opportunity to meet force with force were I so foolish as to start it. I got in the golf cart with Sgt. Pepper and as reasonably as I knew how I began to explain in more detail why I had cut down the fence and tried to free Charlie Brown, that it was a symbolic act basically, a deliberate exercise of civil disobedience—my right, nay my duty as an American citizen—that I had done all this on Earth Day and I was wearing a green arm band to prove it. I held up my arm with the arm band on, smiling pleasantly, I hoped, and nodding my head, but he kept his eyes glued to the road. Speaking very deliberately and as if underscoring each word, I said: "And it's not at all unlike what the late Dr. Martin Luther King, Jr. did." I thought this would get a rise out of him because he was black, too, but he responded not at all. I smiled warmly. "You know what the late Dr. Martin Luther King, Jr. did, don't you?"

He acted as if he hadn't heard a word I said. He ground his teeth, the muscles bunching on each side of his face.

"I do have my rights as an American citizen," I told him.

He turned his hateful mask of a face toward me. "You not in America now, mon."

Without another word we went slowly through the streets of Bimini to the jail, the deputies following at some distance on foot.

The Bimini Jail, with which I was to become intimately familiar, was a two-story building overlooking Bimini Harbour. The constable and his two deputies lived upstairs. The jail itself was not much used. Prisoners picked up in Bimini were usually shipped directly to Fox Hill Prison on New Providence Island, where Nassau is. The most recent prisoner had been several months earlier, the deputies told me, a Jamaican who was picked up on a charge of drunk and disorderly conduct (relieving himself on a grave) and had spent the night in jail to sleep it off. He would have been put in my cell, the one farthest from the door, because the other one was used to keep a 300-pound pig in. I never learned why the pig was in jail but I assumed that he was in for life. The other cell, the one they put me in, had a window looking out, a barred window about nine feet high so that in order to look out I had to pull myself up and hold on. That they weren't accustomed to having prisoners would explain their amateurish attitudes about food and toilet facilities. The food, though it was probably what they prepared for themselves upstairs, was inedible. Hard bread, bad water, peas and rice. And the peas and rice were cold. I couldn't eat any of it.

I had told no one about what I was going to do before I came to Bimini. They would not have understood and would have tried to talk me out of it. What I did was not only against the law and dangerous— I knew all that—but also, for anyone who didn't feel as strongly as I did about it, idiotic. My one concession to practicality was leaving a note on my front door for Martha Kent, my girlfriend then, my wife now. The note explained that I would be in Bimini to free the dolphin in captivity there. I found out later that someone from Chalk's Airlines tipped off the press about my arrest and the next morning five or six journalists were camped on the front steps of the Bimini Jail. They had a lot of fun with the story but kept a serious eye on it too. One of the headlines said:

TRAINER OF FLIPPER IN FLAP
CAN'T GET DOLPHIN TO FLEE

That same day Martha flew over, and so did Ricou Browning, my movie mentor. They saw the papers, the story was on page 1 of the *Miami Herald,* and they caught the next available plane. My brother Jack came over, too, and offered to help me escape (if I ever got to the water, he told me, they would never be able to catch me), but this had taken more out of me than I thought it would and I wasn't up to such heroics. Also, my civil disobedience was still intact and I wanted to play it out. I complained to Martha about the food, so she took a room at the Bahama Mama and, with the passive complicity of the two deputies, began slipping me delicious meals through the bars from the outside.

A Very Bad Week

I was in jail a week. And it was a very bad week. The whole point of civil disobedience is to be charged with the crime one intends to challenge, but I hadn't been charged with anything at all. In fact I didn't know what the charge was until the day before my trial. There was no preliminary hearing, no formal charge, and thus no way to defend myself. I was also beginning to feel my resolve weaken more and more, and I feared that instead of throwing myself upon the sword of martyrdom in the interest of a just cause, I might settle for mere survival.

Because of the nationwide media attention, I was getting dozens of letters a day. I received several hundred in all, that week. I was allowed to get out of my cell and go to the front desk and sit on the bench against the wall to read the letters. They were from all over and from all kinds of people, many of whom seemed to understand what I was trying to do and who agreed with me. Sgt. Pepper never understood why a common fish thief, which is what he thought I was, should receive such popular support and journalistic interest from the mainland. As I read the letters, I glanced up a number of times and caught him frowning at me, his eyes squinted in puzzlement.

Sgt. Pepper was a devout man. He carried the Bible under his arm almost everywhere he went and really studied it. When I was in my cell, I could put my head up against the bars and see him reading it studiously when no one else was around.

But his piety apparently didn't extend to his police methods. I learned to stay away from him when no one else was in the jailhouse. He had a brutal but effective way of getting at the truth as he imagined it. It began one time when the mail was delivered and when Sgt. Pepper was alone in the office. I yelled up from my cell and asked if I had received any mail.

He was sitting at his desk, reading the Bible. He looked up at me and glowered thoughtfully. "Yes, you have."

"May I read it?"

He glowered even more darkly. He got up, came back and unlocked the door to my cell, then led me back to his desk and indicated the bench along the wall. I sat down, he pushed a bundle of letters over to me. I was reading one of the letters—it was from a young girl who said she loved Flipper and wanted to know if there was anything she could do to help either Charlie Brown or me—when suddenly Sgt. Pepper grabbed my hair and banged my head twice—Bang! Bang!—against the wall. Through clenched teeth he growled: "You come here to steal dee fish! You bess tell me de trut, mon. You come to steal dee fish!"

"Dolphins are not fish!" I yelled back at him.

I was stunned. I didn't know that things like that really happened. I was also embarrassed: it happened more than once. In fact, it happened several times, every time we were alone together—till I figured out the pattern and stayed away from him unless someone else was around. One day I was sitting in my cell, wondering vaguely what would happen next, and when I looked up, there was Sgt. Pepper, gazing down at me, the muscles of his jaws grinding. "Were you sent to Bimini by someone else?" he asked.

"No," I said simply.

"You're not a fish expert, are you, mon? A scientist?"

I shook my head no.

He frowned. "Then what are you, mon?"

I shrugged. "I don't know. I've been called a dreamer."

A look of repugnance formed on Sgt. Pepper's face, he made a hissing sound, "Shhhhh!" and went back to his desk, shaking his head.

As the week dragged on and as the stories and TV footage piled up, more and more people across the country understood what I was doing and awaited the disposition of my case. I, too, began to understand what I was really doing. At first I was merely striking out at something wrong. Then I realized who the bad guys were. They were the free-lance dolphin hunters of Biscayne Bay.

From the deputies, I understood that there was some indecision about what charge should be brought against me. Sgt. Pepper was convinced that he could get a confession to attempted stealing of a fish, a felony because Charlie Brown was worth a lot of money. But each day the headlines grew and, as I learned later, Lerner Lab's parent company, the New York Museum of Natural History, was in daily contact with Dr. Kingsley about it, insisting that the charge be reduced to trespassing or to anything that would stop the publicity and get me off the island.

Or was there more to it than that? Already the newspapers had discovered that Dr. Kingsley was not really a doctor. And because of my background with the Flipper dolphins, the press was taking it seriously when I charged that Charlie Brown and all other dolphins should be released.

Though in a sense I had bungled the job because Charlie Brown had refused to escape, nevertheless my plan was working. The message was getting out. I faced the terrible prospect of prison, but I welcomed it—or so I told myself—because my suffering would crystalize the issue and lead to needed legislation. It was a small price to pay if people would realize that dolphins should not and could not be owned.

To my dismay, I was delighted when I learned that the charge against me was merely one of trespassing.

The Trial Comes Swiftly

Once the charge was made, the trial came swiftly and I had one really fine moment. Sgt. Pepper handcuffed me that morning, then he and his two deputies marched me down the street about a block to the Bimini courthouse. A small retinue of interested observers followed: several reporters and photographers; a writer from *Life* magazine; Martha; and Dr. Henry Truby, a friend and a specialist in interspecies communication at the University of Miami. The courthouse was a stately building, with tall white columns in front, a vestige of the island's British background. The courtroom itself was also in the best British-Bahamian tradition: small but with high ceilings, large windows with West Indies shutters, and a pair of paddle fans on the ceiling. The judge, a large and round-faced man with Ben Franklin spectacles, was as black as his flowing robes, and he wore a big white wig with yellow stains and large curls, just as in a British movie. During the trial he never looked at me in the dock but over my head to the two dozen or more American reporters and TV crews who filled the gallery behind me. The judge had obviously kept up with the running account of my abortive attempt to free Charlie Brown, and was playing it for all it was worth.

My one good moment occurred when the judge asked how I wanted to plead. My hands were still handcuffed in front of me. I stood at attention the whole time in the dock. The evidence against me was spread out on the table before me, my diving gear, the fins and face plate, the bolt cutter and also the green arm band. It was spread out and labeled with tags as if it were a summary of my life. "I plead guilty, your honor," I said, "but with an explanation."

"All right, Mr. O'Barry," the judge said, speaking to the media behind me. "We will accept your plea of guilty. What explanation do you want to make?"

Martha, Ricou, and Jack were not allowed in the courtroom but the press was there, and it had a crazy-happy look in its collective eye. I looked around the courtroom at Sgt. Pepper, Dr. Kingsley, and the Conchy-Joe of a guard, their faces glowering in anger.

"It'll just take a minute," I said, "but I would like to refer to the Bible that the sergeant always carries with him." Sgt. Pepper shot me a hot look and I said directly to him: "Would you let me read from your Bible, please?"

Sgt. Pepper didn't move except for the muscles on each side of his face. The judge leaned toward him slightly and intoned: "Do you have your Bible with you, sergeant?"

He stood up. "No, your honor. It's back at the jail."

The judge smiled. "Then would you mind getting it for us?"

Sgt. Pepper heaved himself to his feet, threw me a dirty look, and marched out. While he was gone, the judge explained piously to the gallery of world press behind me: "I've never objected to reading the Bible in my court." When the sergeant marched back in, the bailiff called the court to order and the judge handed me Sgt. Pepper's Bible. My hands were still cuffed but I could handle the Bible easily. I opened it to the first page, Genesis. I cleared my throat, for I too was playing to the press. This was one of those moments that come but rarely, when you are given the chance to explain yourself. My heart was beating too fast. I took a deep breath to calm myself, then I spoke slowly:

"Please bear in mind that all dolphins and porpoises are of the whale family. Indeed they are whales." I glanced around at the press. "Dr. Kingsley will confirm that for you, I'm sure."

Everyone looked at Dr. Kingsley. He glumly nodded agreement.

"It follows," I said, "that Charlie Brown is a small whale."

Again everyone looked to Dr. Kingsley. He got red in the face and again he nodded. Then I read slowly and with emphasis from the first chapter of Genesis:

21. *And God created great whales,* and every living creature that moveth, which the waters brought forth abundantly, after their kind, and every winged fowl after his kind: and God saw that it was good.

22. And God blessed them, saying, *Be fruitful, and multiply, and fill the waters in the seas,* and let fowl multiply in the earth.

That was strong stuff, and I let it sink in for a moment. The paddle fans whirred above us and someone was ringing a bicycle bell out on the street. Just outside the courtroom a young girl laughed softly. I closed the Bible and said:

"In no way is this what has happened to Charlie Brown."

There was a longish silence. I had said everything I wanted to say, that dolphins are whales, that God blessed them and put them on earth to be fruitful and to fill the waters in the seas, and that we were violating all this. I didn't pretend to be innocent. I had been as guilty of violating God's law as I was of cutting down the fence to free Charlie Brown. But at least I had confessed and tried to make amends.

The judge nodded. "Is that all you wanted to say, Mr. O'Barry?" While reporters scribbled in their notepads, I told him that it was. Then the judge made a brief speech about the abuse of hospitality, which I also was guilty of, and pronounced my sentence:

"I find you guilty as charged and fine you the maximum: five dollars."

I breathed deeply. It was over.

"One other thing," the judge said, leaning slightly toward me and for the first time looking straight at me. "The plane for the mainland leaves at noon. Be on it."

Only then did they remove the handcuffs. I asked for my diving gear back and the judge nodded assent. "Including the bolt cutters," I said. "I may need them again." Again the judge nodded. Sgt. Pepper gathered up the items of evidence from the table and brought them over to me. Our eyes met for a moment. I hoped for a glimmer of understanding from him, perhaps respect for what I had done, but there was none, and I finally looked away. I don't think he ever understood what I was doing, and he hated me all the more for that.

Martha paid the five dollar fine; I had no money. As we walked out of the courthouse and into the sunshine, she tugged on my arm. She was slim and beautiful, with green eyes and long dark hair. "What now?" she asked.

"I don't know." I shook my head. "Back home, I guess. I have no plans beyond this point." We walked down the steps to the street, arm in arm.

It was nearly noon, and fairly heavy traffic for Bimini was going in both directions, mainly bicycles streaming past but also several cars, several people walking by. Down the street I saw Sgt. Pepper's golf cart parked at the police station. It seemed as if this past week had never happened. Martha and I could have been just another pair of tourists. I stopped and turned to her. "Do you think I helped any?"

"Helped the dolphins? Yes, I'm sure you did," Martha said. She tugged my arm again. "And by the way, Ric, I love you."

It hadn't worked out the way I'd planned. Charlie Brown was still in that miserable pen, or what was left of it. And many other dolphins were also trapped in their miserable pens all over the world. They were owned by people who shamelessly sacrificed them to the glory of science or for the amusement of crowds.

I didn't know if my attempt to rescue Charlie Brown helped or not but at least I knew that it was the right thing to do. And I knew that I would keep on trying.

Two years later, Charlie Brown died. According to the post-mortem, he died of malnutrition.

3

Summer, 1944

A boy's will is the wind's will, and the thoughts of youth are
long, long thoughts.

—Henry Wadsworth Longfellow

By nature I am not an exhibitionist nor even very outgoing.
In my private life I'm practically a recluse. I live quietly, sometimes
going all day without speaking to people. I enjoy my privacy and the
world of silence. That's one of the reasons I like diving. Even when I
trained Flipper, it was in silence. Most dolphin trainers use whistles,
but I used hand signals for Flipper to keep down the noise while actors
were saying their lines. Even Flipper was silent. That excited chattering
you hear on the screen when Flipper sticks his head out of the water
and bobs it back and forth is produced by Mel Blanc, who also created
the voices of such characters as Bugs Bunny and Woody Woodpecker.

But if I am so naturally quiet, what caused me to make such a noisy
scene in Bimini? Pondering little else in the Bimini Jail, I realized that
I was probably trying to make amends. For a long time I had been
aware of my own part in the exploitation of dolphins. And like the
song says, I had to speak out against the madness.

This is not so strange as it might seem. Most of the people I know
who have lived closely with dolphins have been affected by them,
sometimes profoundly. I don't mean that dolphins are smarter than
us and are taking over or that they're casting spells, though I wouldn't
be too quick to deny such claims. I mean simply that having known
dolphins, having come to love and respect them and now regretting

my part in their tragic encounter with us, I had no choice.

For years I lived with dolphins. I was in the water with them day in and day out, sometimes around the clock. They're social creatures— far more than I—so I stayed with them just to keep them company, hanging out on the edge of their tank, floating in an inner tube with them or lying on a surf board. Using scuba gear I also spent a lot of time underwater with them, sitting or lying on the bottom and watching the dolphins. I stayed underwater with them till I ran out of air, came up and got another bottle of air and went back down again. I never tired of being with them like that. Looking up from the bottom of the training tank while two or three dolphins circled above me against the sky, the thousand shades of blue and green fusing phantasmagorically, I could only wonder at those amazing 400-pound creatures flying around me with such power and grace.

I was underwater with the dolphins so much that the copper sulfate in the water turned my hair green. Others at the Seaquarium, who called me "The Dolphin Man," used to tell the tourists that the only difference between me and the dolphins was that I had green hair. It was a running joke that when I did come up it must be payday. I ate with the dolphins, I slept with them, and I read the "Flipper" scripts while they frolicked all around me. When they were hungry, I fed them. When they were sick or injured, I cared for them. When there was a new trick to learn, I taught them. And when they had to be moved, I perched on the edge of the box they were in, keeping them wet and reassuring them that all was well.

If I sound like a mother hen to my Flipper dolphins, that's exactly right. That was especially true for me with Susie, the first of the TV Flippers, and of course with Kathy. Susie was a beautiful animal, her skin unblemished, her conformation perfect. She was about four feet long and weighed 100 pounds when we captured her in Biscayne Bay with her mother. We estimated that she was about one and a half years old. Soon after that, Susie's mother, whom we never named, developed light-gray square patches on her skin, an early symptom of swine erysipelas. Caused by bacteria and dirty equipment, this dread disease has no cure. When we discovered it, we lowered the water. Dr. Bob Knowles, a veterinarian, injected them both with penicillin and streptomycin. What we needed, though, was a miracle.

I wondered what would happen to Susie. She hadn't even been weaned yet. The next day I tried to give Susie her first fish by hand.

I was standing on the edge of her tank with a bucket of Icelandic herring, Susie was swimming up to me, saucily wheeling and swimming away. I leaned down to her.

"Come on, Susie, you little flirt. You're going to learn how to eat what's good."

I tossed the herring in front of her. She swam right over it.

"No, no," I said. I reached down and got the fish out of the water. "Look!" I put the fish to my own mouth and made a chewing motion. "It's good. Yum-yum," I said, smacking my lips.

The first thing dolphins must learn when they're captured is to eat dead fish. This is not natural for them; they're not scavengers. Sometimes it takes a while but when they get hungry enough, they learn. And then they seem to like it. But it was doubly difficult for Susie. She wasn't going from live fish to dead fish but from mother's milk to dead fish, which I don't think had ever been done before.

Susie came up to the edge of the tank where I was kneeling down. I opened my mouth, and Susie, mimicking me, opened hers. I put one of the herrings in her mouth, head first so that the fins wouldn't stick in her throat on the way down. I always sampled these fish myself to make sure they were good, taking some of each batch home where I cooked and ate them myself. So I knew there was nothing wrong with this one.

Susie tasted the herring I had put in her mouth, rolled her eyes at me and spat it out. She began lazily swimming in a circle, then stopped. "Come on, Susie," I said. She opened her mouth in a laugh, I put another small fish in her mouth. She held it there for a moment, eyeing me to see if I was kidding. I wasn't, but I might as well have been. She spat it out again and swam away. I didn't push it. In training a dolphin, the main pressure we use is hunger. To put it simply, the hungrier they are, the better they learn. If they're not hungry, there's no way to teach them anything. There's more to it than that but not much more. I had studied dolphins so closely and for so long that I could tell just how hungry they were and therefore just how much longer they could be trained or put through their paces.

Though it was taking a little longer than I thought it might to get Susie used to captivity, she was coming along fine, I thought. Maybe I was trying to rush her too much. Then early one morning a few days later, just two months after their capture, I discovered the mother dead on the bottom of the training tank, the baby trying to nurse.

We lowered the water in the tank, pumping it out into the bay. Almost certainly something in the water had killed the mother. We removed the body and I buried it under a coconut tree behind the dolphin tank facing Biscayne Bay. This is where most of the other animals and fish that died at the Seaquarium were buried. Death is a part of keeping animals captive, perhaps, but the death of this nameless mother seemed particularly pointless.

My thoughts turned to Susie. Now she would have to eat the dead fish. Normally, baby dolphins that were orphans and had not been weaned were force-fed a mother's milk concoction; they always died. I was determined to try something different: fish by hand. It had never been done before but I wasn't sure that it had ever been tried. If the death of her mother weighed heavily on Susie's spirits, it didn't show. In my logs, it's recorded that I fed Susie three pounds of fish that first morning, two at noon and another three that evening. When she ate the first fish by hand, I felt like a new daddy—and I was! I went all over the Seaquarium telling everyone that Susie had eaten a fish! That she would live! The next day, she ate six pounds of fish, half smelt and half herring. And that afternoon she was leaping about five feet in the air.

I didn't want the dolphins to feel that they were in prison, though in fact they were, and it was my job to get them to act like they enjoyed it. This was not simple because I had the distinct impression that they understood their predicament and were trying to help. Dolphins are not little windup toys; they're complex individuals with likes and dislikes, fears, moods and dispositions, good days and bad. In general, dolphins are a fun-loving bunch; cautious, impressionable, sensitive and intuitive, loyal to one another, highly adaptable, curious, willful and yet malleable, easily spoiled and then quite demanding, possessive and apt to throw tantrums, lovable, sensuous, mischievous and highly intelligent. They are almost anything you might say of a human child.

They are also wild animals. With their approximately ninety-six conical (cone-shaped) teeth, they could rip your head off if they wanted to, though the teeth fit into grooves on the opposing jaw for grasping things, not chewing. And with their powerful flukes (the marine mammal's version of a tail) they could beat you to a pulp. But they don't. I have never even heard of a normal dolphin injuring a person. To the contrary, I have heard only of their helping people. Their friendly reputation begins at the dawn of human history, stories from the most ancient times telling of dolphins befriending man.

As the dolphins we had captured tried to adjust to their strange new life, I tried to adjust to them. Sometimes as I sat on the bottom of their pool, the bubbles streaming upward to the surface while they circled above me, I wondered what they must think of this strange new world they were in and of the humans who had put them here. For 60 million years these dolphins had adapted to the sea. Except for sharks and killer whales, they had no enemies in nature. As mammals in a world of fish, the ocean must have been a Garden of Eden to them, the water pure, the seas running thick with schools of small fish to be herded together and eaten—alive!

Now they were here in what must have seemed a teacup to them. They swam in a circle, which bent their dorsal fins. Even worse must have been their psychological distortion. We can only guess at this, but if sonar is the dolphin's main sensory equipment, what must it have seemed like in a steel tank where every shot ricochets crazily back at them like a pool of Babel? I can think only that the tank they were in was to them like a house of mirrors would be to us. And I blush at what they must have thought of us. We made them do such inane little tricks, wearing funny hats and whirling hoola-hoops, rewarding them with dead fish and gawking at them endlessly. No wonder most of them had ulcers!

Although I was a part of that, I was also their friend. Or I tried to be. To them I was necessarily one of the enemy, but at least a friendly enemy. I tried to understand them—their physical needs, their feelings and fears—and to intercede for them. I studied the dolphins. I knew what they liked and didn't like. I wanted to be one of them. That's why I spent so much time with them. But, as I knew, my benevolence was rooted in my own benefit. It was my job to get their trust. Without Flipper's trusting someone, there would have been no TV show. So I did what I had to do to get their trust; and to maintain that trust, I was prepared to go to any extreme—even deception.

For example, when we needed to fly Kathy from the Seaquarium to the Bahamas for underwater scenes, we had to catch her in a net first. This was always traumatic. Dolphins associate nets with the time they were captured and both fear and hate them. It might seem simpler to shoot them with tranquilizers. That's done with lions, bears, and gorillas. But not dolphins. At least five dolphins have been sacrificed trying to find the proper dose to put them under safely. In 1955, neurologists, attempting to map the dolphin brain, administered nembutal and paraldehyde (anesthetics that humans tolerate with ease) to five dolphins and watched in horror as the breathing of each of them became disorganized, and as they gasped and died of asphyxiation. We learned the hard way that there is no proper dose, that dolphins breathe deliberately, not automatically as we and other mammals do, and that dolphins are always conscious. Even when they seem to be sleeping, bobbing just below the surface, their blowholes above water and breathing about three times a minute, they're just catnapping; they never really sleep. If they lose consciousness, they stop breathing and die. That's why Kathy was always caught in a net.

But not by me. Oh, no. I was never a part of that. If I had helped to catch Kathy in a net, she might never trust me again. She thought that I was really something special, that I had clout with my fellow humans. This was an impression I went to great lengths to maintain, for it gave me the control I needed over her. When Kathy had to be caught in a net, I wasn't there. Or so she thought. Actually, I would lurk to one side while others strung the net across the lake. When they drew the net around her and she was frantically trying to get away, I would sneak into the water to be "captured" with her and pulled up just like another dolphin.

We would swing there together in the net above the water, Kathy and I, packed like sardines. "Easy, Kathy," I would say, my voice low and gentle. "Take it easy now." She would become calm. As the net lifted us out of the water over to the special dolphin box for her, we looked into each other's eyes. Dolphins have horseshoe pupils, like a "U." I would put my arm around her and rub her dorsal fin. I could feel the tension. "Don't be afraid," I would say softly. "I'm here and I'll take care of you."

Yes, we were very close, my dolphins and I, and when something went wrong, I took it very personally. Years later when Kathy died in my arms, something of myself died, too. She played the role of Flipper, she and the others, though in large part they were doing only what they had to do to be tossed a fish. If there was a Flipper, it was I more than any of them, but actually we were all in it together.

Exactly when I began having these strong feelings for my dolphins, I don't know. As I sat in the Bimini Jail and went over and over what had happened, I returned to the summer of 1944, a time of innocence when I was growing up in Miami Beach and before I knew anything about dolphins.

Another World—and All Mine

Toward the climax of World War II, we on the Beach felt ourselves involved in the war more than most other Americans. Miami Beach, like the rest of the East Coast, was blacked out. No lights were allowed at night because a favorite trick of the German subs, which patrolled the Gulf Stream in what they called wolf packs, was to zero in on a tanker at night against the haze of Miami's nightlife. Then as now, the Beach had an international flavor, but it was different from what it is today. Russian troops were trained at Government Cut, and from my bedroom window I could see them climb up cargo nets and jump off into the water for abandon-ship exercises. Japanese prisoners were held in nearby camps. They were a common sight cutting grass along the causeway between Miami and Miami Beach. And German submarines would drop off spies on lonely stretches of Florida's coast. This last was what all of us living there were intensely trying to prevent.

South Miami Beach was beautiful then. Except for oil slicks and a tarlike sludge on the beach at times, caused probably by torpedoed tankers, the ocean was as sparkling clear then as Bahamian water is now. Despite the war, those were the best of times because our cause was just and we knew somehow that we would win.

My parents owned the Biscayne Restaurant, next to Joe's Stone Crab, which is at the south end of where the Art Deco section is now, and one day that summer when I was five years old, I was playing on the beach. The water has always held a fascination for me. I can't explain it, but it's always made me feel happy inside. That day on the beach I found a one dollar bill. That was a lot of money in those days and it was the first money I ever had. I went running home. "Look," I yelled, waving the money at my brother, Jack. "Look what I've got!"

Jack was a year older than I. His eyes were as large as saucers. "Where did you get that?"

"I found it! On the beach! It's mine!"

Jack grinned. "Let's buy a ball with it," he said. "We can play catch."

"A ball? No. I already know what I'm going to buy."

I bought a pair of underwater goggles. They were new in those days. I ran all the way to the sports store, bought the goggles, then ran all the way back to the beach. I put them on and stuck my head in the water and looked around. It was another world. A beautiful world. It was quiet. Like a dream. And it was all mine.

I was a little older when I got the rest of my underwater equipment: my first fins, a snorkel with a ping-pong ball that was supposed to keep the water out, and a spear. There was no scuba diving then. Scuba gear (Self-Contained Underwater Breathing Apparatus) came much later from France and Italy. My spear had three prongs, like Neptune's trident, and was propelled through a metal tube by a strong rubber band at the back like a slingshot. At the end of the spear was a ten-foot line so that whatever I shot could be hauled in. My first target was a 2½-foot stingray sleeping on the bottom and partly covered by sand. The stingray is a flat sea creature with eyes on the top, who goes through the water by flapping his wings. He's a cousin of the shark. My heart pounding, I eased up to about four feet away, drew back the rubber sling and, holding my breath till I had my quarry lined up just right, let if fly. I was as surprised as the stingray was when the spear hit. As I watched in amazement, the stingray went straight up, then flapped his wings and took off like a bat—with my spear! I took off in the opposite direction.

Later when I had got another spear, I hit another stingray off the reefs of Virginia Key, which is just south of Miami and where the water was as pure as crystal. I dragged the stingray ashore and was cutting the tail off as a trophy when the stingray flopped one last time and his stinger, a sharp barbed weapon just above the long tail, jabbed into the index finger of my right hand. I had never felt such pain before. I couldn't get it loose. I was scared, my finger was bleeding and it burned like fire and my whole hand was turning numb all at once. I was crying and didn't know what to do, so I picked the stingray up, cradling it in my arms, kicked off my fins and walked up to the road, bawling my eyes out. Stingray barbs are covered with a poisonous mucous. Most people stabbed by them take weeks to recover. A car came along, the driver saw in an instant what had happened, picked me up and drove me down to the toll gate where the uniformed guard, a short man with a big beer belly, matter-of-factly took out a pocket knife and cut off the tail. It was still attached to the stinger, which was so deep in my finger that he didn't dare try to pull it out. He called my parents on the phone and they came and took me to a hospital in Coconut Grove.

The doctor took one look at it. "This is going to hurt a little," he said. But he was wrong. It hurt a lot. He couldn't pull it out because of the barbs, so he pushed it all the way through. I still have the scar of that first battle. And I decided that from then on I would leave stingrays alone. Looking back on it, I think that stingray may also have taught me something important about the sea: that for all its beauty and mystery, the sea is also dangerous.

For a long time my prime target was the parrotfish who lurked along the sea walls. The parrotfish, so named for his brilliant colors, eats coral, which can cause ciguatera poisoning in anyone who eats one. You can also be poisoned by eating any fish that eats the parrotfish, such as the barracuda.

Later, when I had joined the Miami Seaquarium, I discovered that a mucous like that of the stingray also covers the bills of sawfish. I'd been hit accidentally on the ankles by sawfish more than once while feeding them in the tank. Like hungry puppies, they got excited going after the fish I was handing out and swung those bills around with abandon, not realizing or caring about the pain they might inflict. Being hit by the bill of a sawfish hurts as much as being stuck by a stingray, though, and I always took care to feed them first to get rid of them. Mucous of a similar sort also covers the green moray eel. Without the yellow coating, he's dull blue or slate-colored.

A Little Problem on the Atule

My career in diving began in the U.S. Navy. I joined in 1955 when the Korean War was winding down. I was sixteen and, though I looked even younger, I lied about my age. I wanted to become a member of the UDT (Underwater Demolition Team) and was disappointed to learn, after I had already joined the navy, that you must be twenty-one. I knew they wouldn't bend the rules for me—that's not how the navy works—and in fact I didn't dare try to get them to for fear they would find out I was too young even to be enlisted. If I was to become a diver, I decided, I would have to learn it on my own. I had a number of navy assignments, the first aboard the U.S.S. *Tripoli*, an aircraft carrier, which crossed the Atlantic forty times in twenty-two months. Then for a year I was at the Navy Base at Dam Neck, Virginia, a gunnery and guided missile school where the training is top secret. For the final year of my five-year hitch I was aboard the U.S.S. *Furse,* a destroyer in the Sixth Fleet stationed in the Mediterranean.

It was on the *Furse* that I really got started diving. I was chipping paint below decks when I discovered a Jack Brown commercial mask with two fifty-foot lengths of hose. The Jack Brown, now called the Desco, was named for its inventor, whom I met some years later. Standard equipment on all navy vessels, the Jack Brown was a full-face mask with a constant air flow. It replaced the old Miller-Dunn Shallow Water Helmet, which looks a little like a space helmet. The Miller-Dunn worked well as long as the diver stood upright, but if he bent over to look down, the helmet would fill with water. Nevertheless, it's a great-looking diving helmet, which is why it's still used by divers at the Miami Seaquarium. Scuba gear later became the navy standard.

I sent off for the *U.S. Navy Diving Manual* and studied it on my own. I knew it practically by heart. It was my Bible. Several of us used to scuba dive off Italy, Monaco and France, Gibraltar, the Azore Islands, Spain, and Cuba. One day the executive officer of the *Furse* called me to his office. "I hear you're a diver," he said. He was a businesslike, humorless sort of man and ordinarily very solemn, but now he had a conniving gleam in his eye.

"Yes, sir," I said. "You heard right."

The U.S.S. *Furse* and several other destroyers in an antisubmarine–hunter-killer group were tied up together with the submarine *Atule* off Palma, Spain. These ships and the U-boat used to train together. We held war games, destroyers against the sub. But if one of us had a problem, we all had a problem. This was especially true because we were getting ready to head back home to the States. "Homeward bound"—if you've never been at sea for any length of time, you can't know what that means to a sailor. Like being in love, it was the only thing anyone could think about.

"We've got a little problem on the *Atule,*" the executive officer said. He frowned. "A crewman was cleaning the starboard running light and...."

"Don't tell me, sir," I said. "It fell in?"

He nodded. He didn't have to add that we would be stuck there till it was found. Our group didn't have an authorized diver. If we were to go by the books we would have to request a diver from Sixth Fleet's submarine tender ship or the U.S.S. *Everglades,* which was the destroyer tender that traveled with us. Requisitions, explanations, reports, clarifications, perhaps reprimands and rule changes—it could take weeks of paperwork; paperwork that would follow the fleet forever, resting finally as a statistic in the official history of the U.S. Navy.

"If it's down there, sir, I'll find it."

"It's down there, O'Barry. Go to it."

My sidekick on diving expeditions was Seaman Roger Loomis, a baker. We got the Jack Brown mask, the wet suit, the lines and all the rest of it, then over I went, down to the bottom thirty-five feet below. That's as deep as a three-story building is tall but it's shallow-water diving; anything under 100 feet is considered shallow. I had no underwater light and the water was as black as pitch. I was literally feeling my way along the murky bottom in what must have been a thousand-year-old garbage dump. We were at anchor and both ships would swing around in a circle, perhaps as much as a hundred yards as we drifted with the tide and wind. The running light was about the size of a basketball, which meant that I could have stumbled around for a week looking for it. But luckily I found the running light—I felt the wires that stuck out from it—after only a few hours of my first dive. I hooked the line to the running light and signaled for Roger to pull it up. When I came up a few minutes later, at least a hundred sailors lined the *Furse* and *Atule*, watching. They knew that we would be going home now. They were grinning. When I broke the surface, they gave me a rousing cheer, and soon we were under way.

A few days later the ship's company was called to full dress inspection and much to my surprise I was ordered front and center by Capt. B. T. Stephens. I thought that I might be in big trouble. In port while the watch conveniently looked the other way, I had been swimming to shore commando style almost nightly when we had Cinderella Liberty (when you must be back on the ship by midnight). But it wasn't that. Instead of a reprimand, I was presented a commendation. It was for finding the *Atule's* running light and for several other diving jobs, including untangling a net from propellers in 50 feet of water at La Spezia, Italy; repairing a sonar transducer at 25 feet off Sardinia; instructing scuba divers at 120 feet off St. Raphael, France; and recovering gear dropped over the side at 70 feet in both Pollencia Bay and Monaco.

Part of the commendation read: "...and volunteered to perform these acts solely because of your personal interest in diving...."

Personal interest? Yes, that's true but an understatement. I loved diving.

Hurricane Donna, the most destructive storm to hit Florida since 1926, swept through the Keys in 1960. A Category 4 hurricane with winds of more than 131 miles an hour, Donna roared across the state from the Gulf of Mexico and curved out to sea, catching the U.S. Sixth Fleet off Charleston as we were heading in. That was my last voyage as a navy man. And for a while I thought it might be my last voyage of any kind. We pitched and rolled so much we had to strap ourselves into our bunks.

When we tied up in Charleston, I still had the Jack Brown mask and other diving gear. I asked the executive officer: "Where do you want me to stow this?"

He looked at the equipment, then at me. "Do you want that gear, O'Barry?"

"Do I want it? Yes, sir, I want it. I'll even pay the navy for it."

He made a frown. "Forget it. We'll need a new one anyway. Take it. It's yours."

Even then I didn't know where I would go or what I would do as a civilian. I called a family friend, a man who had been my boyhood idol: Art McKee, diver and treasure hunter. Growing up over the years, I had read about him in books and magazines. He owned and operated the McKee's Museum of Sunken Treasure on Plantation Key, which is just south of Key Largo. When I called, Art told me that he had lost both of his forty-foot work boats in the hurricane. The *Treasure Princess* sank at the dock in about twenty feet of water, the *Jolly Roger* was picked up and tossed across U.S. 1 into the mangrove swamps. I asked him if he could use a hand to help him with the salvage.

"Sure," he said. "I can always use a good hand. Come on down."

4

Treasure Diving

> He did not dream of the lions, but instead of a vast school
> of porpoises that stretched for eight or ten miles and it was
> in the time of their mating that they would leap high into
> the air, and return to the same hole they had made in the
> water when they had leaped.
>
> —Ernest Hemingway, *The Old Man and the Sea*

When Art invited me to help him with the salvage, that ended
my doubts about what I would do in life. It was not an auspicious
beginning, cleaning up the mess of a terrible hurricane, but I loved
the sea and felt good about it, as if it were home.

Art was a big, good-natured Irishman from New Jersey, with red-
dish-blond hair, who smiled easily and could make friends in a minute.
Originally a deep-sea diver for the U.S. Navy, who came down to help
lay the fresh-water pipeline to Key West, he had got gold fever and
devoted his life to the quest for sunken treasure. Most people who
dream of finding gold wake up in the morning and contentedly go
back to work. Almost anyone who tries to live this dream soon finds
that his life has become a nightmare. Only the most fortunate few
actually find sunken treasure, and Art was one of these.

Historians tell us that Spanish galleons made 17,000 Atlantic cross-
ings between 1500 and 1820 A.D. That's a longer time than the United
States is old. During that time, they say, the Spanish shipped at least
$22 billion in gold and silver bars back home through the Florida
Straits. If only 5 percent failed to make it back, at least $1 billion in
treasure went down. Although a lot of that treasure has been found,
enough is still on the ocean floor to make a lot of people very rich.

Art was not rich but he lived well and kept the IRS sniffing around

him all his life. In 1948 he discovered part of the Spanish treasure
fleet of 1733, one of Spain's annual "plate" fleets of twenty-one galleons with $68 million in treasure. It had run afoul of a hurricane in
the Florida Keys. Art found hundreds of silver coins ("pieces of eight"),
gold doubloons, and exquisite pieces of jewelry, including several gold
rings, silver hearts and pendants, crosses and religious medals, and
many other items. The dean of treasure divers, Art lavished his expertise on anyone who shared his dream, including Mel Fisher, who
later found the *Atocha*. Art displayed his finds in his museum, which
was built of coral like a Spanish castle at Treasure Harbor on Plantation Key.

Art had a contagious enthusiasm about treasure diving and, like all
adventurers, a sharp eye for the dramatic. An expert on the Spanish
explorations of the sixteenth and seventeenth centuries, he liked telling
stories about the people he had come to know through his research,
especially when he could use the actual artifacts involved. One evening
after dinner at the museum, he launched into one of his tales of incredible derring-do, of pirate gold and dueling. As Art reached the climax
of his story, he got a certain look on his face that I had noticed before,
the look of someone rolling the dice with everything on the line. He
rose dramatically from the table and walked over to a steel treasure
chest against the wall. With a big brass key, he opened the chest and
removed two exquisitely crafted dueling pistols. He held them for a
moment in his big hands, feeling their heft.

"It's true, Ricardo. Here," he said, thrusting one of the pistols at
me. That was not my name—Ricardo—but he liked the sound of it,
I guess, and always called me that. He grinned. "They fought to the
death with these."

Though Art was obsessed with sunken treasure—gold and silver
especially—he was convinced that it was cursed. And so am I. There
was no other explanation, he said, for the danger and hardship that
hung over every attempt to find it.

Art traced the curse to Atahualpa, god-king or emperor of the Aztecs
in Peru. The year was 1532. Invited to the Spanish camp, the king
was captured along with thousands of his men. The men were slaugh-
tered. When Atahualpa realized what Francisco Pizarro wanted—gold
and silver—the emperor promised a king's ransom if he were released.
He would fill the large room he was in halfway to the roof, he said,
once with gold and twice with silver. Pizarro agreed. The word went

out and the precious metal came in. But the Spaniards murdered Atahualpa anyway, strangling him to death, and the struggling Inca empire never recovered.

He Was Coolest Under Fire

Art was cool but I didn't realize how cool till I went on my first treasure diving expedition with him. In 1961 aboard the *El Amigo* ("The Friend"), a 136-foot ex-navy minesweeper that had been converted into a treasure-diving ship, we were headed for the treasure ship *Genovese,* a fifty-four-gun Spanish frigate that sank in 1730 on Banner Reef, a section of San Pedro Bank some seventy miles southwest of Jamaica. The *Genovese* carried three million pesos in gold and silver, including many ten-foot strips of silver, pieces of eight that hadn't yet been cut or stamped.

When tourists visited Art's museum, some of them said they wanted to go on his next expedition. He would write down their names and addresses and tell them that if he got enough interest, he'd be in touch. Twenty-one thrill seekers wanted to go with him on this expedition, including Burt Webber, who later led an expedition that found the *Concepción.* Art charged $1,000 each to go with him. He promised his subscribers eight weeks in the Caribbean searching for sunken treasure. We could come back rich, he told them; we could also come back with nothing but a few memories. Art was the only one who was paid. He received $1,000 and half of whatever was found. I was to get a fourth of Art's share, and the subscribers would divide the rest among themselves.

Art chartered the *El Amigo* from Lenny Lawson Shaw, a tough old seadog with red hair and a red face who looked like a firecracker ready to go off. And with reason. Captain Shaw was a wanted man in Cuba. He apparently had smuggled guns to both sides during the early days of the Cuban revolution, so everyone was after him. The captain and his son Mike, his first mate, had only one reason for taking this charter into such dangerous waters: money.

The first night out, Art and I were in the wheelhouse. Captain Shaw, who was at the wheel, said that his former partner had cheated him out of his part of the pay on a previous expedition and he (the captain) had tracked him to Alaska. He stared straight ahead. It was a dark night, clouds obscuring the sky, the smell of rain in the air.

Art glanced at me—I was sitting behind them—and winked. Then Art said to the captain: "Am I supposed to ask what happened?"

The captain sucked on his lower lip and gave Art a dead-fish look. "I broke every bone in his body," he said.

The next day, a storm rolled in. I was assigned to the crow's nest to keep a lookout. We could see that we were very close to Cape San Antonio, the westernmost point of Cuba. As the sun came up I could see four boats heading for us. Fishing boats, I wondered? I studied them through my binoculars. No, I decided, not fishing. Too many people. I counted them. There were twelve men on each boat. As the boats came closer, I could see the men more clearly. They all had M-1 rifles. I called out my sighting below and everyone lined the rail. By now I could see also that the four boats bearing down on us had .30 caliber air-cooled machine guns. The sea was rough, the crow's nest I was in was swinging wildly from side to side as our ex-minesweeper pitched and rolled. I couldn't have climbed down if I'd wanted to. Then I noticed that all my shipmates had gone below. "That's strange," I thought.

Suddenly they were back on deck again.

With weapons!

No one was supposed to bring weapons on board, but all of them had. As it turned out, Art and I were the only ones who were unarmed.

But that problem paled beside the one confronting us now. We were about to go to war with a fleet of Cuban boats that outnumbered us four to one and outgunned us ten to one. And with me in the crow's nest! I wanted to climb down. To hide. Anything! But that was impossible. The sea was raging and the mast was whipping crazily from side to side; I hung on for dear life to keep from being flung off into the sea.

This was a good time, I thought, to be friendly. I waved and grinned at the oncoming boats. Several minutes dragged by, an eternity. Then abruptly they waved back. Wonderful, I thought. They were not mad at us after all. Had I saved us? I scanned the boat below. I was looking for Art. I wanted to tell him. Where was he? Then I spotted him. He was at the stern. What's he doing, anyway? I stared intently. He was waving at the gunboats with one hand, holding up the end of a flag with the other. The flag? Was it the American flag? I looked more closely. No. Cubans were not fond of Americans. Art was showing them the *Panamanian* flag!

Suddenly all four of the Cuban gunboats turned and headed for shore. Exactly why they headed back, we never discovered. Perhaps the sea was too rough for them. Maybe they thought we were more heavily armed than we were. Or they might have turned back because of my friendly waving. But I doubt all that. I think instead it was because of what Art did, showing them that though we were an ex– U.S. Navy ship, we were of Panamanian registry.

The Knife Uncomfortably Close

That expedition ended in disaster, the subscribers turning on Art in a mutiny that I unwittingly touched off. But it sealed the friendship between Art and me because I made it up to him.

We had been out a while and had found some things, but not the silver we were looking for. We found historical artifacts, mainly: pewter mugs, spoons, and bronze crosses. Art was a master at reading artifacts. He read artifacts of a shipwreck the way a detective reads a murder scene. From his research, he already knew everything there was to know about the ship, including the route, the cargo, and everyone aboard, the number of cannons carried and whether they were of bronze or iron. He had dug up all the known facts about how and when the ship had sunk, which told him about the tides and prevailing winds. He also knew or could shrewdly guess what other divers had already found. When we found mugs and plates and a rat-tailed spoon, this told him where the galley was. And when we found a pile of big rocks, Art knew that they originally came from Spain and were used as ship ballast. Now, resting as they did on the ocean floor, he could tell where the center of the ship was when it went down. We found a brass button, which marked the officer's quarters because in those days only officers wore brass buttons like that. We also found burlap bags of cocoa beans. Like everything else, they were encrusted with coral and preserved deep under the sand. But like the large coils of rope we also found, when we tried to swim them to the surface, they turned to powder. We found ivory combs, crosses, flintlock pistols and clay pots, which told us where the cargo hold had been and confirmed that the ship was indeed heading back to Spain.

Any moment, it seemed, we might find the silver and become instant millionaires.

Unless Art and I had already found it and weren't telling the others.

That's what Captain Shaw apparently thought. Shaw, who was as crudely persuasive as a .44 caliber pistol, told his son Mike and the subscribers that Art and I were cheating them.

We weren't, of course, but people believe what they want to believe. And when treasure is involved, they believe the worst.

You don't have to be a mind reader on a small boat to know what others are thinking. In a thousand ways the subscribers let Art and me know that they didn't trust us, that they were watching us and that they did not intend to be cheated.

On the day of the mutiny, Art and I had been out in one of the dinghies all morning and the carburetor of the 25-horsepower kicker was acting up. I looked in the tool kit for a small screwdriver but it wasn't there. We rowed back to the *El Amigo* and I went below for another one. On my return, Shaw intercepted me, motioning with a toss of his head for me to come over.

"Yes?" I said, glancing at my watch. Art was waiting.

"You remember our little talk, don't you," he said, "the first night out?"

I was in no mood for games. "What are you getting at, captain?"

He sucked on his lower lip. "You remember what happened to a partner of mine who double-crossed me, don't you?"

"You broke every bone in his body," I said. "Yes, I remember."

Shaw smiled. "I didn't tell you the good part."

I glanced impatiently at my watch. "Okay, what was the good part?"

"The good part is that I did it without killing him. And I hope he lives forever."

Later, at a general meeting on the stern of the boat, I noticed that Mike, the captain's son, had edged uncomfortably close to me, the sheath of his knife unsnapped. I remember thinking very clearly: If this is not important, why am I noticing it? Was something about to happen? Was he warning me? Or was I as paranoid as everyone else?

Nothing happened and maybe nothing would have happened. But I gave him a hard look and edged away.

I can understand the subscribers' feelings. The lure of sunken treasure is everything and more that people say about it. They had hired the best in the business to lead them and so far the only thing they had discovered was a truism: work at sea is hard work. Certainly if hard work and hardship meant anything, they *deserved* to find the silver. The food was worse than mediocre. There was no shower except the rain. The weather was unbelievably hot, the air so thin that breathing had become an act of will. Our drinking water, stored in large, black bladders up on deck, tasted like rubber.

Though Art never promised anyone we would find treasure, the pressure was intense to find something that would make it all seem worthwhile. Art and I didn't talk about it but I think we both wanted to prove ourselves to the others, and the quickest way to do that was to find the silver.

Art and I and Art's brother-in-law, Bob Soto of Grand Cayman, were going back and forth in the dinghy over a 100-yard-square grid. Art steered, Bob and I took turns bent down with a black hood over our heads, looking through a glass bottom. The glass bottom is actually a Plexiglas plate covering a one-foot-square hole amidship. Looking through it, I could clearly see the bottom of Banner Reef twenty or twenty-five feet below. If something looked interesting, I tossed over a buoy to mark the spot. The buoy is bright red and has a fifty-foot line attached to a lead sinker. Later, we went back to the buoys and I dove down to check them out. If I thought I had found something worth investigating, I tied the line of the buoy to it. Sometimes when I spotted something interesting, I would free-dive down and check it on the spot, and swimming up again I could see Art's face through the glass bottom, grinning at me from ear to ear.

What do you look for on the bottom? Anything unusual. That could be a mound of sand, a pothole, anything sticking up, but especially straight lines. There are no natural straight lines at sea, so when I spotted one I tossed over a buoy. Craters indicate that something has disturbed the bottom; so do mounds. The only way you can find out for sure is to dig.

The *El Amigo* had edged up to within hailing distance of Art and me. When I went down to check out one of the buoys, I saw several long strips on the bottom. They were six feet long, maybe longer, encrusted by coral like white stucco. Ocean currents cover things up one moment, expose them the next. These strips—or what I could see of them—were sticking out in a bundle and looked very interesting. I swam up to the surface. The subscribers, their faces gray with fatigue, noticed that I had swum up earlier than usual. They lined the rail, suspiciously watching every move I made. How I wanted to prove them wrong!

"What do you need?" Art asked.

I took my mouthpiece out. "The hatchet."

Art nodded and handed me the hatchet. The subscribers grumbled and became restive.

I dove down with the hatchet and found the long strips again. Probably metal. I drew back and chopped. It clanged. Yes, it was metal. I looked more closely and could hardly believe my eyes. It had the dull-shiny and soft, wonderfully lustrous sheen of silver. This was it! We had found the *Genovese*'s silver!

I chopped several more places to make sure, chipping off a chunk of it. This was it! We had found it! I pushed off the bottom and a moment later broke the surface.

They yelled from the ship: "Find anything?"

I spat out my mouthpiece. *"Silver!"* I yelled, thrusting my arm skyward like an Olympic champion.

The cry went around the ship like a cheer. "We found it! We're rich!" Exhausted divers were jumping up and down, hugging each other and some even jumped over the side in their joy.

Art looked skeptical. "What have you got?"

I handed him my sample.

He looked at it, frowning. "Steel," he said with disgust, then tossed it carelessly into the water.

"But Art—"

"Steel," he spat out, shaking his head.

As Art and I went on to the next buoy, the celebration continued aboard the *El Amigo*. They thought they were rich.

Hours later when Art, Bob and I returned, they couldn't believe it when Art told them that I had been mistaken. There were harsh words, accusations, threats.

Art was tired. It had been a long day. He was emotionally drained. We were all gathered at the stern. They were getting nasty. Angrily, he challenged them: "If you want someone else to lead this expedition, damn it, go to it. That was *not* silver, it was *steel*." Then he added wearily, "As for myself, I'm going to lie down in my cabin." He pushed his way through the circle of men.

The subscribers elected Burt Webber to lead them. He was at least the most enthusiastic of the subscribers. The first thing they wanted to do was to check for themselves what I had found, so they came to me.

"Sure," I said with a shrug. "But it was only steel."

"You said it *was* silver," Shaw charged.

Mike chimed in: "Yeah!"

"I thought it was silver," I said lamely, "but—"

"But what?" Shaw had a mouth like a shark's. They all crowded around me, twenty sweaty men who thought their fortunes had just been stolen from them.

"But I was mistaken."

It occurred to me that they hadn't already tossed me over because they thought I might lead them to the silver.

"Not silver, huh?" Shaw said. His eyes were squinty. He sucked his lower lip a moment, apparently in deep thought. "And how do you know *that*?"

That made me mad. I exploded: "How do I know? I know because it's *so*. And it's so because Art *said* it was so."

"Art said it was so," Shaw mocked me. They all laughed.

It was uncanny how *they* had suddenly become the expert divers.

"We want to see for ourselves," Burt Webber said. "Come on." He took me by the arm, the others crowding around. "Show us where it was." Everybody but Art squeezed into the two little dinghies and we went back to where I thought the spot was. It was getting dark. We couldn't find the buoy.

"What's the matter?" Shaw demanded. "Didn't you tie the buoy to the metal strips?"

"Of course I did."

He looked at me with skepticism. "And what kind of knot did you use?"

I didn't like this kind of questioning. "A bowline," I snapped. "What kind would *you* use?"

He rubbed his chin. "A bowline? And it pulled loose?" He looked around at the others as if this clinched his case.

"I don't know what happened to it," I said. "All I know is I can't find it now."

I knew he didn't believe me, none of them did. Early the next morning we went out again and searched all day in vain. Back on the *El Amigo,* it was very tense. Nobody spoke to Art or me. And suddenly I realized that we hadn't found the buoy because it wasn't there. How I could have forgotten, I don't know, but I recalled now that when Art said my sample was steel, I went down and released the buoy. It was automatic. But it was also not the right time to say anything about it, so I let it ride.

We were near the Cayman Islands and when we pulled in at Georgetown the mutineers offered to let us off. Art took them up on it. "Come on," he said to me. But I shook my head. I felt responsible for what had happened and decided to stay with his equipment— several boxes of dive gear, the air lift, two compressors and air lines— and the artifacts.

"Stop blaming yourself, Ricardo," Art said. Then he told me I ought to fly home with him. "Anything could happen aboard the *El Amigo*," he said, shaking his head miserably. "Some of those guys are not very happy."

As it turned out, I was right to have stayed with the ship. I think my staying convinced the subscribers that they might have been wrong about us. When we docked in Miami two weeks later, they helped me carry Art's equipment ashore and lock it up.

If Dolphins Dived for Gold!

We returned to the museum and life went on. By now, working shoulder to shoulder with the most famous treasure diver in the world, the lure and luster of his fabulous artifacts always around us, I had caught gold fever, too. It wasn't as bad as Art's but it was just as real. I could think of nothing else.

How much the precious metal itself was worth, the melt-down value, I don't know. But whatever it was, the value as artifacts was greater still, not percentages greater but magnitudes greater. Some of the things that Art found, and that I found, too, may have been priceless. Tourists from all over the world came to see and touch these treasures, to relive the history and feel those magic times. Because I worked there, I could come and go as I liked. And I did. I gazed in wonder at those pieces that spanned the centuries, living beyond their own time, beyond the dreams that had created them, precious artifacts that had popped up suddenly into a totally different world. I knew every piece in that museum, and I knew how Art McKee had recovered them.

Though there is money in diving for sunken treasure and there is no greater thrill than finding it, treasure diving is an uncertain life and the work is as hard as it is frustrating. There are no street addresses neatly lined up on the ocean floor. The sea is forever moving, the winds shift and so does the sand below. To hold fast in one spot at sea, you set your anchors, four and five at a time. And when the tide changes or the winds shift, you set them again. Lines break, cables snap, pumps wear out. And they must all be fixed. Immediately. Treasure diving is an endless emergency. Though nothing can tarnish the thrill of striking sunken treasure, I never worked so hard and for so little in all my life.

I was about to get married at the time, or so I thought, and it was obvious that I would need a regular job and a regular paycheck, so Art spoke about me to his old friend Captain William B. Gray of the Miami Seaquarium. He hired me on the spot as a diver.

But I always kept in close touch with Art McKee, occasionally going on treasure-diving expeditions with him. Later, when I became Flipper's trainer, what intrigued Art most, as I knew it would, was the prospect of using dolphins to find sunken treasure. Every time he came to town from his castle on Plantation Key we talked about it. Once he came by to see me at the Seaquarium and we strolled out on the dock at Flipper's Lake, the salt water lake where the TV films were shot. I noticed Kathy in the lake, swimming effortlessly and watching me.

Art was talking: "The important thing, Ricardo, is to use your dolphins for something really worthwhile."

I knew what he was getting at, but this was a litany that we enjoyed playing out. "Oh? Like what?"

"Like training your dolphins to find gold." He looked at me and I felt the old magic, the flash of daring in his eyes and the guttural lust in the way he said "gold." It was like all the gold the Spanish had ever lost at sea was rightfully his and all we had to do now was stake the claim. "With that sonar of theirs," he said, "dolphins are natural treasure finders. It's true! They could be better than any electronic instrument we could build. Think of the work we could save. And the time. You might be wondering if it would pay. Would it pay? Ricardo, we could be millionaires." He looked at me with fiercely squinted eyes and hissed: *Millionaires!*"

Kathy was watching me. I knew she was eager to show off. Actually, she hadn't been fed and was ready to do a trick for a chunk of fish. I said: "You ask if I could train a dolphin to find gold. Art, that's simple! Give me your watch. That's gold, isn't it?"

"My Rolex!" His right hand went to his watch protectively and he shook his head. "This watch is solid gold."

"Good!" I said, grabbing his big hand. He protested with a grin but let me pull the gold watch off. "You want to know if I can train a dolphin to find gold?" I wound up like a baseball pitcher.

"Oh, no!" Art moaned. "That watch keeps perfect time."

I let it fly. The watch went up, a rainbow, and came plummeting down with a splash. I held Kathy up with a signal to "stay" till the watch had time to sink to the bottom, then, as she watched me eagerly, I gave her the "fetch" signal, arm thrust out, and shouted: "GOLD!" Kathy streaked across the water seventy-five feet away. She dove. Art looked at me quizzically. "You yelled 'gold.' What was that about?"

"Art," I said with mock-exasperation, "I have to tell her what I want her to find."

He looked at me skeptically. Kathy popped to the surface and came racing back to the dock with the watch in her mouth.

I bent down and removed it from Kathy's mouth and patted her on the head. She wanted a fish but I didn't have one and she squealed with indignation. I whipped out a handkerchief and dried off the watch, using big movements like a magician showing that there's nothing up his sleeve, and presented it to Art with a flourish. "Does *that* answer your question?"

Art made a sour face and held the watch out in front of him for a moment. He looked at the second hand to make sure it was still going. Then he put the watch on with great deliberation. "That's not exactly what I had in mind." He sighed. Then, frowning in thought, he started to walk off. He stopped and turned to me solemnly. "You know, Ricardo," he said, pointing at me, "if God hadn't meant for us to find that sunken treasure, why did He put dolphins in the sea? Ever think of that?"

Swimming with Wild Dolphins

A few years later on our last treasure-diving trip together, something happened that was to transform my life.

We were in the northwesternmost part of the Bahamian Out Islands looking for the fabled *Maravillas*—the *Nuestra Senora de las Maravillas*. This ill-fated treasure ship collided with another galleon during a storm that struck the Little Bahama Banks in 1665. These shallow banks, ranging from twenty to fifty feet deep, border the Gulf Stream. They're forty miles from the nearest land, Grand Bahama Island, about fifty miles due east of Stuart, Florida. One moment the water is a couple of thousand feet deep, a dark-blue river moving 3½ knots north, and the next moment you've run up on a bank covered by barely twenty feet of water. The *Maravillas* went down at the edge of the Banks with 650 passengers and crew, all but forty-five of whom drowned. One of the survivors, a priest, told of his fellow clergymen charging 200 pesos to hear confessions. When the ship ran aground, according to the survivors' reports, the priests went over the side to save their skins, but because their pockets were so filled with gold and silver, they sank and never came up again. The ship's cargo included four million pesos in gold. The bars were cast in the size and shape of Hershey bars. There were also several million dollars worth of silver and emeralds. Most of it is still there.

Art McKee was at the helm of the MV *Falcon,* a forty-two-foot pleasure boat equipped with diving gear. It was the tippiest boat we had ever used. Top heavy. There was too much diving and salvage gear on deck and it was badly placed: compressors, an airlift, hoses and tanks, lead weights, fins and wet suits, everything. Clouds were building and Art anchored the *Falcon* in twenty-five feet of water. We had a crew of six, including two U.S. Navy divers. While Art stayed with the *Falcon,* two of the navy men and I took the small Boston Whaler and crisscrossed in a grid, looking for certain holes in the bottom that would mark the wreck. While one of us steered, the other two were pulled through the water on the end of a line, feet hooked in bowlines. We were near the *Falcon* and I could see Art, his hair now quite white, watching hopefully as ever. Suddenly the two navy men let out a blood-curdling shriek.

"Shark!"

It's a cry that freezes the blood.

I stopped the dinghy and looked back. The water was alive with fins. They sliced the water all around the navy men, slashing, diving. I ran to the stern and pulled the men aboard. They clambered into the boat, out of breath and scared witless. But something was wrong here, I thought. I put on my face plate and stuck my head in the water.

They weren't sharks; they were dolphins! As far as the eye could see in every direction—spotted dolphins! They're like bottlenose dol-

Adolph Frohn, the first man to train a dolphin, performs at Seaquarium.
—*Miami Seaquarium*

ABOVE: Scene during
production of "Flipper"
show.—*Donn Renn, Ivan
Tors Studios*
RIGHT: Ric O'Barry rides
Hugo the Killer Whale.
—*Miami Seaquarium*

LEFT: Swimming with wild dolphins in the Bahamas.
—*Richard O'Barry, Dolphin Project Archives*
BELOW: "The Magnificent Seven" wild dolphins stop to check out Liquid Music.
—*Richard O'Barry, Dolphin Project Archives*

Joe and Rosie loaded aboard Army helicopter.—*Craig Kasnoff*

Jimmy Kline during Top Deck Show, Seaquarium.—*Miami Seaquarium*

Scene from "Flipper" show.—*Donn Renn, Ivan Tors Studios*

Abigail Alling, *left*, and Gigi Coyle, with R/V *Heraclitus* in background.—*Virginia Clark*

TOP: Joe, Rosie, and O'Barry, during un-training.—*Abigail Alling*
BOTTOM: Un-training Joe and Rosie at Dolphin Research Center.—*Abigail Alling*

Ric O'Barry and Hugh Downs' dolphin DeeDee, swimming free in the Gulf of Mexico.—*David Kent*

phins, but their bodies are covered with spots. With a yell of delight, I leaped into the water with them. *And the dolphins didn't swim away!*

I'd jumped into the water with wild dolphins before but they had always disappeared. Not these dolphins, though. These dolphins didn't seem to mind me. I popped to the surface and yelled: "Art! Look! Dolphins! My God, Art, the water is alive with dolphins! Hundreds! Look!"

Art nodded matter-of-factly. He had been studying the sky, which had suddenly darkened. A storm cell to the east was moving toward us and we needed to head south, out of the way. The wind was whipping up sudsy whitecaps. The last place you want to be during a storm is exposed like this. "Let's go!" he yelled down at me.

The dolphins were brushing past me in every direction. It was as if I were one of them and also as if I weren't even there. "Look at this, Art!" I held my hands up as if to show that it wasn't a trick, that it was real. "This is something wonderful, Art. I've never seen this before. Ha! Never! No kidding!"

Art clamped his teeth together. "And I'm not kidding you, Ricardo. Let's get outa here!" He jerked a thumb at the sky. "See that?" I glanced at the sky and Art revved the engine as if to go off without me.

Reluctantly, I climbed aboard. But the whole world had changed. From then on, I dreamed only of swimming freely with wild dolphins again.

For a while I was puzzled about why there were so many dolphins, why they didn't swim off when I jumped in with them. Looking back, I think I know. Like Indians following a herd of buffalo, they must have been feeding on a huge school of fish and were simply too busy to bother with me. Nevertheless, being with them and having them all around me and treating me as if I were one of them—that was an experience with no equal. Since then, several other divers have reported the same thing, the same spotted dolphins in the same place, who allowed people to swim with them freely.

We were heading back, catching the storm and indeed justifying Art's decision to leave immediately, and Art, holding the wheel, yelled above the roar of the wind that he thought I must have flipped when I jumped into what they thought was a school of sharks. We laughed. As a trainer of dolphins, I have always thought that despite my feelings for them, they would have left me if they could, that if they weren't held captive they would have had nothing to do with me. But these dolphins were different. They could have left—but didn't. I couldn't get over it. It was as if I had been one of them.

As often happens at sea, you can live almost in someone else's back pocket and yet be in a totally different world. Speaking from his own world, Art yelled above the wind, framing each word with great precision: "Do you think, Ricardo, that you could really train a dolphin to find sunken treasure?"

He had asked me this before, many times, but each time it seemed to be a fresh, new question for him. We were pitching and rolling with the waves, both of us holding to the wheel, and I waited for a break in the howling wind before replying. Then I answered as I always did, yelling and cupping my hands to my mouth: "Big enough budget, Art, yes." I nodded with certainty. "We could." I let a beat or two go by. "Man on the moon"—I pointed upward to where the moon would be if we could see it—"train dolphins to find treasure"—and I pointed downward into the sea, nodding broadly.

Art nodded. The weather had been quite nasty, angry eight- to ten-foot seas, waves breaking over the bow, and gale-force winds, the sky a black-purple with low, scudding clouds. It was all we could do to keep the bow into the waves.

"Who knows," I yelled, "but those dolphins out there might have been jumping for joy because they had just found the *Maravillas*."

Art cocked his head and looked at me oddly, raising one brow. I didn't often joke with him and he didn't know if I was kidding him or not.

Neither did I.

Saved by a Dolphin

If dolphins usually flee when they discover someone among them, how could I ever effectively study dolphins in the wild as I wanted to? Simply this: dolphins are attracted by certain music.

From early Greek times, legends have told us that dolphins are attracted by the music of the lyre, a kind of harp. The most famous legend, recounted in 400 B.C. by Herodotus, is about Arion, a Greek poet who lived a couple of centuries earlier. The poet had won an armload of gold prizes in a singing contest in Corinth and was returning by ship to his native Lesbos when the crew, which had got a glimpse of the gold, turned pirate and was about to make him walk the plank far at sea. He asked if he might play one last song on his lyre; the pirates consented. For his last show, the poet dressed in his finest robes and sang an orthian hymn, a shrill song to the gods, accompanying himself on the lyre. Whether the gods heard him or not, we can't be sure; but a dolphin heard him. A few moments later when Arion went over the side, the dolphin saved his life by keeping him afloat and pushing him to shore. Records show that Arion later gave thanks at the Temple at Taínaron for being saved by a dolphin.

It's common for dolphins to help one another. That's the way they're brought up. If a dolphin is sick or injured, other dolphins help him stay at the surface of the water so that he can breathe. I have seen dolphins keep other dolphins at the surface of the water long after they have died. When baby dolphins are born (tail first so that they won't drown), the mother dolphin and attending midwife dolphins push the baby to the surface for its first breath of air. It should not be strange that they would help humans the same way. Sailors have always told stories of dolphins saving drowning men by pushing them to shore.

But I never saw anything like that myself—except once.

Art McKee had brought his family out to see me and Susie at the Seaquarium. Kevin, Art's son, was about five years old then and was wandering out on the dock to look for Flipper. Art and I were standing off to the side, Art facing Flipper's Lake and keeping an eye on Kevin. I was facing Art. We were talking about something—probably gold— when all of a sudden, the unflappable Art McKee got a look of horror. I turned. Kevin had slipped and fallen in. But before any of us could move, Susie had pitched the child back onto the dock.

She did this—no doubt of that. But why she did it is the important question. To me it's simple. She did it for the same reason you or I would have done it: to save the child.

The Sound of Liquid Music

When I was training the dolphins who played Flipper, musician friends of mine used to come by: Fred Neil, Joni Mitchell, David Crosby, and some of the Mamas and Papas. I play the guitar a little myself and Fred noticed that when a chord was played and sustained on the twelve-string guitar, the dolphins became very attentive. The sound seemed to soothe them. Any chord would do but especially, he discovered, the D chord. The dolphins stuck their heads out of the water and listened attentively. Occasionally they would also come over to the guitar and very gently rub the tips of their snouts along the vibrating strings.

The dolphins' gentleness is what struck me as much as anything else. When they handled the props that were part of their repertoire of tricks—the hoola-hoops, the balls, and the hats that they were made to wear—the dolphins were quite rough, acting as if they held them in contempt. But when Fred played the twelve-string guitar, the dolphins approached the vibrating strings almost in reverence.

Did they want to feel the vibrations more closely? And if so, what did it mean to them? Or were they trying to play something for us?

Can dolphins compose music? Could we build a musical instrument for them? If so, we never learned what it was. The twelve-string guitar is not set up for the blunt snout of a dolphin.

Later I talked with Doug Trumbull, a Hollywood director now but then a special effects man for the movie *Close Encounters of the Third Kind*. He had looked me up because he was interested in interspecies communication. Since my career had been devoted to dolphins and the problems of communicating with them, I was one of a number of people Doug was questioning about how we might relate to creatures intelligent but totally different from us. I didn't know which movie he was working on then—I got the impression it was about an airplane—but when I saw *Close Encounters*, which is about man's first contact with an alien intelligence, I realized what we had been talking about.

We were at my home in Coconut Grove and I was telling him that I had thought I must be very clever to train dolphins so easily until it dawned on me that it wasn't my brilliance, but theirs.

"If we were ever to communicate with dolphins," I told him, "it probably wouldn't be in a conventional language, but with something neutral or something we had in common."

"Like what?"

I shrugged. I had a guitar in my lap at the time and I gave it a thrum. "Like music." I smiled as if this idea had just occurred to me. "Why not?" Then I told him about the twelve-string guitar and the dolphins' peculiar response to it.

Doug nodded. "And the music—how do you think it would go?"

No, I don't remember what notes I suggested. But I did toss off three or four pure whole notes and didn't think about it again until I saw the movie. His musical encounter with alien beings was beautifully done.

They "See" with Sound

Since then, I have gone a step further. I have lowered special waterproof speakers into the ocean and played music to attract dolphins. Captain Joseph A. Maggio took me and my sound equipment out into the Bahamas aboard his seventy-foot Bahamian schooner *William H. Albury,* which he renamed *Heritage of Miami.* We found the sandbar near the wreck of the *Maravillas* where I first swam with spotted dolphins. I lowered the speakers and turned up the volume. The sound going through water is heard—no, you can feel it—for half a mile in all directions. I call it Liquid Music and dolphins seem to love it. They come, they listen, and they stay.

Dolphins don't like all music. They are repelled by hard rock and other raucous sounds. They like the classics, though. They like full orchestras playing Strauss waltzes, for instance, or live music of the guitar, flute, clarinet, harmonica, African finger piano and various bells, also Ravi Shankar and other East Indian musicians using the sitar, which makes high-frequency pings like those of the dolphins.

Could music be our bridge to the dolphins? Why not? We live in a world of sight, they live in a world of sound. Compared with humans, dolphins are auditory geniuses, their aural capabilities light years beyond ours.

The dolphin is sensitive to vibrations ranging from 200 to more than 150,000 cycles per second through water, their most acute hearing between 30,000 and 60,000 cycles per second. That's a much higher range than we can hear. We hear from about 20 cycles a second to 20,000, most acutely around 3,000. What sounds are we talking about? If you play the bottom note on a piano, it vibrates about 27 times per second; the highest note on the piano, about 4,200.

Does that mean we're cut off from the dolphin's world of sound? No, we can pick up the full range of dolphin sounds with electronic equipment, then play it back at a slower speed. What we hear are very complicated sounds, rich patterns, sometimes two at once. And when dolphins are with one another, we hear the sounds going back and forth as if in conversation. The sounds themselves can be described roughly as blats, mews and yelps, wails and moans, whistles and pings, clicks, and even Bronx cheers. Some investigators have claimed that when they've slowed the dolphin sounds down, they can hear them imitating us: words, phrases, laughter. Unfortunately, this fascinating claim has resisted verification.

The interesting thing about the sounds that dolphins make is that they use them not only to communicate, but as sonar, an acronym for *SO*und *NA*vigation and *R*anging. It's also called "echolocation." The dolphin shoots a beam of sound through the water and when the echo bounces back, he can "see" what it hit.

Bats do the same thing. Lazzaro Spallanzani, an eighteenth-century Italian scientist, first suspected something of the sort with bats. He noticed that they could maneuver quite handily in crowded spaces, even when blindfolded. He thought that they must have an unusual ability to hear. But he never got much beyond that. His colleagues laughed at his theory, calling it "Spallanzani's bat problem." But in 1899, a hundred years after Spallanzani's death, electronic equipment was developed that verified what he suspected: that the bat uses echoes from high-frequency sounds he produces himself.

In 1947, the same idea was suggested about dolphins by Arthur F. McBride, first curator of Marine Studios in St. Augustine. He noted that when dolphins were being caught, they would charge at seines with large meshes but not the ordinary small-mesh seines—even in dirty water.

Indeed, tests show that they can "see" with their sonar as well as we can with our eyes. In one set of tests, a dolphin named Alice could distinguish between two steel balls, one 2.25 inches in diameter, the other 2.5 inches. She did this blindfolded. People given the same task need their eyes—and calipers. Dr. Kenneth S. Norris, one of the most astute of marine mammal watchers, says that when we truly understand the sounds of porpoises and their meanings, we'll find that they have an incredibly refined capability of "seeing with sound," even to the point of "forming sonic images" of their environment.

When I told Art that Susie could distinguish between gold and silver and other metals, I wasn't kidding. I've tested dolphins and they can assay metals. Other investigators have come to the same conclusion. Dr. Norris notes that dolphins can "hear the composition and texture" of things. Various metals and other materials reflect sonar waves differently, which means that dolphins, when they know what they're expected to do, can almost invariably tell the difference between plastic and aluminum of the same size and thickness, between copper and steel, gold and silver.

The most astonishing insight into the world of the dolphin is that their high-frequency sounds don't bounce off of living things. The vibrations are so small, they go through flesh and blood, right through skin, muscle and fat as if it were water. But the sounds reflect from air-containing cavities and bones, which means they would "see" one another, fish, or humans, as an x-ray machine would.

We keep putting quotation marks around "see" because we have no idea what sorts of images dolphins might create, if any. This is not just because they're dolphins. We don't really know about our fellow human beings, either. Or at least there's no way to have direct evidence of what imagery anyone else creates, if any. This is because there's no direct way for one person to compare mental processes with those of another person without becoming the other person. But if we can't do it directly, we can try to do it indirectly, with language. We can describe our experiences and compare the description with the way others describe theirs, and while that's not perfect, it's as good as anyone can expect. Our contact with other minds, be they human or dolphin, is through words, which is why we're all so interested in speaking the same language, whether theirs, ours, or something we make up.

The high-frequency sound of the dolphin has an interesting ethological ramification. If they can see through one another and presumably see the internal states of others first hand, what's the need for facial expressions, for example, to let others know how they feel? If others could read their internal state, there would be no point in hiding their feelings from others. Or pretending. They would be completely open. Transparent. They wouldn't know how to be dishonest or to lie. Their faces—it wouldn't matter what their faces were like, but they might as well be pleasant. It could be a mask that never changed. A smiling mask.

And that's the way it is!

In fact, all the comparable muscles that other animals use in expressing feelings are in dolphins concentrated at their blowholes.

Besides their hearing, dolphins can also see quite well, both in and out of the water. They have a highly developed sense of touch and they can taste things. Dolphins cannot smell, however. Though as a foetus, a dolphin has vestigial olfactory equipment, it withers away as the foetus develops, an echo of the atrophication of that sense during the dolphin's evolution.

Most of our human talents are visual. If we were to make contact with alien beings, we would know it because we had seen them. Consider what you would think of someone who merely *heard* alien beings. Or felt them. To us a thing is real only if we can see it. When we see it, we can describe it in words, which we can write down, using the symbols of one language or another, including math, or we can draw pictures of the thing we've seen. When *Voyager* 2 took off for deep space on August 20, 1977, it did include gold-plated phonograph records of music as well as photos. But mainly it had a gold picture of what humans look like and the location of Earth in our solar system. Inspired by Carl Sagan of Cornell University, the message assumes that alien life forms who might receive the message would respond visually as we would.

But what would happen if contact with alien beings were made by dolphins? That contact would almost certainly have to be in terms of sound.

Speculation beyond this point has got to be labeled science-fantasy, but it seems reasonable that if sound is to dolphins what sight is to us, then if alien beings produced the right kind of sounds, dolphins would respond by being friendly. If, on the other hand, the alien beings made a sound like a school of mullet, who knows what dolphins might do? In the same way, if alien beings looked like artichokes to us, we might boil them and eat them with melted butter; but if they looked human, we might be friendly—at least until we got to know them better.

If dolphins made contact with alien beings who made the right kind of sounds and if dolphins were enlightened enough to understand what was going on, they might very well treat the aliens the way they, the dolphins, would like to be treated themselves: with respect, kindness, patience, and love.

Indeed, they would treat the alien beings just as they have treated us.

5

The Hunt

They that go down to the sea in ships, that do business in
great waters; these see the works of the Lord, and his wonders in the deep.

—*Psalms* 107: 23, 24

I had been a member of the Miami Seaquarium Collecting
Team for about three months when we went on a collecting expedition
I will never forget. We headed the yacht *Seaquarium* to St. Helena
Sound off Beaufort, South Carolina, to capture the only known albino
dolphin in the world. This expedition was carried out like a secret
military mission. I didn't know where we were going until we were
under way. Later I realized why the secrecy was so necessary.

Captain William Gray was the Frank Buck of the sea, the best in
the world at bringing fish and sea mammals of all kinds back alive.
But twice before he had tried and failed to capture the white dolphin
off Beaufort. It's tempting to speak of Gray's quest for the white
dolphin in terms reminiscent of Ahab and Moby Dick. But there wasn't
a mystical bone in Captain Gray's body. Although there was more
than a little professional pride involved, our main interest was commercial. The white dolphin was one of a kind, the single most valuable
water creature in the world and certainly the most important quarry
Captain Gray had ever sought. Theoretically the albino was worth
whatever it took to capture her. In fact, though, there are limits.
Wometco, Inc., which owned the Miami Seaquarium, decided to give
Gray one more shot. Either way, Wometco officials told the good gray
captain, after this trip he must hang it up. He would be expected to

spend his time in the front office, a figurehead, meeting and greeting visiting dignitaries.

He loathed that prospect, and when they finally beached him, he used to steal away from his office and hang out with me and the dolphins at Flipper's Lake. He would sit in the shade of the coconut palms, skipping stones across the surface of the lake. He liked to work on nets, too, which were always in need of repair. At times when we were there together, they would page him over the public address system. He would shake his head mournfully, haul himself to his feet, and brush the sand off his suit. He would stand there a moment, pull out his big, heavy gold pocketwatch and check the time, then trudge back to his office.

The Vanderbilts had given him the watch when, as a young man, he captained their schooner *Pioneer* and led them on fishing expeditions around the world. The watch was magnificently ornate, engraved with mermaids and anchors. He once showed me the solid gold anchor chain that went with it. The chain was a little much, though, so he had replaced it with a simple monofilament fishing leader. After he had been beached and I had become Flipper's trainer, he used to bring special visitors back where I was working and tell them that this was where the Flipper films were made. Invariably they would look eagerly across the lake and ask: "But where's Flipper?"

Captain Gray would grin. It was the opening line of his standing joke. I knew what was coming so I looked up and grinned back. "That's Flipper, right there," he said, pointing his big square hand at me. "He's the *real* Flipper."

Capturing dolphins was just part of my job as diver aboard the yacht *Seaquarium*. We worked our tails off in the hot subtropic sun, setting the nets and pulling them in. It was not as hard or as frustrating as diving for sunken treasure, but it was backbreaking work nonetheless, the kind of work that turns your hands into big, strong lobster claws like Captain Gray's.

I had wanted to work at the Miami Seaquarium from the first time I saw it. That was during the Christmas holidays of 1955, just a few months after it opened. Home on my first fourteen-day leave from navy boot camp, I took my mother and two brothers, Jack and Terry, there, and it made an indelible impression on me. When I saw the diver in his Miller-Dunn helmet striding slowly around on the bottom as in a dream and feeding huge, dangerous, exotic fishes, I said to myself, "That's it." How we're supposed to pick out the goal for our whole life, I don't know, but from that moment on, my life had a goal. A few years later when I was actually working at the Seaquarium, it amused me that they should pay me for doing what was so much fun.

The biggest problem I had as a diver was feeding the sawfish without getting cut up. The sawfish, a strange creature, grows to the enormous size of 900 pounds and up to sixteen feet. A member of the ray family, the sawfish has a cartilaginous snout with twenty-five to thirty-two pairs of teeth. But it's the very sharp "teeth" on its long, flat bill that make this fish so dangerous. They're coated with poisonous mucous like that of the stingray's stinger. The sawfish's feeding style is (1) to rake the bottom with its bill, stirring up anything that lives there as a potential meal, and (2) to swim into a school of fish swinging its bill back and forth like a chain saw. Oddly enough, one of the safest places to be is at the sawfish's mouth. When the bill swings, the mouth, which is at the base of the bill, stays relatively still. To feed the sawfish and keep away from its menacing bill at the same time, I almost had to be a contortionist. I straddled the sawfish, facing the same direction it was facing, and got the food to its mouth by thrusting it between my legs from the back. And by *feel,* too, because if you look down wearing a Miller-Dunn helmet, it fills up with water.

Feeding the fish was quite a show for the spectators. It was one of the many shows we staged at the Seaquarium. The Seaquarium offers educational entertainment of the best sort, a circus sideshow and a college education rolled into one. The specimens we collected sometimes served in medical research, especially anatomical studies, and in research on underwater sound techniques. Some specimens were also used in research to develop shark repellents.

We Are the Bad Guys

Our quest for the albino of South Carolina was notable because for the first time we were the bad guys. The South Carolina State Legislature had passed a law against "netting, trapping, harpooning, lassoing or molesting genus *Delphinus* or genus *Tursiops* in the waters of Beaufort County." There have been marine mammal protection laws on the books for many years, going back at least to New Zealand

in 1904 and 1956, and even to Russia in 1966. But this was one of
the first marine mammal protection laws on the books in this country—and it was aimed directly at us!

We were the best dolphin hunters in the world—and proud of it.
But the albino was smart. She knew all the tricks. And she was lucky.
She eluded us at every turn. Frustration at sea becomes mysticism if
you let it, and I began to think we had met our match. Could she be,
I wondered, the dolphin who couldn't be caught?

The public hue and cry against us didn't help. Later I was to join
them in committing myself to the welfare of dolphins and other
whales, but then I thought that the people who were criticizing us
were weirdos. They acted like they owned the albino. I couldn't
understand it. We weren't going to *eat* the damned dolphin, we were
trying to catch her and put her in a show where millions of people
could enjoy seeing her. And what was wrong with that? The funny
part was that most of the people who were objecting to us had never
even seen the albino.

Their criticism stung, nevertheless, and we kept a low profile. We
never went ashore and we never talked to others about our mission.
There was a lot of talk on the shortwave radio, though, and we knew
how hot they felt about us. We hung around, waiting in the waters
of the adjoining county where it would be legal to capture the albino.
One group of protestors came out in boats and hoisted a sign that
said:

LEAVE OUR WHITE PORPOISE ALONE!

And from another boat, this one:

SOUTH CAROLINA'S WHITE PORPOISE, YES!
MIAMI SEAQUARIUM, NO!

They wrote letters to the editor of the local newspaper and they
vented their feelings on radio talk shows. Some of them followed us
in boats, and on the CB wavelength, we could hear them reporting
our position and heading. They planned to get in our way when we
set the net.

Not everyone was against us, though. A few of the commercial
fishermen, who dreaded pulling in their nets one day and finding the
beautiful white dolphin dead, were on our side.

*   *   *

To understand the difficulties of capturing the albino, consider first how we usually went about our job. The yacht *Seaquarium,* which we called the collecting boat, was designed by Captain Gray himself. Fifty-five feet long, the steel-hulled craft was powered by two 892-horsepower General Motors diesels and had a top speed of ten knots. What made it special was its live-well. A live-well, which is open to the sea, is where you put fish you've caught so that they will stay alive and fresh. In our case, the well kept specimens alive so that they could be put in the Seaquarium. It measured eight feet by twenty-one feet and was three feet deep. The well was open to the sea not amidships, as most live-wells are, but at the stern. This allowed us to haul in huge specimens, like small whales and large sharks. For collecting smaller specimens, which was more usual, the well could be partitioned by three sliding panels, including one at the stern of the boat.

Though Gray designed the *Seaquarium* to his special requirements, I never thought he felt comfortable on it. He liked the *Sea Horse* and *Sea Cow,* smaller but more easily handled work boats that the yacht had replaced.

Most of our collecting trips were to stock the twenty-six corridor tanks along the walls at the Seaquarium and the 235,000-gallon reef tank. The reef tank, our favorite, reproduced a Bahamian reef, complete with most of the species that live there. Fifty feet across and seventeen feet deep, the reef tank holds hundreds of species of tropical fish; thousands of individuals. We also supplied other large oceanariums around the world.

Usually there were only three of us aboard the collecting boat: Captain Gray; Captain Emil Hanson, his old friend but some years his junior, who was gradually taking over from him; and myself. We had two main collecting areas: (1) the Bahamas, especially around Turtle Rocks and the Berry Islands, south of Bimini, and (2) Miami's Biscayne Bay, which was in the Seaquarium's back yard. We went on all sorts of collecting trips for certain species like green turtles, jewfish and grouper, sea cows, snapper, snook and moray eels, or we trawled for sea horses and set lines for sharks.

Our trips ranged from excursions of half a day to, occasionally, a month. Some of our one- or two-week collecting trips to the Bahamas were scheduled, I suspect, simply because Captain Gray needed to get out on the water again.

Collecting in the Bahamas usually took two or three weeks. Captains

Gray and Hanson both had an uncanny feel for finding fish. Usually they needed only a glance at the water, but sometimes they would study the water through glass-bottom buckets for hours, searching for exactly the right spot to lay a trap or to string the shark line. I learned a great deal from both of them.

Hunting reef fish in the Bahamas, we often baited the traps with conch, a delicacy for fish and man alike. When we spotted a field of conchs, sometimes thousands of big, pink-shelled creatures crawling at glacial speed, I would go over the side with my face plate and fins. Captain Gray would cast off in the thirteen-foot skiff and drift across the grassy flats, his net on a six-foot pole held casually over the side. I'd swim down to the bottom, ten or fifteen feet below, gather an armload of conchs and bring them up. Captain Gray would extend the net over to me, and I would put the conchs in the net. He would empty them in the dinghy, and then down I would go again. Usually we filled the dinghy almost to the gunwales with conchs in an hour or so. Hundreds of conchs. Later, back on the collecting boat, we would knock off the heads of the shells with a hammer. Then we'd dig the conchs out with a rigging knife and put most of them on ice. We never wasted the conchs. Those we didn't use for bait, we ate ourselves. Conch fritters, conch chowder, conch salad, cracked conch, and even live conch or Bahamian sushi. Conch is widely known as an aphrodisiac, too, and recipes for it are legion.

The wire-screen traps we used for tropical fish were about three by two feet and had a funnel entrance. It was easy for fish to get in, but virtually impossible for them to get out. Besides conch, we used various other things for bait, sometimes a fish head or octopus (which we also caught on the reefs) or just a can of sardines with a few icepick holes in it. A few days later we came back and pulled up the traps. If we had caught anything we wanted, we dumped it in the live-well. If not, we dumped it over the side.

We also used a fine-meshed net to catch tropical fish, and sometimes, for special species, I swam down with a Slurp Gun. This is like a large syringe with a clear plastic barrel. Many of the fish we most wanted lived in tiny crevices in the coral. The yellowhead jawfish, for instance, is only four inches long and swims through the water like an appar-ition, fins and tail of gossamer blue on a pale white body topped by a blunt yellow head with big, black, round eyes. Another was the threespot damselfish, which is full grown at only three inches. This petite golden fish has vertical stripes from top to bottom behind the gills, and a large blob of black at the tail, designed to look like the eye of a larger fish. At the threespot's other end is an amazed expression. The little royal gramma is a vividly colored red and yellow fish with a purple head. As rare as he is beautiful, he sold for more than fifty dollars apiece then. The spotfin butterflyfish, which is eight inches long at maturity, has a stripe cutting deceptively through his eyes and a large black dot at the other end, no doubt designed to make him appear to be going the other way. Other reef fish include the crested goby, the darting brown chromis, the grunt and the angel fish.

When they saw me—swoosh! They were gone. They disappeared into their holes where they were safe.

Or so they thought. I would swim over to their lair, put the butt of the Slurp Gun over the hole and pull the handle back, sucking the little creatures out. Then I carefully transferred them to our floating holding tank.

Sometimes I took down an injector of ammonia. It works like tear gas. When I came to a likely crevice in the rocks, I squirted it with ammonia, and whatever was in there would come swimming out— mad as hell, usually—and into my net.

An Unfortunately High Mortality Rate

Unfortunately, many of the fish we caught died. Nobody kept close tabs on the actual numbers, but I would guess that about one out of ten survived. If we captured a thousand fish on the Bahamian reefs, for example, 450 of them would die before we could get them back to port. The 550 that survived to this point would be transferred to the corridor tanks of the Seaquarium. Despite all of our efforts, most of those would be dead by the end of the first week. Perhaps 100 of the original 1,000 would survive the ordeal of capture and go on living—sometimes for years—in the reef tank, making it their home.

I don't know how much the mortality rate could have been improved. One out of ten is probably pretty good. We tried to keep them all alive, of course, but I'm sure that if that priority had been higher, we could have tried a little harder. Keeping wild fish alive in captivity is not easy, especially salt water fish. They are such fragile creatures. Even the stress of being captured can kill them. So can even the slightest environmental change. Though the Seaquarium water is filtered at a rate of 3,000 gallons a minute and chemicals are used to fight harmful bacteria, the water is never as good from a fish's viewpoint as the water it was born and reared in.

If we lost nine out of ten fish we captured, we saved nine out of ten dolphins. We were more selective in capturing dolphins. We captured young females, usually. Being young, they were more tractable; being female, they were less inclined to be aggressive. And, as a kind of bonus, they reproduced themselves.

The dolphins we caught in Biscayne Bay and didn't want—the males, the older females and any of them with scars of shark bites—we turned loose. It got to the point where we caught some of them rather regularly. It was as if they thought getting caught was a game.

Sometimes when we went after dolphins we came away empty-handed, but that was rare. Usually we caught four or five at a time. Once we caught ten. We tried to be gentle with them and to keep them from thrashing about so much that they might hurt themselves. They were valuable animals; a young female was worth up to $400. A trained dolphin like Susie or Kathy, by contrast, was priceless. But that was then. Now, because of the change in the Marine Mammal Protection Act of 1972, you can hardly find a dolphin to buy, and if you can, it will cost you around $20,000.

The dolphins we collected went not only to Miami Seaquarium but to similar marine aquariums all over the world. They all wanted their own "Flipper." The dolphins ended up in all sorts of places: side shows, carnivals, state fairs, zoos, scientific labs and traveling circuses. They fell in with sharp promoters who used them to attract crowds at shopping centers or featured them in little sideshows at gas stations or to serve in a tiny, collapsible pool as the mascot of a football team. Susie was finally sold to a European promoter who carted her around in a trailer and showed her off at political gatherings. Some dolphins would also live, however briefly, as so-called pets in the chlorinated horror of someone's swimming pool.

The Miami Seaquarium Collecting Teams caught a great many dolphins, usually in Biscayne Bay just off Mercy Hospital. By collecting mostly females, which give birth only once a year, we were burning our bridges ahead of us, reducing the supply of dolphins that we would depend on in the future. But who thinks of the future when you're having the time of your life? The supply of dolphins seemed endless. If I had bothered to think about it at all, I would have assumed that someone else had already decided that it was okay to do this.

Catching a dolphin is like catching no other animal in the world, because the dolphin is the only animal in the world that rides the bow wave of a boat. When we saw a pod of dolphins, five to fifteen in-dividuals swimming as a group, in Biscayne Bay, we headed over in the collecting boat and before long they were riding the V of our bow wave. They probably do this because it's fun and they love games. Dolphins play very much like kittens and puppies. When they find a steady bow wave, they ride it. All day. When the boat changes speed or direction abruptly, however, they drop off.

Riding the bow wave of the collecting boat, they have no idea that they're about to fall into a trap. We used half a dozen or so kinds of nets to collect various specimens, sometimes making up special nets on the spot to fit the situation: the tide and wind, depth of the water, and condition of the bottom. Our dolphin net was made of nylon, twenty feet deep and a mile long. The top of the net was lined with cork so that it floated, the bottom had lead weights. One end was attached to the mother ship, the so-called bitter end, and most of the net was carefully piled up on the stern. I was in the dinghy with the running end of the net and when Captain Gray, who was watching the dolphins line up on the bow wave, gave me the signal—a chopping motion of his hand—I cut loose from the yacht and took off, dragging the net off in a wide circle. At the same time, the yacht began making a big slow turn. When the boat turned, the dolphins on that side of the bow were caught. By the time the collecting boat had made its turn, the dolphins on the inside began to realize that they were trapped. They fell off the bow wave and raced around, confused, or gathered in the middle.

You might wonder why the dolphins didn't leap over the net to freedom. And so did I. They could have. But they never did. Dolphins do jump in the wild, of course. In swimming, they leap forward out of the water all the time. The spinner dolphin (*Stenella longirostris*) even jumps and spins at the same time. Captain Gray, in his book *Creatures of the Sea,* noted that when a pod of dolphins is surrounded and discovers that it can't break through the net, one of them throws himself on top of the net, pushing it down and letting the others escape. We saw this occasionally, but whether it was done deliberately is another question.

As the net drew more tightly around this pod, and as the full im-plication of their plight became apparent, they swam more and more frantically, not knowing what to do. All of them were almost certainly shooting out sonar signals, reading them or trying to read them when they came bouncing back in a garble of noise from the net, from their fellow dolphins, and from the collecting boat. If they happened to hit the net, they struggled, twisting and turning. If we lost one dolphin out of ten during a capture, this was how it happened. They charged the net and thrashed around in panic, becoming entangled underwater, and drowning. I watched for that when hauling in the net. When dolphins got snagged by the net, I pulled them over to untangle them or I leaped in if necessary and freed them—even if it meant cutting the net.

Running Out of Time

This happened while hunting the albino off the coast of South Carolina. We were having problems with the bottom. It was covered with oyster shells, which snagged the net. A number of streams or rivulets emptied into the sound, making gullies at the bottom and gaps under the net.

The water of St. Helena Sound was as dark as coffee. We had spotted the albino swimming in unprotected water with several other dolphins. She was following one of the shrimp boats, and we had laid the net but had missed her. The albino saw what we were up to and scooted off with her baby. We spent the rest of the day pulling in the net. Halfway in, I saw a dolphin tangled in the net, belly up. He was dead. Captains Gray and Hanson saw it about the same time. We all stopped. Catching dolphins is not easy even when you know how. Catching them in strange waters is doubly hard. And trying to catch a particular dolphin in strange waters is—well, you've got to be lucky. Besides that, we were running out of time. The local people who had organized against us were getting on everybody's nerves. And if that dead dolphin washed up on shore, it would add fuel to the fire.

On a ship, the lines of authority are well established. Nobody wonders what to do. When I saw the dead dolphin, it was obvious what had to be done and who had to do it. I leaped in the water—clothes and all—and swam back to the dolphin. He was almost full grown. Probably five years old, 300 pounds. He had got caught in the net and drowned. I cut the net away with my rigging knife and cradled him in my left arm. Then I ripped open the gullet from below his chin to the belly, aiming for the air sack. There was lots of blood. Blood in such dark water is not red. Depending on the light, it is some shade of dark blue or black. Because the blood is warm, it rises, and when it touches the surface it becomes bright red. The dolphin's blood hit the surface like a surrealistic red splash and almost covered me. I let the dolphin go. It sank like a rock. Then I swam back to the dinghy, climbed aboard and continued pulling in the net. The whole thing happened swiftly and without a word.

I didn't think much about it at the time; there was no time for thinking. Besides, I wanted to prove that sinking the dolphin was no more to me than cutting up a mullet for bait. But there was more to it than that. I dreamed about that moment, the black blood curling up from the dead dolphin, becoming bright red and covering me. I still dream about it.

I See the White Dolphin

Before Capain Gray became a collector of fish, he had been a fisherman, once having caught a world-record marlin. Fishermen liked Gray. They felt comfortable with him. And like all seamen, they told tales, including the one about the albino.

Fishermen know dolphins well because dolphins follow the trawlers and eat the fish that fishermen don't want and toss back into the water. They also eat the fish that fishermen do want. They dive into the nets for a fish and dive out again before they can be caught. Some of them do get caught, though, and sometimes they drown—hundreds of thousands of them. Fishermen of ancient Rome called dolphins "pig fish" because, or so the speculation goes, either (1) their beak of a nose was like that of a pig or (2) they ate too many fish that fishermen thought should have been their own. The Latin term for "pig fish" was corrupted to "porpoise," the term that many people still use. Captain Gray always called them that. And in Europe that's their name.

The shrimpers and fishermen of Beaufort for years had watched the albino dive into their nets for fish and shrimp. One day, they knew, the albino would dive in for a fish and not come out again. Then the criticism directed now at the Miami Seaquarium would be directed at them. Quietly, therefore, some of them helped us. Beaufort County was off limits. But St. Helena Sound lay in both Beaufort and Colleton counties. It was only a matter of time before the albino would follow a shrimper across the line into Colleton.

That happened on August 4, 1962, the sixteenth day of our trip. We got a message from Sonny Gaye, one of the fishermen:

"Yacht *Seaquarium*. She's right behind me to starboard."

Captain Gray smiled and nodded. Captain Hanson was at the wheel. Our ship picked up speed and turned slowly, heading toward the trawler, which was a few miles away.

Another message: "She's got her baby with her."

We eased into position behind the trawler; the albino was now on our bow wave. I slipped back to the Boston Whaler where the net was. I could see the white dolphin, her pup swimming easily alongside. My heart was beating very fast. Suddenly Gray signaled me, the chopping motion of his hand. I dropped off and gunned the motor in reverse. The net spilled out. The *Seaquarium* made its big, slow turn. I looked for the albino. Already she had fallen off the bow wave and was trying to make her way to freedom. But she didn't know about me and my net. She hit the net and backed off. I closed the circle. She raced off to starboard, her baby right beside her. There was a gap there. I gunned the motor and closed it off. We had her. She hit the net and thrashed around. I leaped in and grabbed her; she was caught! Captain Gray beamed with delight. None of us had ever seen such a dolphin before. She was nearly eight feet long, about 375 pounds, pure white with pink eyes, a pink mouth—and black teeth! Like ebony. Her only flaw was a shark bite on her dorsal fin.

In all, it had taken Captain Gray fifty-eight days of actual pursuit over ten months to capture the albino—his last expedition. She was named Carolina Snowball. A $100,000 tank with a picture window was built for her and her baby, who was named Sonny Boy in honor of Sonny Gaye, the South Carolina fisherman who had led her into our trap.

Carolina Snowball's trainer was Adolph Frohn, but she proved to be an intractable sort, learning only one rather simple stunt: swimming in synchronization with Gay Idema Ingram, who still lives in Coconut Grove. Despite her refusal to learn tricks, which I secretly admired, Carolina Snowball was the Miami Seaquarium's star attraction, drawing millions of people from around the world to see and admire her.

*   *   *

Three years later she developed an infection at the base of her tail. She began swimming erratically one day and, to the horror of tourists watching, she veered into the picture window with a sickening thud. Despite the heroic efforts of Robert Baldwin, director of operations at Miami Seaquarium, she died.

In an autopsy, doctors discovered all sorts of problems. She had a tumor of the stomach as large as a tennis ball, cirrhosis of the liver, emphysema, cysts embedded in several organs, and muscles full of parasites. Nothing could have been done for any of this.

To mark the delight she brought to so many people who came to see her, Carolina Snowball was mounted in a playful pose at the entrance of the Main Tank of the Miami Seaquarium. She's in a place of honor on the wall near the popcorn stand.

6

Glory Days

There is only one success—to be able to spend your
life in your own way.

—Christopher Morley

When Captain Gray stepped down to become a figurehead,
his power at Miami Seaquarium devolved to others like spoils of war.
Captain Hanson was now in charge of the collecting boat, Warren
Zeiller the curator in charge of exhibits. Warren was a role model for
me. He, too, had been in the navy (submarines), and loved working
at the Seaquarium almost as much as I did. Everybody seemed to be
changing except me. I mentioned this to Captain Gray one day. "Everybody
else is moving on," I said. "I feel like I'm going backwards."

He just nodded and I thought I might be stuck there my whole life.
But the next day he asked if I would like to join the Underwater Show
as a diver. Usually I try to keep from showing how I feel about things
but I couldn't help myself. I broke into a big grin. Gray was grinning
back at me.

Going from the collecting boat to the Underwater Show was an
incredible change for me. It was like night and day or, more exactly,
work and play. On the collecting boat, you worked. In the Main Tank
feeding the fish, it was play.

We all enjoyed our collecting expeditions in the Bahamas, naturally,
but much of the time we spent at the dock, working. A seventy-two
foot boat needs constant upkeep. Cleaning, fixing, and replacing gear.
Chipping paint and painting. Repairing nets. Checking supplies, ordering
equipment, stocking it, and forever working on the engine. It

was like working in a garage; the moment you finished one job, there was another one to do. But it was not a new job. It was the same job you did a month ago and six months before that. And when all that was done, you chipped paint and painted again. There's no end to the work at sea. The salt, the subtropical sun, the restless wind and the constant strain of the sea work their implacable will on men as well as boats. It was exhausting. Endless. Frustrating. And solitary.

Becoming a diver in the Underwater Show had been a dream of mine since the moment I first saw one. The Main Tank was a world in itself, an arena full of enchanted monsters. Eighty feet from side to side and seventeen feet deep, it held more than 600,000 gallons of sea water. Every day the Seaquarium used about a million gallons of water from Biscayne Bay, which was filtered at a rate of 3,000 gallons a minute and monitored by the lab each day. Although I worked on the collecting boat at the bay side of the Miami Seaquarium grounds, I occasionally walked through the show areas, usually en route to the main office, and couldn't help but notice the divers. They looked sharp: black wet suits, the diving helmet with the hoses coiling upward, a diving knife strapped to the ankle. Very Hollywood. The girls noticed them, too, and I noticed that.

Who noticed me? Nobody. I wore work clothes because I worked. On the collecting boat we really worked, all of us, even Captain Gray, sweat pouring off us, our fingers and hands hardening like shells. Most people didn't even know we existed, and nobody gave a damn.

By contrast were these play-acting divers in the Main Tank, their every movement followed minutely by adoring crowds, including swarms of girls dripping over them and over every word about them. This was not real. They were drugstore divers. As they dream-walked about on the bottom of the Main Tank, feeding and caressing exotic species, the hollow-voiced announcer explained their every move to the crowds:

"And now, ladies and gentlemen, if you will direct your attention ...you will see the moray eel slithering around the diver like a snake. The moray eel is hungry. See those teeth? Yes, those needlelike teeth are real, all right, and just as sharp as they look. You see the moray eel opening and closing his mouth constantly, not to threaten the diver but to breathe. That's how he forces water through his gills, which extract oxygen from the water. If he ever got mad about something— but don't worry about the diver, folks. The diver and that moray eel are on friendly terms. And now...."

And so it would go; the crowd, usually from mid-America where sea creatures were found only in books and movies, would gasp in disbelief and admiration.

Was I willing to exchange my difficult and dangerous but honest work aboard the collecting boat for something this frivolous, where sweat in the sun was replaced by fun, exhaustion by exhilaration, pain by thrills and the dull ache of loneliness by admiring crowds and girls with fluttering sighs?

I've never been one to rush headlong into momentous decisions. I considered my options carefully. This took about a second, which was twice as long as necessary. Did I want to become a diver? Yes, I did. Desperately so. As soon as possible. After years of backbreaking work at sea, yes, I would do almost anything to become one of the drugstore divers. Yes, yes, I could hardly wait.

And I got a 15 percent raise to boot!

Dave and Clown

You would expect some cruelty in people made subservient to animals. It's probably human nature, a way to assert their alleged superiority. But some people need to assert themselves more than others. You'll find cruelty at zoos, prisons, and virtually everywhere else: at hospitals, lawyers' offices, at work, on the road and at sea, on the golf course and at home, anywhere authority and resentment mix.

You could argue that aquariums in themselves are cruel. For a while I tended to think that way. But if they are, it's a very subtle cruelty, and in fact I no longer think that aquariums are necessarily cruel. By "cruelty," I don't mean something less than ideal for the specimens on display. The kind of cruelty I mean is the crude kind, the deliberate, physical injury or humiliation of another being.

Miami Seaquarium had very little of that. We lived in a fish bowl, after all, and our secrets were few. Also, this was show business, and we were dependent on the happiness and joy that we could bring not only to our patrons, who were sensitive to the slightest sign of cruelty, but also to our wondrous wards.

But cruelty, nevertheless, sometimes did flare up. I remember it happening one time when we fed the fish. Feeding the fish is a three-man job: one man hand-feeds the fish, the second guards the feeder from marauding dolphins, and the third is the divers' tender, manning the air supply and acting as lifeguard topside. Head diver Jack Bacerra was in charge, but we alternated the jobs and this day it was my turn to feed the fish, Dave's to guard, and Jack's to be tender. Dave was big and strong and blessed with athletic quickness. He had dark-blond hair, a flashing smile and a temper to match; but he'd been doing this too long, and may have got his priorities mixed up.

Dave and I, wearing wet suits and Miller-Dunn helmets, were on the bottom of the main tank, our air hoses coiling upward. During the Underwater Show, we circled the tank twice, which tended to snarl the hoses. Keeping them straight was Jack's job, but that was simple compared with what happened when the sea turtles hit the hoses. These clumsy 400-pound monsters seemed to be drawn to the hoses. Sea turtles have but a tiny brain, and only a tiny part of that do they ever use. Their idea of fun was to take a deep breath and go down to snooze for an hour or so. When they hit our hoses they swam off in a wild tumult of frantically paddling legs, twisting the hoses and sometimes cutting off our air or simply yanking the helmets off our heads. Though this happened with some regularity, none of the divers was ever hurt that way.

The feeder went down with a wire basket of fish, blue runners usually, and fed all the specimens except the dolphins. Dolphins were fed only in the Top Deck Show so that they would perform more eagerly. A dolphin that's just been fed has little interest in jumping through a hoop. According to theory, since the dolphins had already performed and been fed by the time we went down for the Underwater Show, they wouldn't pester us for more fish. But they always seemed to be starving. Captain Gray in his writings described the problem like this: "The porpoises [dolphins], not satisfied with their own meal, try in every way to get their snouts into the basket for a second helping."

Fair enough, but there was more to it than that. I think the dolphins didn't like the idea of the fish being fed while they, the stars of the show, were not. They devised a little game. It was called "Get the Fish." And that is exactly what they tried to do. With all their speed, their power and their oceanic wiles, the dolphins tried to steal the fish from the diver.

It was the guard's job to keep this from happening.

Big and fast and sleek and powerful, a dolphin could swim the whole tank before we could take three steps. Like wild torpedoes, the dolphins could slash in from any angle and knock us off our feet with their wake. And they did, too, especially me, because I was the smallest of the divers. The dolphin, king of the seas, also could have mauled and maimed us with powerful flukes and mouth, but never did.

The dolphins used ingenious tactics. Sometimes they came in squads, two or three together like World War I fighter planes; but more often they came alone. Sneak attacks. They came swooping past us, whirling us around with the force of the swirling water. Or more directly, they struck the arm that held the fish bucket, trying to knock the bucket loose and cause a wild scramble for the spilled fish. When they darted in and went for the fish, sometimes they got our hands by mistake. We wore steel mesh under yellow gloves of heavy rubber, but being nipped by a dolphin is still like being hit with a ball-peen hammer. Dolphins are natural tricksters: clever, strong, relentless. Moreover, these dolphins could get away with anything, and they knew it. They had been in the Main Tank for years, most of them. They were tank wise. Four times a day, this bizarre spectacle took place, the most graceful of sea creatures in the world dazzlingly outwitting us poor plodders of the deep.

A Vicious Jab

I had almost finished circling the main tank the second time when I remembered something. "Did I feed the large nurse shark?" I asked myself. I looked around for the seven-foot creature, turning slowly as everything underwater is done. "No," I answered, shaking my head. Talking to oneself and more especially answering oneself is considered odd on land. But in diving, when all is silent and there is no one else to talk to, it's okay. Almost all helmet divers sing underwater. The resonance is even better than in the shower. One also tends toward broad gestures underwater as in pantomime, acting out everything for the faces pressed against the glass. "Nope," I continued, "haven't seen the nurse shark. And where-oh-where could he be?" Actually I hadn't fed him in a couple of weeks and didn't know for sure if anyone else had. Sharks can go for weeks without eating, but they shouldn't. "Maybe I should look around for Mr. Nurse Shark," I said to myself. "All right. Don't mind if I do." I plodded across the sand to the intake pipe where the big nurse shark usually hung out. And there he was.

The nurse shark is sandy colored and looks like a big catfish. He even has long whiskers like a catfish at each side of his mouth. These are actually tasters. The nurse shark sleeps a lot. He can be dangerous, though, if you're not careful. Like the jewfish, the nurse shark inhales his food. He creates a suction in his mouth, then opens his mouth and sucks everything in, grinds it up with his row upon row of tiny teeth, and spews the scales and other refuse out through his gills. Once I got a little careless and a nurse shark inhaled my hand, but I pulled it out in time. A 500-pound jewfish once sucked up my whole arm, which startled him, I think, as much as me. Sharks and jewfish hung out near the intake pipe because the jet of incoming water flowed through their mouths and out their gills, a cheap way of breathing.

"There you are," I said to myself. The nurse shark had stuck his head under a pile of rocks near the intake valve. I grabbed him by his tail and dorsal fin and pulled him out, turned him around and shook a blue runner under his nose. Sharks actually have taste buds in their skin. When you're in the water with them and they brush against you, they are actually tasting you. "Come on," I said to the nurse shark, shaking the blue runner in his face. "Wake up and have a bite." This was the kind of moment dolphins looked for. Normally when I fed fish, I did it quickly, my hand darting into the stainless steel basket, grabbing the blue runner and thrusting it out so that dolphins couldn't sneak in and get it. I looked around. No problem this time, I thought. Only one dolphin lurked near. It was Clown. She was the star of the Top Deck Show. Bright, cooperative, and fun-loving, Clown did the cigarette jump (leaping up and snipping off a cigarette in the trainer's mouth), the double jump (leaping in unison with another dolphin), and wore a hat (she put on a straw hat the trainer tossed into the water). But Clown was not a saint. She did enjoy sneaking a forbidden snack. From about fifteen feet away, like all the dolphins, she watched, hovering about five feet off the bottom. She was near Dave. Too near.

The Miller-Dunn helmet has round glass ports on each side. You can turn your head inside the helmet and look out of them. I had turned my head and was looking out of my left port to see what Clown was doing when, to my horror, I saw Dave suddenly lunge with the pole and jab her viciously in the lower belly. Startled, Clown swam off. She was hurt, I could tell. She swam erratically, this way and that.

I could hardly believe it. "Why?" I said. It made me sick. "Damn you, Dave," I said. I wanted to look for Clown but she was gone now.

Later, she had a miscarriage. Had Dave caused that? I don't know. I looked at the blue runner in my hand. A dead fish. "And for this?"

Always Borderline

I put the fish back in the basket. I was in no mood to spoon-feed an indifferent shark. I headed for the ladder, walking as fast as possible but still as slowly as if I were on the moon. Dave followed me. I wanted to yank the pole away from him and jab him with it. What a show *that* would have been for the spectators. I could feel their eyes upon me. Had they seen Dave plunge that pole into the defenseless dolphin? Were they watching to see what I would do about it? Would there be complaints?

When you walk up the ladder, there are hooks to hang your helmet on. The helmet weighs about fifty pounds in air, and by craning your neck just right, you can look up through the small top front port and get an idea where the hook is, which you have to line up with the handle on top of the helmet. When they're engaged, you lower yourself out of the helmet and walk on up the ladder and out of the tank. When both of us were out, I was still fuming. "What was all *that* about?"

Dave looked puzzled. "Huh? Do what?" He brushed his blondish hair back with his hands.

"Clown. You were a little rough with that pole, don't you think?" I waited a moment for him to explain but he was pretending not to know what I was talking about. "She wasn't doing anything," I said. "I saw the whole thing. She was just watching."

"Clown? Watching? Oh, that. Ha!" he said, wagging his head. "You don't know Clown." He tossed a conspiratorial glance at Jack, who bent to the task of rolling up the hoses.

"I *saw* it," I said. "What the hell, Dave. What do you think we're doing here, anyway?"

"Wait a minute." He laughed and held up his hands in restraint. "Why am I getting the feeling that you're mad about something?"

"Because I am mad."

"Hold on a minute. I like to look at things from both sides because, well, that's just the kind of guy I am, I guess"—he grinned disarmingly—"but in this case, Ric, I don't see another side. Nothing."

"Then listen to me! You jabbed Clown with that pole! You didn't have to!"

"I popped her, sure. But whatever else you think I'm doing, I'm doing for you. I'm the guard, remember? If we don't keep 'em in their places," he shrugged, "they'll walk all over us." He nodded vigorously. "Yeah, man. Up one side and down the other."

I was speechless.

He went on: "What do I think we're doing here? I *know* what we're doing here." He gave me a sympathetic look. "But you have no idea what's going on here, do you?"

I was shaking my head. I knew that I was right but I had the feeling that I was losing this argument. "She's pregnant, Dave. You know that."

Dave looked amused. He had been a diver in the Underwater Show for years and years, yet here I was, the new guy, trying to tell him how to handle a dolphin. It was funny, too, because I weighed 120 pounds dripping wet, and he weighed nearly twice as much. "If she was half as smart as you seem to think they are, she wouldn't have been that close to me, now would she? Don't let it bother you," he drawled, starting to turn away.

I pushed my face up to his and my voice got reedy. "But it *does* bother me, Dave. I want to know just one thing: why?"

He grinned lazily. "Why did I pop her?" He shrugged. "'Cause I wanted to. Okay with you?" He nodded approval of himself and hunched forward, that big tyrannosaurus jaw of his hanging in my face. I have had sharks do this to me and it felt about the same. Dave wasn't smiling. He had no expression at all.

I was still mad as hell about it but I wasn't stupid. I was scheduled to feed the fish in the reef tank, so I traded Jack my nearly empty basket for the full feeding basket, and headed over to the ladder at the reef tank.

Jack finished rolling up the hoses. He had said nothing but he'd been listening. As I left, he looked up at Dave. "Like the song says: 'Don't be cruel.'"

That's about as much as anyone ever lectured anyone else. There was never any heavy talk among the divers, certainly not about how to treat the fish and dolphins. There were better things to talk about. Girls, for instance. There was an endless stream of starry-eyed, pubescent girls who seemed to be fascinated by guys in wet suits feeding monsters of the deep. We talked about that at times, but never about the job. It was always assumed that we knew what to do and what not to do.

When I became a diver in the Underwater Show and first saw Dave roughing up a dolphin, I realized that he was not like the rest of us. The first time I noticed, it wasn't flagrant—it was almost like a joke—and I didn't say anything. A new, young dolphin got too close to Dave and got bopped on the snout. It was borderline. Then I noticed that Dave was always doing something like that. He pushed the dolphins around every chance he got, jabbed them with the pole, kicked them— I thought that he must hate the dolphins. Dave probably began by just trying to intimidate them, then it became a habit. He did intimidate them, incidentally. The dolphins were afraid of him. When he was in the water, they usually kept their distance.

It might seem strange that one guy could get away with acting like that. But I think he was acting out what the rest of us at one time or another wanted to do but didn't. We tolerated Dave's cruelty without approving of it because we did have a problem with the dolphins. The dolphins, in fact, were our only problem. Except for the dolphins, the job of feeding the fish and other creatures in the Main Tank would have been a snap.

War of the Dolphins

But viewed from afar, we divers were just part of the show, and a small part, at that. It was the dolphins' show; divers were like supporting actors, comic relief for the clever stars. Dave didn't realize this. And because the dolphins did realize it, their relentless opposition was like the War of the Dolphins. It was like Vietnam, which was going on then; there was no way we could win this war, and this must have galled Dave.

The struggle with the dolphins had been going on long before I joined the divers. Most of what we did was aimed at frustrating the dolphins. Wearing the steel mesh glove, for instance, didn't just happen, and neither did the stainless steel basket with the snap top. And the guard—there was no guard the first time out. That came later. When that wasn't enough, the guard armed himself with a pole. But except in Dave's hands, the pole was hardly adequate. We discovered that a blast of the compressed air from a spear gun scared them off. So the guard began taking down a spear gun and blasting the dolphins with the bubbles. This looked good to the spectators and kept the dolphins at a distance. But it only worked for about two weeks. Then we tried shooting little rubber-tipped spears at them. This had no effect at all. Finally, in desperation, we jabbed at the dolphins with the spear gun as we had with the pole. But still the dolphins played their game.

This same sort of game goes on in the wild, too. Fishermen off the Kona coast of the big island of Hawaii have been struggling for years with one device after another, trying to discourage rough-toothed dolphins (*Steno bredanensis*) from stealing the live skipjack tuna bait. They have tried a variety of booby traps: wrapping the bait with wire, coating it with pepper, using extra hooks, inserting a stiff wire—even poison. But nothing works. The dolphins figure it all out and go on stealing the bait. This began in 1949 with a single dolphin, a Pacific bottlenose dolphin (*Tursiops gilli*). It was a curiosity, the fishermen thought. Now all the dolphins do it.

In the Seaquarium's Main Tank, I was always aware of the people on the other side of the glass watching us feed the fish and battle the dolphins. It was like being on stage. Being underwater has always had a cinematic quality anyway, like being in a dream or in the movies. It's as if you're sitting in the audience, eating popcorn, say, but then you really get involved. Suddenly you're on the stage, then as if by magic you're in the silver screen itself, arguing with the actors in the movie. I never got that carried away, but with everybody watching, it was tempting. From the inside we could see the spectators clearly, their faces pressed against the glass, their eyes wide with wonder.

Though they always reacted strongly to anything that seemed cruel, they might never know about the real cruelty: neglect. If a specimen died because it hadn't been fed, for example, nobody said a word. Nobody in the crowd would ever know. No grave, no marker, no fine last words. But let a single spectator complain about a single act that seemed cruel to him, whether it was cruel or not, and we heard about it from on high. There had been several complaints like that about Dave.

Most cruelty was a result of ignorance. We were all ignorant to some extent of the dolphins' needs, but some were more ignorant than others. Once, in Brazil, I checked on the condition of several dolphins that had been captured by a licensed dolphin hunter off Key Largo. The dolphins were all blind. I knew what had happened. In shipping, the boxes that the dolphins were packed in were not kept clean, and the dolphins were blinded by their own urine.

We were all blind at times.

7

Seaquarium Show Biz

> This is the common porpoise found almost all over the
> globe. The name is of my own bestowal; for there are more
> than one sort of porpoises, and something must be done to
> distinguish them.
>
> —Herman Melville, *Moby Dick*

There were two dolphin trainers at Miami Seaquarium when
I became a diver there: Adolph Frohn, who came from Germany, and
Jimmy Kline, of Fort Walton Beach, Florida. Both came to the Sea-
quarium when it opened in 1955; Adolph from Marine Studios in St.
Augustine, Jim from an aquarium in Gulfport, Miss. They never spoke.

To say that they disliked each other would be an understatement.
They not only never watched each other's shows, each also pretended
that the other didn't even exist. Occasionally as I crossed the grounds,
I noticed them approaching the snack bar from different directions,
and I stopped to watch. It was always the same, each of them looking
the other way or straight ahead.

Adolph Frohn was the first person ever to train a dolphin. A large
man with an ego to match, Adolph taught a dolphin to jump through
a hoop just as he had taught other animals the same thing. Dressed
in starched whites head to toe, his uniform trimmed in epaulets and
the bill of his captain's hat resplendent in "scrambled eggs," Adolph
Frohn enjoyed center stage at the Golden Dome, which was the major
show for tourists at Miami Seaquarium. A natural impresario, Adolph
had a florid style with large flourishes like a magician. He had a thick
German accent and never spoke during his show. While Adolph and
his animals went through their silent choreography together, an an-

nouncer told the audience what was going on. The show was billed as an animal act—sea lions, seals, pelicans, dolphins, and penguins—but it was really the Adolph Frohn Show. He was a proud man and moved on the stage with a precision that suggested each moment of his act had been hewed and polished through the generations. And that was probably so, for he was the last of a long line of German animal trainers.

Jimmy Kline was practically the opposite of Frohn. When Jimmy poised on high at the Main Tank and held a blue runner aloft for Pedro's climactic leap, he looked like a high-school football star. He was a handsome, all-American boy with sandy-blond hair, rather bright but narrow-minded, and the unfortunate victim of his own success. He had worked himself into a comfortable niche and now it bored him. Jimmy appeared to be friendly and outgoing, but he wasn't. When not on stage, he was phlegmatic and kept to himself, spending most of his free time between shows in the air-conditioned snack bar drinking coffee. I never saw him wear anything but white clam-digger pants, which are cut off at the calf, and a red Banlon shirt. His shoes, when he wore them, were thongs. His passion: orchids. He found orchids in the wild and brought them back to grow in his own greenhouse.

Mankind's relationship with animals over the years has been studied rather carefully. A trained-animal act is amusing at best these days, but not too long ago the sight of a dancing bear, for example, was almost incredibly funny. Dancing? A bear? Turning nature on its head was always amusing. But nature is not viewed the same way these days. People's attitudes change with each generation, sons seeing little of the humor their fathers did in things like dancing bears. In some ages, as depicted in ancient fables, animals were our friends or at least equals. Animals and people talked together. Gods sometimes took the form of animals, including the dolphin, and some societies either deified or defiled certain animals. Dolphins were the sacred "fish" of the Greeks. Apollo took the form of a dolphin to lead settlers to Delphi, which was later the seat of the Delphic Oracle.

With the triumph of Christianity, all that changed. Nature became the bad guy. And animals were a part of nature. When the soul was attributed to man and not the animals, the pious decided that if we didn't keep tight rein on our passions, we too could return to the level of beasts. The animal nature in each of us was like the Devil himself

waiting to snare the unwary. Man pictured himself as a sort of amphibian, one foot in heaven, the other in nature with the animals. He
considered passion, emotion, and feelings as signs of his animal nature,
the beast in each of us that must be restrained. To many people,
civilization itself is but the restraint of animal emotion on the largest
scale. Without laws, they say, we would all revert to the level of savage
brutes.

Are Animals Just Machines?

From some viewpoints, a straw hat on a billy goat has got to be
about as funny as anything can get. And a straw hat on a dophin?
Wow! That's about as funny as funny gets. Jimmy Kline certainly
thought so. This is usually called anthropomorphism. But not by me;
to me it's mockery. We are not just attributing human qualities to
animals, which is what anthropomorphism is, we're making fun of
them, expressing our speciescentricism as scorn and ridicule. Most of
Jimmy's tricks involved this. And so did Adolph's. This is not to fault
them. Their job was to amuse the crowds. When the dolphin leaped
high in the air and did its flips, walked backwards on its tail-flukes
and then put on a straw hat and begged for food, the crowd roared
its appreciation. It amused the crowd to humble such a mighty and
graceful being.

I don't know what Adolph Frohn thought about animals; I never
talked to him about it. But he treated them like machines. The early
behaviorists thought that if you pushed the right button, you could
get an animal to perform. The animal-machine idea has been traced
to the French Christian philosopher Descartes in the early seventeenth
century. He said that animals have neither souls nor consciousness.
How could he be so sure? It said so in the Bible. And if that were so,
then animals couldn't feel or think. And obviously they had no language. That's why talking to animals seems so strange to some people.
Immanuel Kant proclaimed that animals were merely a means to an
end, and the end is man.

Jimmy Kline clearly subscribed to the animal-machine idea. Most
people did. It was common sense. Jimmy's views were narrowed even
more by his deep belief in religious fundamentalism, which taught that
animals were placed on earth to be used. And that included making
fun of them.

Adolph and Jimmy are probably guilty of nothing more serious than pandering to boorish tastes. And I must plead guilty to that myself, for I too have put my share of straw hats on dolphins.

How could I do such a thing?

It was my job. And I was ambitious and sometimes very stupid.

The Top Deck Show

Adolph Frohn had five assistants at all times, dozens of them over the years. Not one of them ever learned how he trained his animals. When he needed to teach the animals a new trick or, more often, when he needed to teach a new animal the old tricks, he locked the door and drew the curtains. Day after day, sometimes for weeks he worked, and when finally he emerged, the animals were trained. Then he or anyone else could do the show. He almost always did the show himself, though, because he enjoyed it. His assistants' main job was to clean up after the animals. Pelicans and sea lions are especiallly messy.

Though I was still a diver in the Underwater Show, I also became Jimmy Kline's assistant, taking over the show on weekends and whenever Jimmy couldn't do it. Technically I was a dolphin trainer but I never trained the dolphins to do anything. Jimmy Kline had already trained the dolphins to do the show and they did it automatically, as Jimmy Kline did: the same show, four times a day, day after day.

If you thought that animals were machines, this show would do nothing to dissuade you. But if the dolphins were machines, so was Jimmy Kline. He was more of a cog than the dolphins were, for at least the dolphins received their payment immediately after doing a trick; Jimmy had to wait till the end of the week.

At showtime, the dolphins started whether Jimmy was there or not. They knew exactly when it would begin, because of the sounds the crowds made as they filed in and ringed the top of the Main Tank. The dolphins would jump with joy, stick their heads out of the water and chatter at the crowds, and do a practice jump or two. Most of all, the dolphins probably felt hungry. It was feeding time for them. As they leaped around like a circus gone wild with joy, the trainer's main job was to keep up with the dolphins and aim the fish he threw them well. They were supposed to get twelve pounds a day; he had to keep track of that, too.

The First Show

All of us divers in the Underwater Show knew Jimmy Kline's narration by heart. Waiting to go on—or down—when Jimmy had finished, we sat on a bench against the wall and heard him four times a day. It never varied. When Warren Zeiller, Jimmy's assistant, was made curator, taking over part of Captain Gray's role, I took Warren's place. I was promoted over several other divers who had been there longer than I had. In fact I was going up the Seaquarium's ladder faster than anyone else ever had. Why me? I loved the job and I followed the work ethic invented by Ben Franklin. I showed up for work earlier than anyone else, I stayed later than anyone else, and I worked seven days a week. I wore a coat and tie to work and said "Yes, sir" and "No, sir" to everyone in authority. That was surely the main key to my meteoric rise in the ranks.

But it couldn't have hurt that earlier I had saved a life during a filming of the capture of tropical fish in the reef area of Turtle Rocks near Bimini. It was winter—very cold—and we were all in wet suits. Captains Gray and Hanson and I were all in the water with Ted Sack, president of Reela Films, not swimming but walking on the reef in big clumsy rubber boots, all of us wearing about twenty-five pounds of lead to keep us from being washed away by the strong tide. We were busy capturing small tropicals with our Slurp Guns and small nets while Ted walked around us with his 16 mm. underwater camera. He ran out of film, headed toward the skiff to get some more and simply walked off the reef. The current got him and carried him into deep water. He hit the quick-release buckle on his weight belt and it fell between his legs out of reach, but it was caught on the harness of his scuba tank backpack. Captains Gray and Hanson and I didn't see any of this, but Larry Witt, the cook aboard the collecting boat, saw what happened and yelled.

I'm certified to teach snorkeling and scuba diving. I tell my students that in a situation like that it's your gear or your life, because you'd be surprised at the number of people who try to save their weights. I was about 100 feet away, which in that current seemed like a mile. I dropped my weights, kicked off my boots, and swam over as fast as I could. How I got there in time, against the current without my swim fins, I don't know, but I did and managed to pull him with all his gear back to the reef—he wasn't blue but he didn't look good, either— then I got up to shore where I could pump him out. When we got back to port, Ted wrote a letter about it to officials of the International Red Cross and to the late Mitchell Wolfson, who owned Wometco, Inc., which in turn owned Miami Seaquarium. I got a nice letter from Mr. Wolfson and, at a large and formal ceremony of the Red Cross, a commendation.

But if Jimmy Kline hadn't wanted me as his assistant, I wouldn't have gotten the job. When I arrived for my first show, Jimmy Kline checked out my uniform. He didn't smile. "You're not nervous, are you?" he asked.

"No," I lied.

"Well, don't be nervous." The crowd had gathered and the dolphins had begun leaping, a sign that the show was about to begin. He glanced out at the crowd, a big one, then back to me. "You know the routine, don't you?"

"By heart."

He nodded. "Just do it like I told you." Our eyes met for a moment and slid away. "If anything goes wrong. . . ." He didn't finish but he made a gesture, pointing generally to himself. He would be right behind me. He couldn't be in the boat with me; it would have confused the dolphins. "Ready?"

I nodded.

"Go ahead! You're on!"

When I took my place in the prow of the boat over the Main Tank, my heart in my throat, it was even more wonderful than I thought it would be: dolphins leaping to the left of me, dolphins leaping to the right, dolphins doing tailwalks and dolphins making up new things to do, anything they could think of to attract my attention. The crowd gasped in wonder, and so did I. I was thinking: "At last! At last! This has got to be what life is all about."

The show went well except for one thing: I must have been talking too fast. At this pace I would run out of Jimmy's narration and have nothing to say for at least five minutes. So I began to improvise. Digging into my bag of dolphin facts and trivia that I'd gathered over the years, I ad libbed:

"If you were to x-ray the pectoral fin of a dolphin," I said, "you would see that it looks very much like the x-ray of a human hand."

I held out my own hand to illustrate, turning it this way and that. "Four fingers and a thumb."

"Do It Like I Told You"

The crowd seemed to approve, but behind me, I could sense an astonished Jimmy Kline shaking his head. Not only was I using his show to promote an idea that he detested, evolution, but I also used the term "dolphin." Like everybody else from Captain Gray on down, Jimmy said "porpoise."

One time when I persisted in using the term "dolphin," he asked me: "What do you call 'em dolphins for?"

I said: "Well, they are, aren't they?"

And he said nothing more. He stared for a moment, then looked away, glowering. I wished he had said something. But he could probably tell that I had a number of citations ready to throw at him and he didn't want to get involved.

Standing in the bow of the boat, tossing blue runners left and right to the leaping dolphins and searching for information the crowd might find as fascinating as I did, I announced:

"The pelvic structure of the dolphin indicates that they left the land some 65 million years ago and returned to the sea, from whence all life is said to have originated. And in that sense," I told the crowd, "they seem to be ahead of us, for we too in many ways are evolving back to the sea."

I'm lucky that Jimmy didn't have a hook. If he had, I'm sure he would have yanked me off the boat and carried on himself. When I finally finished the narration, I came down and there was Jimmy, glumly shaking his head. "No, no," he said. "Do it like I told you."

I knew the crowd had enjoyed the show. They roared their approval. To me it seemed a lot louder than when Jimmy did the show. "They seemed to like it," I said.

He kept shaking his head, his jaws locked. "Don't change anything."

"But—"

"Do it like I told you."

What really ticked him off, I think, was my farewell to the crowd. As a parting gesture and wanting to include everything I knew in the act, I told them where they would go from here: to the Reef Tank, the Shark Channel, the Lost Islands and finally to the Golden Dome, "where Adolph Frohn," I said, "the first person on earth ever to train a dolphin," would entertain them. As they began filing out, I knew something was very wrong. And then it came back to me. Hanging in the air was that phrase:

"Adolph Frohn, the first person on earth ever to train a dolphin...."

How Jimmy restrained himself, I don't know. He said nothing to me about it immediately after the show. But later we managed to meet in the Fish House, where we prepared the fish that we would use next.

With a studiedly casual air, Jimmy brought his fish over next to mine and we worked them together for a minute or so, separating the frozen fish. Then he said: "During your narration, don't refer to the Golden Dome."

"Oh?"

"The announcers can do that if they want to. That's *their* job."

I nodded.

Nothing more was said. Jimmy finished his fish and headed out. He walked through the maintenance shed where there was a big drum of motor oil, used for oiling pumps and generators. As was his custom, Jimmy touched the spigot, got a drop or two of oil on his hand, and then, deep in thought, massaged it into his hair. The rest of us all noticed this but never said anything about it. Later when nobody was watching I tried it myself. But it was not for me. It made me smell like a motorcycle.

8

The Lilly Factor

Within the next decade or two the human species will establish communication with another species; non-human, alien, possibly extraterrestrial, more probably marine; but definitely highly intelligent, perhaps even intellectual.

—Dr. John C. Lilly, *Man and Dolphin*

Dr. John C. Lilly, a fascinating combination of characteristics, had the mind of a scientist, the heart of a mystic, and the vision of genius. Unfortunately it never really came together. A neurologist, Dr. Lilly spent much of his life mapping the brains of various animal species, particularly dolphins, in an effort to understand how communication could take place between man and a nonhuman intelligence. In mapping the brains of dolphins, he drove metal electrodes into the brain itself, then measured the electrical response to various stimuli. Much of Dr. Lilly's work was done for NASA. The United States had begun blasting rockets into space, and contact with an alien intelligence was thought to be imminent. The question arose: How do you talk to an alien intelligence? Nobody knew. So the problem was given to Dr. Lilly, along with lucrative government grants.

Dr. Lilly's driving passion was to communicate with animals. He wanted to discover their language, if they had one, and to learn what they had to say. His first book, *Man and Dolphin,* suggested that dolphins might be our intellectual superiors. Dr. Lilly's speculations were based on brain measurements and tests, plus an imagination reputed to be enhanced by hallucinogenic drugs like LSD. Later, elaborating on this theme, he said that dolphins probably have an oral tradition and culture, meditations, the equivalent of our poetry, mathematics and a very creative philosophy, all of this passed on from one generation to the next. And if we could understand it, he was saying, think what a boon to mankind that would be.

When I read Dr. Lilly saying that dolphins might be smarter than humans, it touched a responsive chord. I had considered the same thing. In fact I was almost sure of it. Most people who work closely with dolphins have had the eerie feeling that the dolphins were reading their minds. I know how strange that sounds, but I know of no other way to explain their uncanny ability to anticipate my signals—not just once but all the time, as if they not only understood English but were clairvoyant as well.

In a 1962 lecture, Dr. Lilly told how he first realized that dolphins might be speaking English. "The feeling of weirdness," he called it. "It came on us," he said, "as the sounds of this small whale seemed more and more to be forming words in our own language. We felt we were in the presence of Something, or Someone, who was on the other side of a transparent barrier which up to this point we hadn't even seen."

Though I had lived around the sea most of my life, I had never thought of dolphins as aliens. But as Dr. Lilly pointed out, they *are* aliens. At least they are from our viewpoint. Actually, I think Dr. Lilly got it backwards. Dolphins are not the aliens, we are. Humans obviously rule the land; in their own way, whales (including dolphins) rule the oceans. But this is an oceanic planet, three to one. Though we tend to think of earth as made up by land masses, three-fourths of the globe is covered by water. More than 97 percent of all the water on earth is in the ocean. Glaciers and polar ice have less than 2 percent, and all the rest—the water underground, lakes and rivers and water in the atmosphere, in soil and in living things—makes up less than 1 percent. We call our planet Earth, but a more appropriate name would be Ocean.

Dr. Henry Truby, a communications expert who worked with Dr. Lilly for several years in the Communication Research Institute at Coconut Grove, Florida, said that he and Dr. Lilly originally talked about working with elephants, another animal with a brain larger than that of man. They switched to dolphins, he said, because they were easier to handle and because Dr. Lilly, a sailor, liked marine life. Dr. Truby, whose specialty was communication, speech, and spectrographic analysis, said that he drew no conclusions from the work they did with dolphins. More work was needed, he said. But at least some of the basic problems of interspecies communication were addressed in the research.

Dr. Lilly was slightly built, a birdlike man (sandpiper) with a tiny voice, the kind you have to strain to hear, and he acted as if he didn't care if you heard him or not—except it wasn't an act. Like most controversial people, Dr. Lilly had the ability to attract and repel at the same time. One of his coworkers said with unconcealed envy that people practically threw their money at him—and half the time he insulted them.

Like Socrates, a Gadfly

If Dr. Lilly did insult people, he probably was unaware of it. Virtually a caricature of the intellectual, he seemed oblivious to others. His true realm was the abstract, or perhaps the alleged connection between theory and the real world. Dr. Lilly's ideas were orchestrated on a grand scale. Some people loved him for his ideas. They were bold. Imaginative. Daring. Best of all, he dared to be wrong. And he never looked back. Others hated this about him and hated him— especially scientists. Many called him a charlatan. How can you be a scientist, they fumed, and speak in such an oracular style? Most people who worked with dolphins laughed at him. And those who took the trouble to study his work encountered a puzzling contradiction. On the one hand, Dr. Lilly characterized dolphins virtually as superbeings, on the other he was driving spikes into their brains. He called for whales, including dolphins, to be given "complete freedom of the waters of the earth." Then added, in effect, "but not now, not till we've done our research."

Genius or kook—who knows? Dr. Lilly's own assessment of himself might be closest to the truth. Like Socrates, Dr. Lilly referred to himself in the third person as a gadfly, stinging his fellow scientists into wakefulness. He liked to say outrageous things, he said, because it made people think.

Dr. Lilly was limited in his experience with dolphins. He rarely got into the water with them. He watched them avidly, though. Hour after hour at the viewing ports of the Miami Seaquarium's Main Tank, Dr. Lilly leaned on his elbows and studied the dolphins. When the tourists flocked to the Top Deck Show to see the dolphins do their tricks, he stayed below to watch them underwater.

I tried a few times to strike up a conversation with him but couldn't. Over the years, people we knew in common would introduce us to each other, and it was always as if for the first time. It was strange.

"But we've already been introduced," I said once. We were at the world premiere of *Flipper's New Adventure*, and I was determined to put him on the spot.

He looked quizzically at me. "We've met? Tonight?"

I smiled indulgently, as if we were both playing his game of absent-minded genius. "No, it was right here at the Seaquarium. Two months ago. They called me in to the office to meet you—and we met."

He pursed his lips thoughtfully and shook his head. "Afraid not. You must be thinking of someone else. I haven't been here in nearly—" he shrugged to show that it didn't matter—"oh, a year, at least."

But of course it had been him. I let it go. I shrugged back at him. "Doesn't matter," I said.

"No," he said deliberately. "It doesn't matter at all." Then he turned and joined someone else and I'm sure that he'd already forgotten me.

Later in my career as a dolphin trainer I read another of his books, *Mind of the Dolphin,* and was gripped again by the old magic. I wanted to tell him some things that I was sure could help him in his research. I had probably spent more time underwater with dolphins than anyone else and surely I knew something more about training dolphins and their mental capabilities than most people. That was my job. I did it all the time. And here I was in the same town. You'd think that *he* would look *me* up. But he didn't. So I tried to call him on the phone. In fact, I called him several times at the lab, but not once did I get through to him. I even went by the lab a few times, a dank and dark little place with lots of electronic machinery and a dolphin or two, lonely guinea pigs in a gloomy stench, but he was never there.

The really strange part is that I lived right across the street from him in the Grove, and the closest we ever came to speaking as neighbors was sometimes a brief nod. I continued to read his books, though. I admired him. I didn't care for his methods all the time, but I thought he was generally right or at least I thought he was doing what had to be done. I thought I could see what he might have picked up by watching the dolphins; their skins rippling as they swam, for instance. I used to watch them swim myself. Walking past the Main Tank, I always stopped and watched. It was irresistible. I always had the feeling that something beautiful or incredible would happen. The story is told, for example, about a man at another aquarium who used to watch the dolphins underwater from a viewing port. The man was smoking a cigarette when a baby dolphin swam up to the port and gazed out. The man nonchalantly blew a puff of smoke at the baby dolphin. The dolphin swam away to his mother, got a mouthful of milk and came back to the port, then blew the milk out at the man, making the same white, puffy cloud with the milk that the man had made with the smoke.

Answering Questions

The three-ring circus of a Top Deck Show was so fascinating to me that I wandered around almost like a tourist myself. I was always there. I liked working with dolphins so much I came every day of the week. Jimmy told me: "You've got one day off a week, take it. Don't come around here on your day off." There were times when he hung his head to the left and showed his teeth in what was not a smile. He did that now. "And don't," he said, "go to the front office. Stay away from there."

But I loved being at the Seaquarium. I would have paid for a ticket if I'd had to. I liked to talk to the spectators, mingle with them. When tourists recognized me (the clam-digger outfit was my uniform) they asked me questions about the fish and the dolphins and I answered them. This was not just part of the job, I enjoyed it. How wonderfully different from anything I'd ever done before! I liked people and I liked seeing first hand what people liked and didn't like.

One day I followed the crowd to the Reef Tank and could feel that my own show with its provocative suggestions of dolphin intelligence had made a point. It was a sunny day, with white, puffy cumulus clouds. Whitecaps began breaking over the bay, a light chop. That happens when the wind is at least twelve miles an hour.

From the Reef Tank, I moved with the crowd over to the Shark Channel, where they began asking me about the dolphins.

A family group—the father, mother, three kids—came up to me. They were probably from Iowa. They were all overweight, pink from the sun, playing the role of typical tourists: the camera, the fixed smiles and wild Miami colors. "Excuse me," the father said, making eye contact. "Real interesting place you got here." He was not one to rush into rash statements.

"Thank you," I said. I tried to nod in the same solemn way. Everyone likes to be treated as an individual, even in a huge crowd. At Disney World the young guides are instructed to treat each question as if it were the first time they'd ever heard it. I tried to do something like that myself but it wasn't easy. The questions from the crowds were mostly rather obvious, and after the first few weeks I'd heard them all.

But there's an urgency each time a question is asked. That makes it different. In this case, the urgency was in the man's daughter, about five, who pulled at his big hand. He bent down obediently and she hissed in his ear: "Go ahead. Ask him."

I smiled.

"Yeah," the father said, straightening up and shoving his free hand down into his hip pocket. He planted his feet firmly, standing his ground. "We were wondering—you were talking up there about how smart the dolphins are. . . ."

"Yes," I said, nodding.

"How smart *are* they?"

I've heard the same question a thousand times in a thousand variations. "They are really very smart," I said, nodding with assurance.

He gave a slow, deeply considered nod, and turned to his daughter. "You see?" he said. Then he turned back to me, smiling with relief. "Well, we thank you very much." He smiled and started to say something more. I thought he was going to tell me that if I was ever in Iowa I should drop by and he'd show me around, but he didn't. He smiled instead, then he and his daughter walked off hand in hand toward the Golden Dome. Suddenly she pulled free, wheeled and yelled back at me. "Are dolphins as smart as my dog?"

I cocked my head and pretended to give the question serious consideration. Then I yelled back:

"Yes. A lot smarter."

She said nothing for a moment. "But you don't even *know* my dog."

"Dolphins are smarter than *all* dogs," I said simply.

"Oh," she said with a slow nod.

A Seminole Indian youth had been watching. Wearing dungarees and a colorful Seminole jacket, he advanced on me.

"I've got one for you. If dolphins are so smart," he said, "how could we catch them? And why do they do these silly tricks?"

That question I had heard a thousand times, too. For me, the hard part was to hear it as if for the first time.

"If we're so intelligent," I countered, "why do we do these things to them?"

His mouth fell open. He had never thought of that. He was with two Seminole girls about his own age, they in their colorful long dresses, their hair like shiny black lacquer, all of them, like me, barefooted. They giggled at him. "Come on," he told them, taking their arms and tossing me a smile. "White man talk with forked tongue."

Serious, But Not Deadly Serious

A young blonde woman with Nordic eyes stood in front of me. "I'm next," she said. "And I hope you'll treat my question more seriously."

"I thought I was serious."

"You know what I mean." She had dimpled cheeks.

"I'm not so sure of that," I said. "What's the question?"

"Same question they asked. But I would like a real answer, if you don't mind."

"What was the question again?"

"How intelligent is the dolphin?"

I liked her. Serious but not deadly serious. In another situation, I thought, she would be wonderfully nonsensical. "You really want to know?"

"Of course. I'm in anthropology. Or at least I'm studying that." She shot me a smile and cocked her head slightly. "Tell me something I can use and I might put it in my dissertation. With credit!"

I made a face to show how impressed I was. And I was impressed. I finished high school in the navy and never went beyond that formally except for a few courses at the University of Miami, but I studied all the time, adding to my stockpot of oddball data and learning something from everyone I met. In short, I was self-educated, which means that I could follow my own nose through academia. My education would seem to be unstructured, my path of interest wandering willynilly. But there was a structure to it. It was internal discipline. I discovered who I was. And who I wasn't. I knew that I had gaps, a weakness in certain fundamentals. So I tried to watch what I said very carefully.

I had studied dolphins for some time now. I had caught them in nets, cured them when they got sick, stood by to help when they gave birth, and fed them a million times; I had swum with them in the wild, I had watched them endlessly in the Main Tank, never tiring of it, and had worked with them as trained animals; I was a trained animal as much as they were. The Miami Seaquarium had every book ever written about dolphins and I had read them all. The Miami Seaquarium was an excellent school for me; it was my alma mater. I used to visit the University of Miami Marine Lab, a large research facility that was practically next door. Everybody there had a Ph.D. I wanted to pick their brains or at least just hang around and absorb things by osmosis. This could be like a graduate school for me, I thought. I wanted to talk to them about Dr. Lilly, for example. I thought the scientists at the marine lab might know him personally. In any event, it would be wonderful, I thought, to meet people interested in discovering the truth about the sea. We had a lot in common, I thought. To me they were like monks, their lives devoted to the most holy of missions. Then I met my first marine biologist in his lab. I introduced myself, we tried to talk and soon I realized that he could sum up his entire academic experience in two words: the damselfish. This is a little fish about two or two and a half inches long. I asked him about dolphins but he knew nothing about them. He had never heard of Dr. Lilly. And in fact it seemed to me that he knew nothing about anything that didn't relate directly to the damselfish. Years later I discovered that Dr. Arthur A. Myrberg's interest in the damselfish was like my own interest in dolphins: communication. And after fifteen years of research, he cracked the damselfish code. I wish I had known what he was working on at the time.

I repeated the young woman's question: "You want some good stuff about dolphin intelligence, huh?"

"Yeah. But it's got to be real good." Dimples again. Every time she smiled or frowned or looked puzzled or said something or even thought of saying something, there were those dimples.

"Mind if I ask you a question first?"

"Please do."

"What do you mean by intelligence?"

She turned away with mock exasperation, then back. "You've done it again."

"Done what?"

"Equivocation." Her hands went to her hips.

"What do you mean?"

She pressed her lips together and frowned. She had Betty-Boop lips that went with the dimples. "Don't you know anything? It means," she said, "that you're playing with words. You're using ambiguity to conceal the truth. It's a form of lying." She laughed. "And don't deny it." She blinked her eyes brightly at me. "I was standing right here and heard you answer the *same* question two ways—and now *three* ways! You *do* speak with a forked tongue!"

I stared at her dimples. They seemed to come and go with certain words. I knew what she was talking about—it made sense in a way— and yet it was all wrong. "Okay," I said finally. "Let me try to explain. You think it was the same question, right?"

"It *was* the same question."

"It sounded like the same question," I said. "But it wasn't. You ask about the dolphin's intelligence and you have something very definite in mind. And so does everyone else who asks me about it—but it's not the same thing at all. Know what the problem is? The problem is the word 'intelligence'. Too many meanings." My voice was getting brittle. I couldn't do anything about it. "Don't bother to give me a dictionary definition. I know what the dictionary says and it doesn't help."

A crowd had gathered around us. About 1,500 persons had gone from the Underwater Show to the Reef Tank, but some of them must have thought that this impromptu question-answer period was part of the show. The young woman shook her head helplessly, playing to the crowd. There were thirty or forty people there. "It's not a tricky question," she said. "It's really very simple."

"You *think* it's simple," I said. "But it's not. By intelligence you probably mean the intelligence of intelligence testing, the good old IQ or intelligence quotient. Well, forget it. That's about people."

"That's not what I mean," she said softly as if trying to placate a lunatic.

"Then what?" My hands went out, palms up. I told myself that I should give her time to answer. And I did. I waited all of two seconds. "You saw the show, didn't you?"

She nodded.

"Could you have done any of that?"

"Could I have held a fish up for the dolphin? I think so."

"You know what I meant." I turned to the crowd. "She knows exactly what I meant, but I'll spell it out for her." I turned back to her, arms akimbo. "*Could you have jumped up for the fish?*"

"Like the dolphin?"

"Like the dolphin. Of course."

"I haven't really given that any thought."

"I have," I said. "You could *not* have jumped up for the fish. You saw Clown do the cigarette jump, didn't you?"

She wiped a wisp of blonde hair from her brow with the back of her hand. "How did I get involved in this?" She turned to the crowd and gave a shrug.

"Never mind that," I said. "You saw the cigarette jump?"

She gave me a long, stony look. She would have walked off if we'd been alone. But in some way, with the crowd watching and all, we had become a part of the act and we couldn't just quit. "Yes," she said. "I saw the cigarette jump. And no. If you're asking me if I could have done that, no, I could not have done that. So what?"

"So this: You just failed the Dolphin IQ test."

The crowd did not cheer exactly or break into applause or anything like that, but I had the feeling that it was smiling and quietly approving.

She grinned to herself and nodded. "So that's where you were going with this? I asked you for intelligence, remember? The dolphin can jump better than I can. I don't deny it. It can swim faster and hold its breath longer than I. I can live with that. It can do lots of things like that better than I can, including jumping up and snipping off a cigarette in your mouth. But I was asking you about intelligence, not skill."

"And what I'm saying to you is that there is no skill without intelligence."

"That's not what I meant—or I don't think it was." She held up her hand to stop me from interrupting and went on as if thinking aloud. "Hold on a minute. I said intelligence, you gave me skill. A dolphin jumping up for a fish is skillful? This is intelligence? Jumping up for a fish?" She was smiling like it was a joke. "Is that what you're saying? No, don't stop me. I've got something here. You say that there is no skill without intelligence. Take away the intelligence, in other words, and there is no skill. Or maybe, just maybe you're saying that skill is a form of intelligence." She looked at me quizzically. "Is that it?"

"Something like that, yes. What kind of test would you give them? True-false? Multiple-choice?" I smiled benevolently at her. "Or what about jumping? Not just jumping, though, but jumping *exactly*. Jumping at an exact place and touching an exact spot at an exact moment. And almost never erring. I don't say that they never make a mistake. If they couldn't make a mistake, then we would have to say that they couldn't do it right, either. That's what the words happen to mean. Machines don't make mistakes, or at least we don't think of them that way. Machines do what they have to do, not necessarily what we want them to do or what they were designed to do but the only thing they can do. If a machine doesn't do what we think it ought to do, then we figure that it's got a crossed wire or some other physical malfunction. But not that it's made a mistake. Not ever."

I turned to the group that had gathered round us and explained to them. "I have gone into a little detail about machines here because some people, and maybe some of you, really believe deep down that animals are just machines, that they don't have feelings, they don't think or anything else like us. But I'm here to tell you that the dolphin, like any other animal, makes mistakes just like humans.

"Let me tell you about it," I said. "One time Clown jumped up for the cigarette between my lips. I would trust Clown over anyone or anything else in the world. And much more than a person, even the most acrobatic, jumping up off a trampoline, say, with a pair of hedge clippers to snip the cigarette in my mouth. Clown grabbed my face by mistake in her jaws. She got my cheek. I didn't have time to be scared. It happened too fast. But later, I realized that she had simply miscalculated. She grabbed me by mistake at the top of her leap—and let go without pulling my face off. That's the only time it ever happened, but it did happen and it's clear to me that if she didn't care, if she didn't pay attention to the details of the jump, if she couldn't concentrate on what she was doing, there would be no cigarette jump. And what I'm saying is that if that doesn't take intelligence, then I don't know what intelligence is."

There was a scattering of applause. One old gentleman patted me on the shoulder, nodding approval.

The anthropology student looked puzzled. "Are you saying that the dolphin is more intelligent than I am?"

"It's possible. He has a much larger brain than you do," I said, recalling one of Dr. Lilly's recurring themes. "Brain size is not directly correlated with intelligence. We all know that. But the dolphin has had a large brain like this for at least 180 times as long as we have. Maybe that means something, maybe not. I'm surprised you didn't say something about language. I expected you to say that dolphins are not as intelligent as we are because they don't have a language. Well, don't be too sure of that. I'm suggesting not only that they do have a language but also that they've gone way beyond us in terms of communication. Consider this: If we found a race of beings in space 180 times older than we are, wouldn't we assume that they had something to teach us? Or turn that idea around. If you were arriving on earth for the first time from some distant galaxy, if you could communicate with any species in any language, if you knew only that dolphins had bigger brains for a lot longer time than people did and your mission was to contact the most advanced form of life on earth, who would you contact?"

Nobody said anything for a moment, then the dimpled girl with the cool-gray eyes said: "I know who I *wouldn't* contact." She turned on her heel and flounced off, the crowd giving way.

I couldn't resist. "Who?" I yelled.

"You!"

9

Going Hollywood

The lunatic, the lover, and the poet,
Are of imagination all compact....

—William Shakespeare, *A Midsummer-Night's Dream*

Like Art McKee, Ricou Browning was my mentor and a
legend in his own time. I had heard of Ricou Browning before we
met, and he had heard of me. He was the brilliant associate producer
for Ivan Tors Studios and cocreator (with Jack Cowden) of "Flipper."
Earlier he had directed the underwater scenes of "Sea Hunt," starring
Lloyd Bridges, the TV series that opened the world of undersea adventure. As a stunt man, Ricou had been the creature in *The Creature
from the Black Lagoon,* one of my all-time favorite movies. He had
cowritten, coproduced and directed the underwater scenes (second
unit) of *Flipper,* the original Flipper movie, at Grassy Key, about eighty
miles south of Miami, and had moved to Miami Seaquarium for the
second one, *Flipper's New Adventure,* a pilot for the Flipper TV series,
because he needed larger facilities.

Ricou had heard of me because our names—*Ricou* Browning and
Ric O'Barry—sounded alike over the Miami Seaquarium public address system and we were always picking up phone calls for each
other.

Ricou, the straightest arrow I ever knew, was married and the father
of four: two boys, two girls. They were the Norman Rockwell family
down the block with the big house and station wagon, the successful,
good-looking couple with the happy kids, all wonderfully optimistic

and uncomplicated by doubts about who they were. They were a beautiful family, the kind that watched "Flipper" together on TV. Families like that don't just happen; they're planned. Especially in Ricou's case. Nothing just happened in his life; he planned everything. Cautious, balanced, four-square in every way, Ricou's idea of reality began and ended in what he could see and touch. I don't think he ever had an unconventional idea in his life—except in the water. There, where he was as much at home as I was, we both went a little wild sometimes.

Like his idol Walt Disney, Ricou was the kind of genius who could see through the humbug of the way things were done. Without even trying, for instance, he was doing the most innovative work with dolphins in the world. Dolphins were customarily trained topside, the trainer working on the edge of the tank. That made sense because dolphin acts, like other animal acts, were for spectators who watched from topside. Everything that happened was above the water: jumping through hoops, leaping up and biting cigarettes in two, tailwalking and all the games like baseball, basketball, and bowling. But Ricou needed to show Flipper going from one place to another underwater. The script might call for Flipper to retrieve a compass from the bottom of the sea, for example, to affix a tracking device to a submarine, or to free someone trapped in a car at the bottom of the bay.

The problem was: How do you get a dolphin to swim for fifty feet underwater in front of a camera? Solution: Ricou got in the water with them. He wasn't looking down on them; they were on the same level, making eye contact. That *sounds* simple, but it had never been done before. When I first saw Ricou doing it, I was amazed. And even more amazing to me was that he didn't make a big secret out of it. I had assumed that all animal trainers were a secretive lot and insecure. But not Ricou. He was always open about everything.

I had finished my Top Deck Show late one spring morning and, still in my clam-diggers and red Banlon shirt, was wandering around barefooted. It was a beautiful day, a light breeze coming off the ocean, puffs of cumulus against a cerulean sky. With a couple of hours to kill, I wandered over to the tank where Ricou was training Susie. She was a big girl now: 250, maybe 300 pounds. The tank was round, fifteen feet across, and ten feet deep. It was next to the bay near Bear Cut where the collecting boat docks and where I felt very much at

home. Ricou, treading water, was throwing a green coconut and signaling Susie to retrieve it. He threw the coconut and then pointed,
thrusting his arm outward.

When I walked up, we nodded to each other. I think he knew that
I was the one picking up his phone calls. "Hey," he said with a smile,
"you see that other coconut over there?" He pointed to the ground
near my feet at an old brown coconut on the rim of the tank.

"This? Sure."

"Slap the water, will you, and give it to Susie when she comes over."

I got the coconut, bent down, and slapped the water. That was the
signal to "come." Susie dove eagerly and came up in front of me. I
held out the coconut and she took it gingerly in her mouth, then swam
with it back to Ricou, who gave her a piece of fish.

"Good," he said with a smile. "I want her to retrieve things no
matter who gives the signal. See that rock over there next to the towel?"
There was a chunk of coral rock in the grass by his towel and tennis
shoes. "Try that."

I slapped the water, Susie came over and I gave her the rock. She
took it to Ricou and he gave her another piece of fish. Rewarding the
dolphin with just a piece of fish was another of Ricou's innovations.
It's obvious, yes, but in the Top Deck Show we gave the dolphins a
whole fish when they performed. That meant they wouldn't perform
as long before they got filled up.

Ricou swam the coconuts and the rock over to me again. "Try it
again," he said. So we kept doing it, passing various things back and
forth. When I slapped the water, Susie came over and I gave her one
of the things. She took it in her mouth and swam it back to Ricou,
who gave her a bite of fish. When he ran out of fish, Ricou swam over
to my side of the training tank. He was a powerful swimmer, with
long, smooth strokes. He had taught synchronized swimming to the
"mermaids" in the "Underwater Ballet" at Weekee-Watchee Springs
on Florida's West Coast and had ended up marrying one.

"Thanks," he said with a grin. "Training a dolphin underwater is
really a two-man job."

"Great!" I said.

He squinted up at me. "Are you going to be here tomorrow about
the same time?"

I looked at my wristwatch for some reason. "Sure," I said.

He put his hands on the edge of the tank and pushed down, propelling himself out of the tank and onto the edge in one smooth, easy motion. He stood there a moment, letting the water drip off of him, then picked up his white towel and rubbed it briskly over his face and arms. "That's good," he said. He slipped his feet into his tennis shoes. "See you then." He gave me a curt nod and walked off toward the shark channel. He looked like Tarzan in tennis shoes to me, except that Ricou was a lot browner. Suddenly he stopped and turned. "By the way," he said. "Wear a swimsuit if you have one. We both ought to be in the water with Susie." He grinned and waved and I waved back.

"Tomorrow!" I called after him.

"Tomorrow, sure," he said. "See you then."

There are times when things click into place and you know that something new and important has happened in your life. This was one of them for me.

When I showed up the next day, wearing my black tank suit and a little earlier than before, Ricou was already in the water with Susie. "Hop in," he said with a grin. I eased into the water. Susie came over, frolicking. We went through some of the signals Ricou wanted to practice: jumping, swimming to a certain place, swimming underwater, presenting her dorsal fin to pull one of us. Susie caught on fast. We went through the signals twice and got to a stopping point. "Let's take a break," Ricou said. We stopped but stayed in the water, both of us holding on to the rim of the tank with one hand.

No one has ever accused me of engaging in social chit-chat, but I have a feel for certain moments, and this was clearly one of them, I thought, when someone should say something. So I said: "Susie and I go way back."

He nodded acknowledgment.

"You might say that I weaned her." I glanced at him for recognition. Nothing. "I was the first one to feed her by hand."

Susie was romping around us, then surfaced between us, expelling air, and dove again. Ricou seemed not to care about Susie's early life but I, caught up in the social demands of the moment, went on: "We caught her and her mother in the bay." Ricou raised his brow and I waited a moment. Again nothing. "Just off Mercy Hospital," I said, pointing and becoming aware of the ridiculous aspect of all this. Here we were, two guys and a dolphin deep in a tank of water, and one of

the guys, the one known for his long silences if for anything, bab-
bling like a brook and pointing to things that neither of them could
see. What had got into me? Was I trying to impress Ricou? "That's
where we catch most of our dolphins these days," I babbled on.
"Anyway, her mother got sick. Swineiferous. Ever heard of that?
Well, anyway, Susie was still nursing. The mother died—she didn't
even have a name—and I took over. Fed her by hand." Susie popped
up between us again. "She probably thinks of me as her surrogate
mother."

Ricou nodded pleasantly and ran his hand along Susie's back as she
swam by.

"What are we doing here, anyway?" I asked finally. "I know about
the movie, but I mean. . . ."

Ricou laughed lightly. "I'm glad to know that *you* are Susie's surrogate mother. I thought she thought it was *me*." He laughed again.
"What are we doing here? Good question. The general idea, Ric, is
to get Susie to respond to commands under conditions of great confusion. Have you ever been on a movie set before?"

"I helped wrangle the tiger shark in *Flipper*," I said. I glanced at
him to see if he might have remembered me.

He looked at me for a moment, his face a blank. "Anyway," he
said, "when a movie crew moves in, everybody has got to know *exactly*
what he's doing. There's no time to stop while someone learns how
to do his job. And when Susie is playing Flipper, the star of the show,
she has got to know exactly what to do under *any* circumstances, *any*
distraction. And how do we tell her what to do? These signals. The
way I see it," he said, "these signals are a kind of language. We use
hand signals so that we can tell her what to do when the cameras are
rolling."

"Hmm," I said thoughtfully. "Ever consider ultrasonics? Sounds
that she could hear but we can't?" Was this me talking? I never talked
like that before. And if I'm not mistaken, I didn't look like myself,
either. My voice was a little strange, too; darker than usual. I was
grinning in a lopsided way with one brow lifted as if I thought I had
said something extremely clever. It was obvious even to me that I was
trying to impress Ricou, make him realize that I knew something,
perhaps quite a lot, about dolphins, too.

"Yes," he said, nodding and frowning slightly. "I've considered
that." Susie popped up between us and blew a plume of wet breath

into the air. Ricou and I both patted her as she went by. "But if we went to ultrasonics, Ric, how would we know that we'd given Susie a signal if she didn't do anything? We couldn't hear it. We wouldn't know if our signal had failed or Susie had failed." He made a face, wrinkling his brow and turning down the corners of his mouth. "Maybe down the road we'll try something like that. But right now, it's new and we don't know much about it. It could cause problems. For instance, though we wouldn't hear the signals, our electronic equipment might hear it and cause glitches." He squinted up at the sky for a moment, then he turned back to me. He had dark-brown eyes. "Maybe the real reason I'm not doing it that way is psychological. The biggest problem on a movie set—especially on location like this— is noise. Airplanes, cars, boats, people coughing or laughing half a block away—you name it. We don't hear all of it, maybe we don't hear most of it, but our recording equipment does. So we try to get rid of noise. All our thinking is to get rid of it, not produce even more. And we already know that hand signals work. We've done it. Ultra- sonics might work perfectly—maybe better than hand signals—but we don't have time to train the dolphins all over again in case it doesn't. And what about us, Ric? I don't know how to do it. Do you? No, you see? We'd both have to take a course in electronics or something before we'd know what we were doing."

I nodded solemnly. Why hadn't I thought of that? At the moment my brain suddenly was spinning out because for the first time Ricou had included me in his plans.

"Let me see your hands," he said suddenly.

I held out my hands to him. I was flutter-kicking in the water to stay afloat.

"Uh-huh," he said.

"See mine?" He held his own hands out. They looked normal to me. "See the nails?" I studied the nails. They looked normal, too. "They're short and smooth," he said. "Susie shows marks easily. All dolphins do. Just a scratch and it could show up on film."

"You want me to—"

He smiled. "If you don't mind."

I had never paid much attention to my fingernails before. But that evening when I got off work I went to a fancy barber shop and ordered a manicure, the full treatment.

*   *   *

Though Ricou was not technically an animal trainer, he probably knew more about training dolphins, especially underwater, than anyone else in the world. Long before the Flipper films, he was training dolphins. He and his friend Ross Allen, celebrated collector of snakes and alligators at Silver Springs, Florida, once went to the Amazon River in Brazil and captured a pair of white fresh-water dolphins (*Inia geoffrensis*). They brought them back to Silver Springs and Ricou trained them to jump and fetch things. They were the first in this country. Unfortunately the two dolphins died about a year later. The water was probably too cold.

One day after a workout at the little training pool, Ricou and I were walking back together toward the office. It was one of those days that sometimes happen when everything is just right. It was uncanny. Susie had been perfect, as if she knew in advance what we wanted her to do. I didn't want to break the spell, but I had to know: "Is there a name for the way you train dolphins?"

"Yes," he said. "There is."

We walked on in silence. Is this the way Ricou kept his training method secret? I had to know: "What do you call it?"

"Common sense," he said.

I looked at him to see if he was putting me on. "That's it? That's a method?"

He looked at me in a funny way. "You asked me, I told you. That's all there is."

Wrangling the Tiger Shark

Indirectly, I had worked for Ricou earlier when he shot some of the underwater scenes for *Flipper*. As a diver in the Miami Seaquarium's Underwater Show, I worked as a shark wrangler and, as such, helped make the big tiger shark look like he was swimming menacingly toward Sandy, one of the stars of *Flipper*, who was adrift in a small dinghy.

Shark wrangling is manhandling the sharks, overpowering them and pushing them into underwater scenes, then catching them as they swim through the scene to the other side.

Ricou needed a big tiger shark for the climax of *Flipper*, and the Miami Seaquarium just happened to have one, a thirteen-footer. Tiger sharks that size can weigh from 850 to 1,500 pounds; the one we had weighed at least 1,000 pounds. By comparison, the world-record great white shark caught on a rod and reel off Montauk, New York, in August of 1986, was sixteen feet, eight inches long and weighed 3,450 pounds. Bruce, the mechanical monster of a great white in the movie *Jaws,* was said to have been even bigger: twenty-five feet long, two tons. Ricou wanted a tiger shark because they're not only more photogenic than other sharks but scarier, too. They're striped like a tiger, their heads are larger, their mouths more angry looking, and they have big round eyes.

Despite their menacing size and appearance, however, in captivity they're pussycats. Even the biggest of them can be manhandled with relative ease by a trained team. We got into the water and walked them when they needed it. This is like giving them artificial respiration because swimming is the way sharks breathe. Water flows through their gills, where the oxygen in the water is absorbed.

The Miami Seaquarium catches big sharks all the time: the great white, hammerhead, and mako. It tries to keep about fifty sharks on display, but rarely does that collection include a tiger shark. The sharks that survive best in captivity are the nurse shark, the bull shark, and the lemon shark. They're tough and adaptable, common in shallow water along the coast. We had no problem keeping them alive. The Miami Seaquarium has a circular shark channel about half the size of a city block, fifteen to twenty feet wide and about five feet deep. Two bridges span the channel, and from them, to the delight of tourists, attendants feed trashfish to the sharks: amberjack, bonito, and barracuda. The sharks are fed four times a day, occasionally producing the fabled feeding frenzy, when they snap at anything, including one another and themselves.

Tiger sharks are usually not in the shark channel because they're particularly hard to keep alive. In captivity they may last a week or a month. But then they slow down and die. Nobody knows for sure why the tiger shark doesn't make it in captivity. Tiger sharks, great whites, and others in the mackerel family are pelagic fish. Their home is the ocean, where they swim for miles and miles each day. Maybe that has something to do with it. In nature the tiger shark can go months without eating—as long as three months, according to Captain Gray. But in captivity the tiger shark refuses to eat. I watched with fascination as Warren Zeiller, curator, made a project of keeping one tiger shark alive. I used to see him day and night at the shark channel, holding a fishing pole with a shark liver at the nose of the tiger shark.

He wasn't fishing; he was trying to feed the tiger shark. Shark liver is not only a delicacy to sharks, it's a natural megavitamin. And it worked for a while. That tiger shark lived for fourteen months— probably a record.

When we say that people have lost their will to live, it means that they have given up. They turn gray, their breathing becomes shallow, and they sigh a lot. They can't eat. Nothing interests them. In captivity, tiger sharks are like that. They look droopy and confused, as if in shock.

Shot from Every Angle

That's how the thirteen-foot tiger shark in the movie *Flipper* was. We shark wranglers got on each side of the tiger shark, holding him as best we could by the pectoral and dorsal fins and, on cue, we pushed him through the water in front of the camera. On the other side were three or four other shark wranglers, who caught the tiger shark and held him ready for the next shot.

This was the first time I had ever been behind the scenes of a movie. I had never even thought about movies and how they were made. At first I thought that this had to be a joke, putting all this unreal and unrelated stuff together. Going from the real world of the collecting boat to the Underwater Show, where so many things were done for effect, I not only didn't mind it, I positively loved it. But using a nearly dead tiger shark like that bothered me. Back and forth we shoved the tiger shark while the underwater cameras ground away. They filmed the shark from every angle: up close with the row-upon-row of teeth, close up on the dazed eye, and along the flanks. Occasionally the tiger shark made a weak attempt to swim. It opened its huge mouth extra wide as if gasping for air and the camera operator moved in close and got a shot of it. How sad, I thought. Hold on, old fellow. The movie will soon be over and you can die in peace.

The story was about Flipper's saving Sandy from the tiger shark by charging it at top speed, ramming it time after time in the belly. Was Susie going to be trained to ram this tiger shark? No, there was a better way. For the close-ups of Flipper battering the belly of the tiger shark, we used plastic mockups. A plaster cast was made from a dolphin that had died and had been put in the Seaquarium's walk-in freezer. From that was made a hollow fiberglass dolphin. It had two bung holes that could be opened so that we could fill it with as much water as we needed to give it the right buoyancy. Then one of the wranglers held the plastic shark, I held the head of the plastic dolphin and with the cameras rolling close up, we crashed them together, time after time, as we thought it might actually happen if it were ever to happen.

All of this is pure choreography. These precious snippets of film are pieced together in a dark room in Hollywood. I began to realize that you could make a movie with actors who never even saw each other. That's practically what we were doing here. When the music was added, the tiger shark looked menacing indeed and Flipper's fight was the wildest since that of Ahab and Moby Dick.

For long shots, we used fiberglass dorsal fins of a dolphin and shark; we divers swam just below the surface of the water and held them above us.

10

Thirteen Weeks a Year

Remember guys. Don't buy anything you can't pay for in
thirteen weeks.

—Ricou Browning

The movie *Flipper* was a big success and Ivan Tors signed
to do a sequel, *Flipper's New Adventure*, a feature film that would
also serve as a pilot for a possible TV series. Even before it was shown
in theaters, NBC saw the film, liked it, and signed the TV series for
a year.

In those days, a year-long TV series meant producing thirteen shows.
The "Flipper" crew averaged one a week. The cost: about $100,000.
That was a lot of money in the 1960s. Making the "Flipper" series
was more complicated than most because it was shot in several places
and edited in yet another. Sometimes we were working on half a dozen
scripts at once. Making a TV series is like making sausages, Ricou
used to say. When you get started, there's no stopping till you get to
the end. We did the topside shooting at the Seaquarium and at various
sites around Miami, interior shots in a studio north of Miami and the
underwater shooting in the Bahamas. Typically, while one show was
being shot topside, which usually took two or three days, the next
one in the series was being planned. Ricou directed many of the topside
shows, and all of the underwater sequences. When Ricou finished the
topside shooting of one of the shows, another director stepped in and
did the topside shooting for the next one. Then while he was shooting,
Ricou would be planning the next script. We did the topside shooting

for six or seven scripts in a row, then Ricou and the rest of us flew to Nassau with one or two of the dolphins and did the underwater shooting for all six or seven. This took about a month. When that was done, back we flew to Miami, where we started on the topside shooting for the rest of the series, flying back to Nassau again for the underwater sequences to them.

All of this film was shipped to Hollywood, where it was processed and sorted out, where credits and music were added, and where Mel Blanc added his voice of the dolphin. Thirty-minute TV shows actually run twenty-three minutes. NBC wanted at least six minutes of each film to be underwater.

As the series went on, a fund of stock footage was built up, all kinds of Flipper shots: Flipper swimming to the left, Flipper swimming to the right, Flipper popping his head up out of the water, Flipper nodding, Flipper jumping, Flipper doing almost anything you can imagine. As the stock footage gathered, so did the temptation to use it. In many cases it would have been simpler, faster, and cheaper to use than shooting it fresh. We used it, yes, but we tried not to. Using stock footage is a tipoff that something serious is wrong, because stock footage equals stock story. And stock story equals cliché. Bad theater. But artistic criticism aside, the big problem with stock footage is that if you use too much of it, your series doesn't get renewed.

I don't think any of us ever sat down and discussed the pros and cons of stock footage. All that had been settled in ancient times and we knew it by osmosis. Most of us, who had nothing to lose but our reputations, were against stock footage. I was always suggesting new shots of Flipper, fresh tricks. If Flipper was supposed to carry a message in a bottle from one place to another, which he did on more than one occasion, I made sure that it was a different kind of bottle each time.

Our opposition to stock footage was actually more complex than that, because professional standards were involved. We were doing the films not only for the public but also for network experts who knew when shortcuts had been made. Ratings are important but so is the respect of one's peers. Credibility comes with continuity.

The "Real" Flipper

Like any other fictional character, Flipper existed only in art. Though he seemed as real as life—or *more* real, actually, as art is supposed to be—Flipper was an illusion, an elaborate fabrication, the work of hundreds of talented people who came thousands of miles and spent tens of thousands of dollars, all to create the legend of a fabulous creature, a creature combining both actual and imaginary delphoid powers with that of a family pet specially blessed—as all of them are when we love them—with human intelligence. That Flipper was more imaginary than real can be said of anyone who presents himself to the public. Cary Grant used to say that even he wished he could be Cary Grant, the Cary Grant portrayed in films. In that sense, we're all at least partly imaginary, whether we're politicians or movie stars, lawyers or storekeepers. When I try to nail down who TV's Flipper really was, I think not of the dolphins who played the role or who were perhaps tricked into it, nor of the fictional creation we see on the screen; I think mainly of myself. I knew what Flipper could and couldn't do, how he thought and felt, how he would react to things and everything about him. When I think of Flipper I think of myself not because I was Flipper, but because I was a part of Flipper, a big part.

"Flipper" was family entertainment, a show that children and their parents could enjoy watching together. The "Flipper" stories were about people who love and trust each other and who have a problem that can be solved only by their pet dolphin. There was never an underlying message to the stories, unless you count the basic message that life is good and so are we. Like Ricou himself, the stories were just what they seemed to be and nobody had to wonder what they were "really" about, nobody had the feeling afterwards that they had been preached at. Family entertainment meant that there was no profanity, no nudity or steamy seduction scenes, no needless violence nor anything really ugly. It was entertainment for normal people, or perhaps the term is "ideal" people, which is what normal people try to be, people who don't feel guilty about the world's problems and aren't always agonizing about them.

In "Flipper" there was violence every week, but a healthy violence. It was always important to the plot. Violence is a part of life, after all, and one of the most important parts of drama. That was the key, I think. Our violence was always necessary: a storm or hurricane, for example, a hungry shark, an escaped criminal or a young lad trapped underwater or in quicksand. All of this is violent, but justified because it was part of the story, the problem to be solved by a dolphin of genius.

Another important part of the Flipper stories, which is often overlooked, was the background: Florida's climate. People tuned in from all over the world to see Florida's sunshine, the sparkling blue-green water, the palm trees, the beautiful clear sky and vigorous people with healthy suntans and simple problems to solve. To all those viewers who lived week after dreary week in a bundled-up life of dark-gray clouds, Florida's happy sunshine burst from their television sets like a miracle.

The plots were simple but well crafted. The basic idea was for Flipper to save the young stars, Luke Halpin, who played Sandy Ricks, and Tommy Norden, who played his young brother, Bud. There were many variations, but the young protagonists, who seemed to live in a sea of breathtaking adventure and terrifying problems, always found themselves in dire straits, among them:

1. Trapped in an old junked car twenty feet underwater.
2. Tangled up in a coil of wire while diving to recover stolen money for the police.
3. Marooned on a deserted island with a hurricane bearing down.
4. Attacked in a dinghy by an enraged tiger shark.

Enter Flipper, the wonder dolphin and wonderful friend. Flipper is the king of the sea and master of a world so strange, the world of sound, that we can comprehend it only metaphorically. These talents he uses to solve the Ricks boys' weekly problems, solving them with a high-pitched, staccato giggle and a lighthearted flip of his tail.

It's a bit unreal, perhaps, but charmingly satisfying, because we do want our fictional heroes larger than life, and our villains, too. The only real fictional requirement is that the story be possible.

For example, do thirteen-foot tiger sharks really attack dinghies?

Sometimes, yes. It's news when it happens but it does happen. The rare part by comparison would be a dolphin attacking such a shark. But that too could happen. If the shark, for example, tried to take a bite out of a baby dolphin, the mother dolphin would certainly try to drive off the shark. She would ram the shark at high speed and bang it around with her big, broad, powerful flukes. If that should happen, the dolphin's snout, which is now a blunt instrument of 300 pounds going thirty miles an hour, might catch the shark just right in the gills or underbelly and kill it. A dolphin that big and going that fast would deliver a punch 100 times harder than that of a .38 caliber bullet. The bullet develops about one-quarter horsepower; a 300-pound dolphin, twenty-four horsepower. Scientists once figured that the bottlenose dolphin is seven times stronger than a human athlete.

If a dolphin took on a thirteen-foot shark like the one in the story, I have no doubt about who would win: the dolphin, every time. That's how much smarter the dolphin is than the shark.

Pete the Pelican

The original cast of "Flipper" was a father and his two sons and their pet dolphin, Flipper, who lived in the sea. But halfway through the first season, I caught a pelican, Pete, who joined the cast. Pete, who spent most of his time perched on a piling or waddling along a dock, never solved any of the Ricks' weekly problems, but he was always there, a comic figure like a court jester, chiming in with author's notes to the audience. One of the actors would say:

"Is that right, Pete?"

And Pete would nod "yes." He was a cutaway device, basically. When you end a scene in TV or the movies, you need a way to let the audience know. Otherwise, one scene would run into the next. To end a scene, the camera might come in for a close-up or go back for a long shot. Sometimes the director uses a slow dissolve, a fade or wide-angle shot, all of them just to let the audience know that the scene is over. In "Flipper," we often showed Pete the Pelican. It worked so well that after a while Pete was written into the script.

Like this:

> SANDY: Is that right, Pete?
> (*Cut to Pete.*) Nods yes with enthusiasm.

Which means that the camera would show Pete the Pelican in close-up. And Pete would enthusiastically nod his head up and down, "Yes!"

How did he do this?

I was in front of Pete but off to the side and out of camera range with my yellow bucket of fish. I found early on that Pete watched my "fish hand" like a hawk. When my hand went up, his head went up; when my hand went down, his head went down. So when Sandy said:

"Is that right, Pete?" my hand began pumping up and down, and so did Pete's head. It was as if his head was on a string. I could make it go yes and no or seem hesitant, I could make his head go in a circle, or do almost anything. I remember that the script once called for Pete to "nod sadly." The director read that and laughed. "A pelican?" he said. "Sadly?"

"But I think I can do it," I told the director.

"Ha! Ha!" the director laughed. "If you can do it, I'll shoot a close-up of it!"

He practically wrote the scene off and went on with the shooting, but I took Pete to one side and put him up on a piling and practiced a moment with my yellow bucket and the fish. There was nothing I could do with Pete's expression, of course, but I found that by holding the bucket up about at Pete's eye level and turning the bucket to one side slowly, Pete's head turned the same way. Then, leaving the bucket at that angle, I moved it down slightly, his head and eyes following me intently, and finally, to get his head to go up and down in a nod at that angle, I simply made my hand go up and down. For "sad" I did it slowly. And it worked.

At the first break in shooting, I carried Pete over to the piling in front of the Ricks' home and put him on top. "Look at this," I told the director. Then I went through the same machinations, the yellow bucket at eye level, turned at an angle, then down a little, and finally my hand working slowly up and down to create the nod.

"By God!" the director exclaimed. "You've got it!" He looked at me with amazement. "He does a better sad nod than a lot of actors I know." He grinned. "Let's shoot it!"

Pete was a favorite because he was a pretty wise old bird. Funny, too. And some of us might have confirmed a deep belief that "mere animals" know a lot more than they let on. We trust animals, especially wild ones, and when they flock around, it's a sign that we must be doing something right.

In real life, though, Pete flocked around because he couldn't fly off. I trimmed his wings. With a pair of scissors, I snipped the trailing edges of his wing feathers, where the flaps are on an airplane. The feathers kept growing back so I trimmed them every couple of months.

I caught Pete, a brown pelican, in back of the Seaquarium on Biscayne Bay. I had a bucket of herring and smelt and went down to the sea wall. It was simple. Half a dozen pelicans hung around there, some on the bulkhead, some floating like toy boats in the water. I picked out the best-looking pelican of the bunch and tossed a fish in front of him. He gobbled it down, the bill going up and the fish going down in outline against his neck. Then he twiddled his tail with satisfaction and waited for more. Some of the other pelicans and gulls crowded around and I tossed another fish just in front of him, which he enthusiastically pounced on and gobbled down. Suddenly he was right under my nose. I had been holding the yellow bucket. Slowly I put the bucket down, watching the pelican's every move. I would have taken off my Topsiders but I might have spooked him. Then I froze. There's an exact moment for leaping into the lives of wild animals. You have to feel their life first, how they fit the world around them. It's like the beat of music. Their eyes, the sounds they make, their head movements, their feet and their whole body, the closeness of things around them—all of this and more make up the way they perceive and adjust to their world. When you figure out the rhythm and how it's put together, you can find the seams in it. These are the breaking points, when the eye blinks, the heart beats, the attention jumps from one point to another. The moment you get it down just right and you're living in his world, that's the time to leap in. I leaped, splashing in the water. He let out a bloody-murder squawk: "*Wrrrraaaaccccckkkk!*"

I grabbed his neck with one hand and tried to get my other arm around his wings but couldn't—pelicans are strong—and they were boxing my ears. What I had to watch out for was his big beak, which is lined with sharp serrated edges and has a pointed hook of a tooth at the end for grasping fish.

A gangling, barefooted youth of about twelve with sun-bleached hair, his eyes squinting against the bright sun, stepped out of the mangroves. I didn't know he was even there but he must have been watching me. "Hey!" he said. "Don't you know you can't do that in Miami?" He was a native. He pronounced it "My-*am*-muh."

I was still struggling with the pelican, the issue in doubt. He had got one wing loose and was flailing the water and me alike, squawking. Finally I slid my hand that was around his scrawny neck down around his bill, and my other arm engulfed both wings. I had him. And he knew it. Suddenly he stopped struggling and shot me a look of resignation. "You see," I said to the boy, gasping for breath, "if I'd thought I couldn't do it, I couldn't have."

The boy said, "You know what I mean."

Now that I had the pelican, I had to climb back onto the bulkhead. I shifted the pelican around so that one hand was free, glanced at the boy and, one human being to another, extended my arm. "Give me a hand?"

"Let him go and I will."

"If I let him go, I wouldn't need your help. Look," I said, finally. "I'm not hurting him." The boy was staring down at me in disbelief. I looked around me. "These feathers? Don't worry about it," I said. "He'll never miss them." Knee deep in water and clutching a bedraggled pelican, I grinned as confidently as I could and proclaimed: "I'm going to make him a star."

The boy glared at me. "Yeah? Like yourself?"

"No," I said. "I'll train this pelican the same way I train Flipper and he'll be a big star."

The boy gave me a sour look. "Are you sure that's what he wants?"

From the mouths of babes, I thought. The kid was right but I found it impossible to admit. Nobody told me to capture a pelican. But it would help the show. I was sure of it. Ricou would smile with approval. He would say: "Nice going, Ric." It wasn't as if we were going to hurt the pelican. We were going to feed him and pamper him and treat him like something really special. But I knew as well as the boy did what the pelican would say if he could speak. "Beat it," I said to the kid.

Though Pete couldn't fly away with his flaps trimmed, he could waddle away if he wanted to, so to make sure he didn't, I tied one of his legs to the dock with a monofilament line.

Years later when the "Flipper" series ended, I took Pete out to the mangrove swamps near the set where I had captured him and let him go. His wing feathers had grown back and he could fly as well as any other pelican. From time to time after the series ended, I went back to the set and could pick him out. I looked for a sign of recognition, but there was none. I wished that the kid who had preached such a hard-nosed sermon at me when I captured Pete had been there then. Over the years, I thought a lot about him and what he said. But in Pete's case, at least, I don't think being in the movies affected him in the least. He loved it.

*   *   *

Though Pete was a welcome addition to the "Flipper" scripts, not everything that we tried worked. Off and on for about a year I tried to put a saddle on a sea cow and ride him around. If I'd been able to, we could have written at least one episode about it. But the sea cow threw the saddle off even before I could get on.

I also tried to get Susie and Kathy to pull me in an underwater dolphin-powered sled. Ricou and I designed the sled with round dolphin collars on each side and all the dolphins had to do was put their heads through it and swim. That part of it worked. But Susie and Kathy were not synchronized in their breathing and one or the other was always having to come up for a breath of air, which dumped me off the sled.

11

Alone

We need another and a wiser and perhaps a more mystical
concept of animals. . . . They are not our brethren; they are
not underlings; they are other nations, caught with ourselves
in the net of life. . . .

—Henry Beston, *The Outermost House*

It was December and Santa Claus was in the air. Ricou and
I used to jog around the lake for exercise early in the mornings before
it got hot. It's beautiful then, a time for clearing the head. Sometimes
we said nothing, just jogged. But usually we chatted about the dolphins
and upcoming plans. Usually Ricou talked, I listened. Ricou was waiting for final word on the upcoming series. He was almost certain that
we had it, but final word hadn't come down. The deal was between
Ivan Tors, an independent producer, and Wometco Enterprises Inc.,
which owned the Miami Seaquarium. For use of the facilities at the
Seaquarium, and for five dolphins (Susie and her four backups), Miami
Seaquarium would receive screen credit and would own Flipper. The
deal also included me as dolphin trainer. In effect, I would be the
liaison between Miami Seaquarium and MGM.

We jogged on around the little lake, stopped and caught our breath.
Ricou put his hands on his hips and gazed across the bay, the rosy
dawn splashed with shades of pink, touches of a nameless yellow, and
a copper orange beyond belief. The air, descending on us like a magic
spell, was spiked with the dangerous scents of distant Caribbean jun-
gles. Ricou, poised as if on a mountaintop, drank it in and sighed,
then turned to me and wiped the sweat from his face with a towel.
"If this comes through, Ric, your biggest job will be the four new

dolphins." He smiled. "You know what we need." He tossed the towel to me and I caught it. "Do what you can with them."

I nodded. Ricou wanted me to train them so that they could fill in for Susie. A master of preproduction planning, Ricou had decided that four extra dolphins would cover most contingencies. The cost? Very little compared with the cost of not having Flipper available.

Ricou never preached to me about money; he didn't need to. I was always intensely aware of the cost—not only of things, but of time. Ricou did not have to tell me that he did not want a hundred people standing around waiting for a dolphin to follow the script.

He told me to get the dolphins used to having lots of people around. Susie is a veteran, he said. She's used to the crowd and the noise. Or she used to be. Who knows now? One morning bright and early the trucks will come, he said, the movie people will pull up, pile out, and go to work. It's noisy, people rushing about, lots of confusion. The camera operators, sound men, directors and actors, specialists in a hundred technical aspects of making movies, suddenly would all descend on this peaceful little lake and expect Flipper to do her tricks.

Then all eyes would be focused on me.

"Maybe I'll have some news later," he said as he left.

That morning a cold front came through. Wind, rain, then suddenly it was forty degrees! In Miami, that's freezing. But it was my job to be with Susie and the others. Hot or cold, they had to be fed and looked after. Late that afternoon I was wearing my wet suit, a quarter-inch of black neoprene, with booties and a hat, floating in an inner tube while Susie played around. Ricou, wearing a dark-red windbreaker, came down from the front office. "How's she doing?" he yelled, walking out on the floating dock. He grinned and I knew the papers were signed.

"Okay," I yelled back, paddling over.

"It's all set," he said. "The series is on. I'm going home to play Santa Claus for the holidays." Ricou hadn't been home in ages. Now that *Flipper* would become a series, he could relax with his family.

I nodded. "Okay."

"I'll take my vacation, too," he said. He dug his hands into his pockets and let his shoulders sag a little. "I need to recharge my batteries."

I nodded and splashed some water just to see what would happen. Susie, cavorting around, nuzzled me.

Ricou gave me a lopsided grin. "Aren't you cold in there?"

"Cold?" I shook my head. "No. I'm freezing."

He snorted.

A shiver went along my spine and my jaw chattered uncontrollably. "Susie likes company," I said, "cold or not."

Ricou grinned. "And Susie gets what Susie wants?"

"Always."

"Then I would say, Ric, that Susie has got you well trained."

We both chuckled. It was a joke but also not a joke, as we both knew.

"Want some advice?" he asked me suddenly.

I was surprised. Ricou seemed solemn. I had never seen him like that before. "Sure," I said.

"Don't get attached to them." He was serious.

"You mean Susie?" Almost on cue, Susie popped up in front of me, grinning.

"Susie, yes. And all of them."

"I'll try not to," I said.

"That's good because," he shook his head, "this won't last forever."

"I know." I splashed the water and it made a thousand ripples.

He looked around as if for a final time. "If I had any doubts that you could handle things here—"

"Don't worry about it. This is the easiest job I ever had."

Ricou nodded. "You'll be alone." He shot me a look to see if I reacted. I didn't. "Think you can start training the other four while I'm gone?"

"I'll give it a shot." I shrugged like it was all in a day's work. "How long will you be gone?"

"I don't know exactly." A sailboat went by and we both studied it a minute. The late-afternoon sun backlighted the sails in an interesting way. He turned back to me. "But I'll be in touch, okay? Just do what you can with 'em. And by the way, Ric, Merry Christmas."

He left, waving a final good-bye. Suddenly I shuddered. The cold. I had been in the water too long. My fingers were shriveled up. I had the feeling that something was wrong but I couldn't put my finger on it. I paddled over to the dock, pulled myself up and then pulled in the inner tube. "I'll see you later, Susie. But I've had it for today."

* * *

I was shivering. I went in and took a long, hot shower, rubbed myself down with a rough towel and put on my Levis, my sweat shirt, and Topsiders with wool socks, which was practically my winter uniform. Then I drove home, which was a motel-efficiency near the Miami Seaquarium. Ricou wanted me always to be within a few minutes of the dolphins. What a life! I thought. Living in a motel on Key Biscayne during the height of the season, driving a rental car of my own choice, having an expense account to buy anything I wanted to for Susie. In the navy I'd hardly dared to dream of such a life as this. I sighed deeply and went to the refrigerator, opened the freezer and there, arrayed in frosty rows, was a vast selection of TV dinners. I chose one and scraped off the frost. Haddock. "No," I thought. "I've had it with haddock." I put it back and got another one: creamed chicken. I put it in the oven and turned on the heat, then walked into the living room and flipped on the TV. If I was going to be in the business, I'd better know what it was all about. The news was on. I switched the dial quickly, looking for "Sea Hunt," "Jacques Cousteau" or—ah!—"Lassie." Lassie is like Flipper, or vice versa, and both are like Mickey Mouse, all of them more an idea than a real animal. I watched the show unfold not for the entertainment but to see how they did things. I'd heard somewhere that Rudd Weatherwax, a Hollywood animal trainer, had seven dogs named Lassie. He didn't use the same dog all the time. They were specialized. Some were good jumpers, some were relatively unafraid of fire or falling, some were trained to attack the bad guys, and so on.

When we caught the other four dolphins as backups for Susie, Ricou asked me what I was going to name them. Naming is the trainer's prerogative. I had the right to name them anything I wanted to. "Let's just name them all Flipper," I suggested flippantly. "That's certainly the simplest and probably the cleverest as well." Ricou didn't say anything but I knew that he didn't go for it. Only Ricou and I could tell one dolphin from another anyway, I argued, and the dolphins never knew their own names, so why not? For a while we did call them Flipper 1, Flipper 2, and so on and it worked reasonably well, but then one day Ricou said he wanted to name one of them Kathy, for the wife of his friend Leon Benson, a director who had helped him in the business.

I don't know why this seemed like a challenge to me. "Which one do you want me to name Kathy?" I asked him.

He gave a shrug. "Doesn't matter."

"Oh, but I think it does matter. There could be problems."

"For example?"

"For example, if you want Kathy to be Flipper No. 1, then Flipper 2 would be the first of the numbered dolphins. And that doesn't make sense. It would make more sense, I think, if Flipper 2 became Flipper 1, Flipper 3 became Flipper 2 and—"

"Okay, okay. What is this," he said, "a new Abbott-and-Costello routine? Forget it. It doesn't matter."

I thought I detected a testy note in his voice. "You don't want me to call them numbers, do you? Why not?"

"I don't care, Ric. I don't care at all. It seems a little impersonal, that's all, but if you want to, I don't really care. Call them anything you want. What do you want to call them?"

"Call them a cab," I said. "Or let's call them all Susie." I laughed in a silly way. "Yes. That's it! Then when they ask me if they're working with Susie today, I'll tell them it's Susie today, Susie tomorrow, and always Susie."

"That's ridiculous," Ricou said. "You're not taking this seriously."

"Not taking this seriously! That's a ridiculous thing to say. It's *all* ridiculous! What ridiculous names do you want to call them?"

"Call them anything," Ricou said with a show of exasperation, "anything at all. I don't care." We were at the lake, I floating on a surfboard and he on the dock. He turned on his heel, retreating. "Except for one thing," he threw over his shoulder: "Don't call them late for dinner." Besides Susie and Kathy, the other three were finally named Patty, Scottie, and Squirt.

Lassie was running across a field to warn of fire or something like that. I yawned. Sometimes when I got back to the motel, I fell asleep almost at once. It was a mistake to lie down when I first got home. It was a mistake even to close my eyes. They felt puffed up right now. If I closed my eyes, I would certainly fall asleep and I would not wake up till the middle of the night. I would be starving. That had happened more than once. Now I ate first, or put the TV dinner in the oven to cook. That was supposed to keep me awake but once I fell asleep anyway, waking up early in the morning, a cosmic snow on the tube, my TV dinner burned to a crisp, the peas shriveled up like BB's. Tonight was different. How strange and on edge I felt. Was it connected with Ricou's leaving? It wasn't the responsibility, was it? I got up and flipped the dial again, looking for "Sea Hunt." I got a kick out of seeing Ricou Browning's name in the credits. Would mine be there one day? What a strange, exciting world I was in suddenly. I didn't know exactly where I was going but it didn't matter; I knew it was in the right direction. Except tonight something was clearly askew.

I began to fill out the Flipper log automatically. Times, tricks, food—and then it hit me! Food!

Susie hadn't eaten all day. I hadn't thought about it at the time but she had just played with the food I gave her. This occasionally happens with dolphins. Nobody knows why, but one day every month or two they simply don't want any food. Usually it means nothing. The next day they're hungry again and make up for not having eaten. But not eating is also the first sign of getting sick. And if they go for two days without eating, you may have a sick dolphin. Then you start doing whatever you can think of to snap them back. Would something happen to Susie the first day Ricou was gone? I had his phone number in Ocala. At what point should I call him? If Susie got sick now, would this fabulous lifestyle of mine end?

I threw on my bathrobe, hopped in the car and roared down the highway to the Seaquarium. It was three minutes away; I think it took me about two minutes to get there. I went through the back gate and pulled up at Flipper's Lake, swung out of the car and half-ran toward the dock, then stopped. The moon was nearly full. I scanned the lake. There she was, in the middle. I went out on the floating dock, leaned down and slapped the water. She swam over to me.

"Hello, sweetheart," I said. Suddenly I knew exactly what to do. "Hold on a minute," I said. I stood up, my bathrobe flapping, and snapped my fingers. "Yes. That's it!" I walked quickly to the fish house, went into the freezer, hardly noticed that my teeth were chattering again, and picked out a specially plump Spanish mackerel. "If this doesn't work . . . ," I muttered. I left the thought unfinished because it *would* work—it *had* to work—and in a moment or two I had fixed the fish just the way Susie liked it. I cut off the fish's head and tail, gutted it in a stroke, and in a flash of the knife I had denuded it of fins. Then I held the carcass in the palm of my hands. It was fat and succulent. I held it up to the light. "Beautiful," I said. Then I lovingly placed it in my yellow bucket and walked proudly back to the lake. "This is it, Susie," I said as I walked down the dock. She was waiting, eyeing me with amusement. I got down on my knees at the end of the dock. I smiled as I removed this most appealing of mackerels from the yellow bucket and presented it to her as if it were a jeweled bracelet. "For you, dear Susie." Her eyes brightened momentarily. She took it in her mouth. "Go ahead," I said. "It's good, baby, the way you like it."

I've never looked at myself at times like this, when I'm caught up in the moment. But looking back on it now, I think I must have merged two contradictory feelings, one that I could make a miracle if I chose to, the other that I was completely at the mercy of this whimsical being.

Susie tossed the fish up like a toy. Still kneeling at the end of the floating dock, I implored her: "Please! Please don't play games with me."

She bobbed her head and I got the feeling that I was being scanned by sonar waves. Was she trying to tell me something?

"If we could talk," I said, "what would you tell me, Susie? That you're sick? No, I don't think you're sick. Would you tell me that you realize Ricou is going, that you and I are a team now?" I considered this for a moment. "That's possible," I said finally. "Or you might want to tell me something entirely different. That you're not happy here, that you've had second thoughts, that being a star is not what it's cracked up to be and you want to go back to the sea."

She bobbed her head, smiling as always, as if to make me think she was reading my mind and agreeing. If so, she knew what I really wanted her to do. I wanted her to eat. She picked up the fish and I thought for a moment she would swallow it just to oblige me but she didn't; she tossed it high in the air and down it came with a splash.

"Let me tell you something more," I said, still on my knees to her. "This is bigger than both of us." I glanced up at the sky. It was black but with ten thousand blinking stars. "If you put things in perspective, Susie, what we've got here is big—but not cosmically big. I mean it's not like the world was going to end, right? It's just a TV series, after all. It will affect your whole future, of course, and mine, Ricou's future and the jobs of hundreds of people—that's all, plus hundreds more back in Hollywood, the editors and writers and promoters and investors, so it gets into the thousands, probably, and don't forget the people who love you, Susie. To them you *are* Flipper. Could you let all those people down? No, Susie, you cannot let us down. You cannot turn your back on love, on the love of millions of people, on the thousands of people who need you to make a buck, or on Ricou and—and me, Susie, me!" I reached down and picked up the fish that I had prepared so beautifully and that was now sinking slowly like a piece of trash. Angrily, I shook it at Susie and yelled:

"*You cannot turn your back on this fish!*"

She took the fish in her mouth. "Good girl," I purred. Then she flipped it up with a toss of her head again and it splashed back into the water.

I stood up and glared down at her. "You know, Susie, you've really never had it so good. Look at this. Your own lake. All the attention in the world. Playthings. Food—anything you want to eat. Anything at all!" I slapped the water, she came over and I leaned down and rubbed the top of her head. "But don't take all this for granted." A sudden chill went up my spine and I shivered. "There are four others back there, waiting for their chance. They can be Flipper as well as you. Maybe better. In fact, Susie, I've been meaning to tell you something, that there have been some complaints about you. Sometimes you play a little rough. The tail. Watch it. Know what I mean?" I stood up and dusted my hands. "Yes, damn it, Susie, you better shape the hell up or you're *out!*"

I stomped off the dock without looking back. I have no idea if she ever ate that fish. But at least we both knew who was really boss.

12

The Bamboo Trick

To teach is to learn.
—Japanese proverb

One of the first of Flipper's tricks that I worked on, and one of the most important, was what I call the bamboo jumps. It was the opening shot of *Flipper's New Adventure,* and it set the tone of the whole movie. Ricou called it the "establishing shot" because it established the premise of the story.

Ricou and I were on the dirt road at Flipper's Lake and he was outlining the scene he wanted to get on film. "You know the story," he said.

I nodded. We had talked about it a lot. Porter Ricks, a widower with his two sons, is embarking on a new assignment. He will be chief ranger of Coral Key Park and Marine Preserve in the Florida Keys. Their new house is on a lagoon, which opens on the ocean, where Flipper lives.

"Good," Ricou said. "The opening shot will be through the window of the camper, across the father and two sons to the lagoon, where we can see Flipper following them in the background." Ricou had eloquent hand gestures. With just a few flicks of his hands I knew exactly where the camper would be going, where the camera would be and where Flipper had to be jumping in the background. He glanced at me and I nodded. "That shot depends on Flipper jumping in the background."

I nodded. I was wondering how he planned to do it.

"Got any ideas?"

"Me? You mean about—"

"About Flipper, yes."

I shook my head.

Ricou crossed his arms on his chest and studied the lake for a long moment. Several gulls wheeled in tight formation above us, cocked their heads downward and squealed. "We've got to get Flipper to jump ten—no, make that twelve times in a row, nice smooth picture-perfect jumps and dives." He illustrated a series of jackknife dives with his right hand.

I nodded.

"You want to try that this morning?"

"Me?" I pointed at myself.

He nodded.

"I want to try, sure," I said, crossing my arms on my chest, "but I don't think—just off-hand, looking at it objectively—well, I think I see a problem here."

He nodded again.

"The problem," I said, "is how to get Susie to jump twelve times in a row if she expects to be fed after every jump."

Ricou grinned at me. "If it was easy, Ric, they wouldn't need us." He patted me on the shoulder. "Shouldn't be too hard, actually. Just apply the training method I taught you."

"Common sense?"

"Exactly."

I studied the lake again. Susie was in the lake, watching me. It would not be hard to get Susie to jump once. With a simple signal, a rolling motion of the hand, index finger extended, Susie would jump. But then Susie would expect a fish. And I didn't know a signal that would tell her not to expect a fish. One of the keys to Ricou's common-sense training method was to break behavior down to its simplest element. If you looked at this trick as twelve jumps in a row, it seemed impossible. But what if you thought about twelve tricks of one jump each? I was thinking along that line when Ricou said: "Why not try bamboo poles?"

My face brightened. "I hadn't thought of that," I said. "Yeah!" I looked at the lake anew. I turned to Ricou suddenly: "What do you mean, bamboo poles?"

"If Susie had twelve bamboo poles to jump over—"

"Yes!" I exclaimed. It was fascinating to see the method at work. Besides simplicity, another key element to his method was to consider the obvious, and what was more obvious than to give Susie something to jump over? I said, "I could suspend the bamboo poles just below the surface of the water."

"Exactly," he said. He glanced at his watch. "Oops! They're waiting for me." He regarded the lake abstractly for a moment, one arm across his chest, the other with the hand and fingers cupping his chin. "Bamboo poles," he said with a quiet smile. "Yes. That should do it nicely."

I went out and bought a bunch of bamboo poles, cut them off in six-foot lengths and used diving weights and monofilament lines to hold them in place just beneath the surface of the water. But the surface of the water kept changing with the tide, of course, and so I had to keep adjusting them. Anything new in Flipper's Lake immediately became one of Susie's playthings. When she ran off with one of them, I had to track it down and put it back. But Ricou had the right idea. I put two of the poles out at first, and the problem, as we thought it would be, was that Susie expected to be fed after each jump.

In training dolphins, you must overcome certain almost instinctive reactions. When you want the dolphin to jump over two poles, for example, the temptation is to hold up your hand showing two fingers, and to say "two" very distinctly, mouthing it so that there can be no doubt about what is meant. But that means nothing to a dolphin. He lives in an acoustically different world. Even assuming that the dolphin would notice your mouth, he would probably assume that it was a strangely positioned blowhole. And strangely ineffective, too, for it made sounds that to him were almost inaudibly low like the deepest rumblings of thunder are to us.

One thing Susie always understood very clearly was whether she got a fish or not. When she jumped over one of the poles and came to me so proudly, wanting a chunk of fish, I refused and made the gesture for her to jump again.

This may sound strange, but I deliberately kept Susie confused. She already expected to be rewarded after every jump, so sometimes I did reward her, sometimes I didn't. The result is that every time she jumped one of the bamboo poles, she glanced at me on the shore to see if she was to be rewarded or not. If not, I gave her the jump sign from shore and she jumped again and, when she came up, glanced at me. And so it went, I giving her the jump sign each time she jumped till she had jumped all twelve of them. When I caught on to how the trick could be done, we rehearsed it three times, I called in the director and he shot it.

As it so often happened, Flipper's variation turned out to be better than the one we originally planned. On film it looked as if Flipper was keeping up with the Ricks family by jumping along and keeping an eye on them, though in fact she was watching me and the yellow fish bucket.

The bamboo poles? Yes, they were important as markers, showing Susie where to jump. But as I realized later, I could have trained her much more simply. I could have left out the bamboo poles.

Several years later we needed the same trick, Susie jumping a dozen times in a row and keeping an eye on the road. It took about a minute to remind her and then she did it perfectly.

You Can Take the Director Out of Hollywood, But . . .

Shooting "Flipper" was a lot more complicated than most TV series. If you ask film directors what they want least in their scripts, they will tell you three things: animals, children, and water. The problem is that you never know for sure what any of them will do next. We had all three. So the key to shooting "Flipper" was flexibility, which included accepting the help of the professionals who did the show week after week. In those days, TV series were shot on film, and produced by Hollywood professionals with experience in making movies. Most of the directors who shot "Flipper" understood the difficulties we faced. All of the directors wanted to do a good job. In Hollywood, your future is no better than your last movie. But when time is money, coming in under budget depends on clockwork precision. And when a hundred people are involved, including people with large talents and larger egos, the logistics of getting it done tend to become more important than getting it done. When the new directors came in and read the script, saw how much the story depended on subtleties they had no control over, on whether a dolphin could look "concerned but confident," for instance, they shook their heads and asked in mock despair: "Is this going to look real?"

"A lot of things probably look impossible," I would tell them, "but there's never been anything in the script that Flipper couldn't do."

And then I made sure it worked.

The most unforgettable director we had was an old-timer who had made his reputation shooting Westerns. I could tell from the way he was setting things up that he had some fundamental misconceptions. Trying to help, I suggested: "Dolphins are not like horses."

He whirled on me and glared as if I had just said the forbidden word. In Hollywood, the rules are rather rigid about who may speak to whom. The animal trainer, for instance, never speaks to the director. The director supposedly has so much on his mind that he cannot be bothered by whatever the animal trainer might have to say. If the animal trainer must get a message to the director, he speaks to the first-assistant director, who will then tell the director if *he* thinks the director should be told. We were not in Hollywood, but the protocol was still very strong.

The director looked on me balefully. "And what's that supposed to mean?"

"Dolphins work on the reward system," I explained. "When they've had enough to eat, that's a wrap." I shrugged.

The director eyed me with a frown and I realized that he was playing a role himself, the role of the stereotypical director. Hollywood is full of them. Bald-headed, short, and heavyset, he had a white moustache and goatee, an electric megaphone, and—of all things—a gold cigarette holder with a 100 mm. filter cigarette in it. The only part of his costume missing was a pith helmet, which was probably optional. "Hmmmm," he said as though musing to himself, "like actors, then."

He looked at the Call Sheet he had already made up. The Call Sheet is like a military Plan of the Day, where everything is scheduled in detail—which scenes will be shot, who is involved, where it will be shot and when. Everybody had a copy of the script and when the Call Sheet came out, they compared the two to find out if they were involved. I did this for Flipper, of course, and tried to arrange the more difficult tricks for when she would be hungrier and therefore more cooperative. A tricky shot had been set up for first thing in the morning. Normally that was when I preferred to do the tough shots, but today was different. Susie had eaten like a pig the day before and I knew that she was still full. I said, "Is it possible to make that shot later in the day?"

The director's mouth got ugly. "No," he said, shaking his gleaming head. "It's *not* possible." He was holding the Call Sheet, which he had rolled up into a tube. He bounced this with one hand into the palm of the other. "You've read this, I presume. Well, that's the way it's going to be."

The bald-headed director was probably responding to relationships one usually finds in Hollywood, relationships of time-honored self-interest. In Hollywood, animal trainers are members of the Teamsters Union. This goes back to the days when animal trainers handled horses and cattle in Westerns and, in the process, drove the stagecoaches and wagons, which qualified them for membership in the Teamsters. As such, they work by the hour, and a good deal of their thinking is in terms of extending the time it takes to get their work done.

The situation in "Flipper," however, was quite different, beginning with the fact that I was not a member of the Teamsters. I was paid not hourly but by the season. I was as eager as the director to get on with the shooting. I knew that he didn't realize that Susie had been fed twice as much as usual the day before, that she wasn't hungry and therefore didn't give a flying fig if we ever shot the scene. I tried to tell him. "You see—"

He waved me off, shaking his gleaming head. He squinted his eyes at me, little black dots peeking through the bushes of his eyebrows. "You want me to change my schedule? No, I've planned this down to the second and you will have your beast ready to perform on cue. Understood?"

"I understand, yes, sir," I said. "But. . . ."

He glared and I said nothing more.

"Quiet on the set," the assistant director called out. It was precisely 10 A.M. Everybody was ready, the cameramen, the actors, the directors and all the assorted supporting personnel, including me; I was near the actors but out of camera range, as usual. This was the moment we were all working toward. Then the director spoke to me: "Bring on the creature."

I did.

And then, dramatically: "Roll camera and *action!*"

The scene was between the Father, who is on the dock in front of the Ricks' home, and an officer in the Coast Guard, who has just hurriedly arrived in a Coast Guard launch. In the background, the sky is dark, the waves frothy:

COAST GUARDSMAN: (*Cutting engine.*) There's a bad storm coming in. Have you heard?

FATHER: A bad storm! No, we haven't heard a thing. (*With apprehension.*) And Bud is out on the sandbar, digging for treasure!

COAST GUARDSMAN: (*Close-up.*) It's getting nasty out there. We'd better get word to him. Does he have a radio?

FATHER: (*Close-up.*) He has one, yes, but I've been trying to raise him all morning. It must be on the blink.

COAST GUARDSMAN: (*Medium shot.*) That could be serious.

FATHER: (*Close-up, face brightens.*) Wait a minute! I think I've got an idea! (*He takes out a pen and paper, writes something.*) I'll give this note to Flipper!

FLIPPER: (*Wide shot, appearing between them in background.*) Raising her head above water and nods head eagerly up and down.

The camera grinds away, the actors speak their lines correctly and the camera focuses on the spot of water between the Father and Coast Guardsman.

But there is no Flipper!

"*Cut!*" cried the director. His fat face was like a blunt instrument aimed at me. "That was your *cue!* Why didn't you send in the beast?"

"I tried to explain to you, sir—"

"Speak up! I can't hear you!"

I yelled at him that I had tried to explain about dolphins not being horses. I dropped in a couple of extra "sirs" to make sure he understood there was no disrespect here, either by me or by Susie, of him and his exalted position, but my voice wasn't projecting. The director turned to his first assistant, his face contorted. "What's he say?"

"*He said that dolphins are not horses!*"

The director turned on me furiously, hands on hips and his shoulders hunched forward. The assistant director had told him what I said but not how I said it.

I walked out to the end of the dock, closer to the director, cupped my mouth and yelled again: "I'm very sorry, sir, but I have no control over Flipper when she is not hungry. When Flipper is not hungry, we're shut down."

Jimmy Pergola, camera operator, cut in. "That's what we tried to tell you."

The director's head was bobbing around like it was on a string. His voice wavering, he said: "Do you mean to tell me that I must wait— I must wait for an animal to get hungry?"

"That's about the size of it, sir," I said.

With a heavy twist to each word, he replied: "And when do you think your animal will be hungry enough to perform?"

I looked at my watch. "Around noon," I said.

He smacked his lips. "You *are* the animal trainer, aren't you?"

"Allow me to correct you, sir," I said. "I'm the *dolphin* trainer."

"And allow *me* to correct *you*, sir," the director said with withering sarcasm. "That dolphin is the trainer. He's got us *all* eating out of his hands."

Andy White and the Hula Taildance

"Flipper" episodes were written by a number of talented people, but the most prominent, perhaps, was Andy White, who had written for "Sea Hunt" and "The Undersea World of Jacques Cousteau." He was in his 50s, gray-haired and soft-spoken. I had been told that he would be heading out to talk to me about dolphins, but I didn't know when. The part of my job I enjoyed the most was telling the top people in the "Flipper" organization about dolphins. It was a hot summer day and Kathy was lolling around in the water near the end of the pier where I was hanging out. I was trying to decide whether to keep sitting there or to slip into the water myself when Andy came up, waved from the shore and headed out. I was about to stand up and shake hands, but as soon as he got to me he took off his shoes and socks, sat down and stuck his feet in the water. "Ahhh!" he said with pleasure. "This sure beats L.A."

I laughed. "I hear that a lot. They told me you might drop by to see the dolphins."

He nodded. "I spend most of my time in an office, trying to imagine things like this." He gazed around in wonder. "Just think: no smog!" He laughed. "I thought if I could see what a dolphin could really do, it might help me with plot ideas."

"And you might be surprised," I said, "but I might get some good ideas from you, too. Come on, let's go."

"Ric," he said with a plaintive look, "could we just sit here and talk a minute? I just put my feet in the water." He wiggled his toes.

I laughed and sat down with him and we talked about some of the "Flipper" stories he had written, the ones he liked the best and the ones he was thinking about writing. We're all in this together, he said at one point, and it can only help if we know what everyone else is thinking. I told him that I took special pride in getting Flipper to do any trick he could imagine, and that so far it had all been possible. "Not because of me necessarily," I said, "but sometimes, I think, in spite of me." I hesitated because you don't say things closest to your heart to just anyone. "We work with dolphins all the time, and it may be," I ventured, "that if you understood a little more about them and could get a feel for their amazing potential, you might be open to even more imaginative stories."

His ears perked up. I told him about how quickly they caught on to the little tricks we expected of them and that many dolphin trainers, including myself, had said they had the feeling that there was a lot more to dolphins than what we were making contact with, that sometimes the relationship was—I stopped and glanced sharply at him. You can't talk to everybody like this. Most people maintain such a desperate grip on reality that they don't dare consider the possibility of other worlds. But Andy understood the world of feelings and the world of possibilities. He realized that I wasn't making extravagant claims about dolphins. I had no evidence for that, no acceptable evidence, anyway.

But what if—and this was my point—what if our idea of evidence was wrong? What if we should trust our feelings about some things? What if it were true, in other words, that they could read not our minds, though that's not impossible, but our souls? That they were way ahead of us and urging us on? What evidence would count in proving any of that? I don't remember how much of this I put into words, but Andy was silent for a long moment, then he put on his shoes and socks and said: "Let's go. I'd like to see some of this myself."

We walked over to the fish house, I got a bucket of fish and, walking back to the lake, I said: "I'll show you a few things we can do."

He grinned. "You said 'we,' things 'we' can do."

"I just talk that way," I said. "I meant Kathy and I, of course. Or maybe I should say just Kathy. Or do I mean just Flipper?"

Andy laughed. "I understand, Ric. Or I think I do."

We went back to Flipper's Lake and out onto the floating dock, and there Kathy and I went through practically every trick we knew. It was like the Top Deck Show, but Kathy did it all herself. It was a one-dolphin three-ring circus, with Kathy jumping, diving, flipping and flopping, tossing balls in the air, and playing catch with both Andy and me. Above us were fifteen or twenty seagulls gliding around in various orbits and squealing like pigs. I noticed one especially high that was poised for dive-bombing. I tossed a chunk of fish in his path and he came screaming through, caught it in his mouth and swooped up again into the sky. Andy got a hallelujah look on his face. "That's amazing," he said. "The seagulls, you feed them too?"

"To keep 'em around, sure."

"Beautiful," Andy White said.

"They add something."

"Yes, they do," he said. "Atmosphere." He was beaming at me. "That's the kind of thing I was looking for."

"Here's something else for you," I said. I gave the signal for a tailwalk to Kathy. This signal is a broad movement like a baseball pitcher hauling off to throw the ball. When Kathy sees that, she rears up out of the water as high as she can, all except her tail, which she beats furiously like an outboard motor. Then, still beating her tail, she leans backwards. But instead of falling down, she travels across the water on her tail. The tailwalk is one of the dolphin's most truly amazing tricks. Many of the dolphin's tricks are variations of what they do in nature. But not the tailwalk. To do that, dolphins have to work at it, building up the muscles in their tails. Like any other athletes, they must condition themselves and practice.

"Amazing," Andy said.

"Watch this," I said. Kathy came back and I gave her another signal, both of my hands about head high, palms out, and she did the tail-*dance,* a variation of the tail*walk.* Instead of traveling backwards, Kathy rose up out of the water, beating her tail as she did before, but this time she stayed in one place.

"Incredible," Andy said. "How do you do that?"

The only difference in teaching the two tricks, I told him, is where I toss the fish. In the taildance, I toss it to where she is; in the tailwalk, I toss it slightly over her head. When she comes up on her tail, she's really just trying to reach the fish I throw.

Andy cocked his head and got an impish expression. "Could she do that wearing a hula skirt?"

It had never been done before but if I could get her to wear the hula skirt, it would be simple. "Sure," I said. "Want me to work on it?"

"How long would it take you?"

"Not long."

Actually it took only a few minutes if you don't count the time it took me to get things ready for Kathy. Here's how I did it.

First, I got an old automobile inner tube. In my office I had dozens of things like that, dolphin playthings like floating toys, beach balls, wind-up fish, and anything they might want to amuse themselves with. I kept them busy playing all the time so that they wouldn't become bored. Bored dolphins tend to get sick. My only concern, like that of any parent, was to make sure I didn't give them anything with a sharp point or so small that they might swallow it. I had an open-ended expense account for items like this, and I was forever buying toys and writing Flipper's name on them. What happened to all these things? Souvenir hunters. I didn't mind when they walked off with them. It was the best advertising we had. I got the inner tube and taped the valve so that Kathy wouldn't scratch herself on it. I was on the end of the dock with my bucket of fish. I held one of the chunks of fish a little above the inner tube and Kathy, a very bright girl, got the idea immediately. She poked her snout up through the inner tube and got the fish.

Here's what we were thinking:

> RIC: Good! She's catching on fast. Must be hungry.
> KATHY: Hey! Pretty good! I put my snout in the inner tube and the Fish-guy gave me a fish. Is this another one of his games? And if so, I wonder if it will work again.
> (*She tries it.*)
> RIC: She's catching on *very* fast! Good, I'll give her another one to keep her interest up.
> KATHY: Eureka! This is like a money machine. I poke my head through the inner tube and the Fish-guy gives me a fish. Now the question is: how long, oh lord, how long will this go on?
> RIC: This is easier than I thought it would be. I was afraid at

first she might shy off putting her snout in the inner tube.
But if she was afraid of the inner tube, she's over it now.
Look at her, poking her head up through the inner tube! I'll
feed her again just to let her know that I approve. And now
look! She's doing it twice as fast! But that's not really what I
wanted. I want her to come on through.
(*She sticks her head through and gets nothing.*)
KATHY: Now what!
RIC: If I hold the fish just a little higher above her head,
maybe she'll get the idea.
KATHY: Maybe if I wiggle my head a little coming through,
that'll start things up again.
(*Kathy sticks her snout through the inner tube and wiggles
her head.*)
RIC: That was odd, wiggling her head like that. Wonder if
she's getting tired. Come on, Kathy, don't give up. Here's the
fish. Come and get it.
KATHY: What's he doing, anyway, holding the fish so far
away? Does he think I'll do *anything* for a piece of fish? So,
okay, I'll see if this is what it's all about.
(*Desperately seeking the fish formula, she now sticks her
head a little farther through the inner tube.*)
RIC: Aha! Good! Here's two chunks of fish for you.
KATHY: Aha! I think I've got the Fish-guy figured out.
(*Kathy sticks her head all the way through and Ric tosses
three fish chunks.*)
KATHY: Ah! The magic button! Now watch me get the whole
bucket!
(*Kathy puts her whole head and pectoral fins through the in-
ner tube till it catches on her dorsal fin in back.*)
RIC: What a piece of luck!
(*He tosses her three fish chunks again.*)
KATHY: The jackpot! He's a little cheap but, let's face it, he's
all I've got.

By this time, Kathy was ready for the tailwalk while wearing the
inner tube. When she came up the next time, virtually wearing the
inner tube, I gave her the sign for the tailwalk, which she already
knew how to do. When she saw the hand signal, she knew what she

would have to do for the chunk of fish, so up she went, her tail beating the water to a froth; and then back she went, walking on her tail while wearing the big black inner tube.

At the end of the tailwalk, Kathy usually splashed into the water, but wearing the inner tube, when she fell back, she bounced back to her tail again. I laughed. I always tried to be open with Kathy and the other dolphins. If I felt something, I expressed it. I wanted them to know how things were going. The worst thing that can happen to a dolphin is to perform and not know whether it's any good or not. Like anyone else, they need approval, which means chunks of fish, but it's more than that. Especially in this alien environment, they need constant feedback. I always tried to be with them and to let them know where they stood. When Kathy bounced back to her tail, I laughed to show her that it was funny, sure, but also that I loved her and that she was okay. "Don't be alarmed," my laughter said. She shrugged herself back out of the inner tube and came racing over to me and I showered her with fish chunks.

The inner tube was too fat to be used with the hula skirt but it was good as a training tool. I called the prop room and got a plastic hula-hoop, cut out a section and put it back together so that it was about forty-five inches round, just large enough for Kathy to wiggle into. The prop department also had several hula skirts. I put one of them on the hula-hoop and left it in the water with Kathy so that she could get used to it. She nosed around it a little, making sure it was okay, then with the offer of a chunk of fish, I got her to come up through the hula-hoop with the hula skirt attached just as she had with the inner tube.

She came up through the hula-hoop, got her flippers over it and was wearing the hula skirt, then I gave her the tailwalking sign and back she went, laughing as she always did, which is exactly what Andy White wanted.

That trick appeared in "Flipper Joins the Circus," which was the story of how Flipper and the Ricks boys put on a circus in the neighborhood to raise money for a worthy cause.

300 *Feet Below*

We followed the same principle in "300 Feet Below." The story, originally written by executive producer Ivan Tors himself, is about a doctor sailing in the Keys who happens to fall over the side where he is attacked by a shark. Bleeding profusely, the doctor manages to crawl back into the sailboat, where he radios the Coast Guard for help. He manages to apply a tourniquet to stop the bleeding but he's already lost a lot of blood. On the radio he reports that he needs a transfusion: four pints of type A blood. Time is short, but there's enough time for the Coast Guard helicopter to reach him. The trip by helicopter would take about an hour.

Ranger Porter Ricks is aboard the helicopter when the call comes through, and the crew goes into action. Already near the hospital in Miami, they call, order the plasma, land on the roof and pick it up, then off they fly at full speed down the coast till they spot the doctor's sailboat. But as they lower the plasma to the doctor—disaster! The sailboat lurches and the line gets tangled in the rigging, the package comes loose and falls into the water, then sinks to the bottom, 300 feet below. The Coast Guardsmen are appalled. They can't fly back to Miami for more plasma, then all the way back to the boat. There's no time for that. Indeed, there isn't enough time even to radio for a second helicopter to pick up another package of plasma and make the hour-long trip.

These are anxious moments, but Sandy, listening to the drama at home on his own receiver, has an idea. He breaks in with a suggestion: if they buzz by and pick up him and Flipper, just fifteen minutes away, Flipper could dive down and retrieve the package of blood plasma.

But will it work? Will Flipper understand what they want him to do? That's the story's real question, the problem of interspecies communication.

Earlier in the show, we saw Flipper playing with an ammunition box he had found in the water, a box like the one that holds the plasma. The ammunition box was in the skiff back at the house with Flipper. The rescuers fly back in the helicopter to the Ricks' home, put Flipper in a sling and hoist him aboard, then Sandy picks up the ammunition box and off they fly to the sailboat.

En route, Sandy shows Flipper the ammunition box, then points straight down. Flipper doesn't understand at first. He cocks his head to one side, puzzled. Sandy tries again. And this time, Flipper understands. He bobs his head up and down and chatters excitedly.

"He's got it! He knows what we want!" Sandy tells the Coast Guardsmen. "But I'll go in the water with him to make sure."

The arrival at the sailboat was to be the big scene. The helicopter could have hovered within a few feet of the water and Flipper could have made a nonspectacular dive into the ocean. But that's not very good theater. So we went up fifteen feet, and there I, stunt-doubling for Sandy, and Flipper were scheduled to take the plunge.

I jumped, sure. That was my job. But did we actually drop Flipper out of the helicopter into the bay?

That was never even considered. Not that she would have swum away. I think Susie, Kathy, Patty, Squirt, and Scottie, the whole gang, would have come back. But we weren't about to take such a risk. We needed a stand-in dolphin. We had a fiberglass dolphin and a frozen dolphin we could have used. These were props. The frozen dolphin had been in the fish freezer for years. Where it came from, nobody knew. It might have been found dead on a beach somewhere or it could have died at the Seaquarium. We had used these two props in close-ups before, when Flipper was supposedly charging into the belly of a tiger shark.

But dropping the props from a helicopter? No, that wouldn't do. I was talking to Ricou about it.

"I don't like it either," he said. "But what else?"

"Wait a minute," I said, snapping my fingers. "You don't pay me for bright ideas, but I've got one anyway."

Ricou frowned. He hated unnecessary dialogue.

"Jimmy Kline," I said cryptically, rolling my eyes.

"Well? What about Jimmy Kline? You're not suggesting that...."

"No," I said, half smiling at the thought. "No, we can't dress Jimmy Kline up like Flipper and dump him over the side. But he says he has a dolphin he's going to release. Maybe we can use him."

I happened to have run into Jimmy in the snack bar earlier that week, where he was hunched over his coffee smoking a cigarette, and I had asked him how his new crop of dolphins were. They needed new dolphins from time to time in the Top Deck Show and the collecting boat simply went out and got them. They're all okay, Jimmy told me, except for one. This sometimes happened. Some dolphins simply refused to perform in captivity. Usually they were the older ones. "So far," he said, "all we've been able to train him to do is eat."

That was a standard joke among the divers.

When I told Ricou about it, he gave me the go-ahead, and I called Jimmy and lined it up. "Sure," he said. "He's all yours."

Roger Conklin, a big friendly man with a flare for public speaking and storytelling, was head of public relations at Miami Seaquarium. When he heard about the story we were shooting, he saw a news tie-in. "Miami Seaquarium to Release Flipper," he headlined a release.

A newsman from WTVJ, a television station that Wometco then owned, came out to check on it. He spotted me out by the small training pool and came over with his mike in hand, grinning. His TV camera running, he asked: "Surely you're not going to set Flipper free, are you?"

"That's right," I said. "This dolphin (I pointed at the old male we were going to release) is a stunt-dolphin double."

"He'll fill in for Flipper in the drop?"

"That's right."

"What's his name?"

Nobody had named the dolphin yet so I gave him the first name that popped into my head. "His name is Ricou," I said.

It made the evening news.

When we got aboard the helicopter for the drop, I was ready to double for Sandy. I was wearing his cut-off blue jeans, a polo shirt, and white sneakers. At first when I did stunts for Sandy, I wore a wig. But wigs always look like wigs. My hair is naturally curly, so I made the supreme sacrifice and had my hair straightened and dyed blond.

We caught the old male dolphin and once we were in the U.S. Coast Guard jet helicopter, I covered his eyes with a towel when we took off and rode right beside him. We circled above Biscayne Bay and got into position.

The drop was scheduled for 9 A.M. Aboard the helicopter were the camera operator and his assistant; Ben Chapman, production manager; and me with Ricou the dolphin and a fiberglass dolphin in case something went wrong. Ben, who was in charge of production costs, had the earphones on and was connected by walkie-talkie with everyone else. There were two boats with camera crews, a formula race boat near the drop, a second boat for long shots, each with a two- or three-man camera crew, and the barge, where the real Ricou was, with yet another camera and crew, script clerk, and assistant director, also water-safety experts and a paramedic, who was always available on tricky shots like this one.

As we circled off camera, Ben, getting word from Ricou below, held his hand up as a signal to the pilot, then he made a short chopping movement of his hand and said: "Let's go." We swooped in and hovered about fifteen feet above the spot, then Ben and I pushed Ricou the dolphin out, followed by me, feet first. It worked the first time. It was shown from several camera angles, but on the film it lasted twenty seconds.

Later that night after the drop, Ricou called me on the phone and said he had watched the TV news where I had named the dolphin after him. "I guess that was because he was big and strong and very bright," Ricou said.

"Not really," I replied. "He was stubborn as a mule and just as ornery."

The Most Unforgettable Trick

I'll never forget the day I finally taught Susie to throw a fish into the boat. It was November 22, 1963. I had been puzzling for some time about how to get such a complicated idea over to her. The story in *Flipper's New Adventure* involves Sandy adrift in a skiff far at sea, helpless and dying of hunger. Flipper finds him at last, catches a blue runner and tosses it into the boat for him. This was complicated because usually when Susie had a fish in her mouth, it went only one way: down. The problem was getting her to throw the fish instead of swallowing it. I thought at first we should work with an imitation blue runner, figuring that when she learned to throw the fake fish, I could switch her over to the real one. So I put in an order for some.

The special effects department at MGM sent me half a dozen rubber blue runners, perfect in every detail. Or so I thought. Susie was not impressed. She caught on to the fact that I wanted her to throw it back into the boat, but her performance lacked something—enthusiasm. I began to have second thoughts. If Susie didn't get the connection between the rubber fish and a real one, wouldn't I have the same problem about her eating the fish instead of throwing it when I switched to the real fish? In short, was I wasting a lot of time with this imitation fish?

Determined to settle this once and for all, late that morning I grabbed Flipper's bucket and headed for the skiff.

"Where are you going?" Luke asked as I went by.

"I'm going to try something different," I said.

"You are? Can I go?"

"Sure," I said.

We got in the skiff and I paddled out to the middle, followed by Susie.

"Exactly how are you going to do this?" Luke asked.

"When in doubt, I turn to Ricou's Common Sense Method," I said.

He turned that over. "What does that mean?"

"That," I said, "remains to be seen. But maybe I've made it more complicated than it needs to be. Now let me think this through. In some ways, this trick—throwing a fish into the boat—is like any other trick. When Susie does what I want her to do, I give her a reward. The reward is a fish. And that's what complicates this trick, because in this case the trick is not to *eat* the fish, which is what she does with her reward-fish, but to *throw* it. See the difference?"

Luke gave me a puzzled look. "I'm not sure," he said, "But maybe Susie does."

"Anyway," I said, "I asked myself what I've been doing wrong." Nodding solemnly, I jabbed at my head with my index finger. "And I think—but why talk about it? Let's see if it works!"

Flipper was at the end of the skiff. I had a blue runner in one hand, two blue runners in the other. When Susie opened her mouth, I put one of the blue runners into it. Before she could swallow it, however, I flipped it into the boat. Then quickly, I gave her *two* blue runners to eat.

Susie was amazed but delighted. In my research of what goes on in the mind of a dolphin, I established that one of the dolphin paradigms goes like this: A fish in the mouth is worth two in the bucket. In this case, I was teaching Susie a variation that went: one in the boat equals two in the mouth.

Two fish for one was a game Susie would play all day. I did it several times, putting the blue runner into her mouth, then flipping it into the boat and giving her two fish to eat.

Finally, the crucial moment came. She opened her mouth and I put a blue runner into it and instead of flipping it out, I gave her the signal to "throw" it, both hands straight out, palms up, then bringing the hands straight up to the shoulders. Susie, waiting for me to flip the fish out and give her two fish for the one, didn't know what to think at first. Then suddenly, in a moment of genius or desperation, she flipped her head and tossed the blue runner into the boat. "YO!" I cried. That's what I wanted! And I let her know it! I gave her *three* blue runners!

Then I turned around to Luke, grinning, and he grinned back. "Is that pretty good, or what?" I said.

"That's pretty good!" he said.

The rest was easy. In simple, common-sense stages I gradually changed the trick so that instead of putting the blue runner into her mouth, I put it into the water. Then I worked on getting Susie to throw the fish perfectly into the boat. Suddenly I realized that Susie was not just learning to do a scene in a movie. She was practically fishing for me. If I had wanted her to, Susie would have caught the blue runner herself, a live one, and thrown it in the boat for me.

This was so good I could hardly wait to tell the others. This was more than just a new trick, it was a dolphin breakthrough. Quickly I rowed Luke and myself back to the dock and tied up, then headed toward the snack shop, elated, where I was sure to see some people I could tell. I was walking on air, but on the way, a woman from the front office went by, a handkerchief to her face, crying. "What's the matter?" I asked. She shook her head—she couldn't speak—and walked on hurriedly.

"This is bizarre," I thought. I was almost at the snack shop when a man hurried by, his face a mask of anger. "What's going on?" I asked.

"The president has been shot."

I was stunned. "John Kennedy?"

"Yes," he said, shaking his head miserably. "And I think he's dead."

"Damn," I said. I don't remember what happened after that except that I told nobody about Susie's new trick and the dolphin breakthrough. It didn't seem important anymore.

The Dolphin Who Put Out Fires

Florida was to be represented at the 1964 New York World's Fair with a pavilion featuring trained dolphins from Miami Seaquarium. Eight new dolphins had been captured for the honor and were put into a new tank, which was the same size as the one to be built in New York, twenty by fifty by ten feet, complete with a feeding platform like the one in the Main Tank.

These dolphins could always be taught the old standard tricks—

leaps, jumping through hoops, wearing hats, and playing such games as basketball and bowling—but we were always on the lookout for a dolphin with a special talent, something that could become the basis of a new trick.

One day while working with Susie on *Flipper's New Adventure,* I glanced over into the New York Tank to see what the new dolphins were like and something caught my eye. One of them was playing with a feather. To keep from becoming bored, dolphins play with anything that happens to fall into their tank. And there were always feathers because the tank was near a stand of sixty-foot-high Australian pines, which were full of waterbirds: cranes, pelicans, gosset hawks, seagulls. What caught my eye was not that the dolphin was playing with a feather, they did that all the time, but the way he was playing with it. He was shooting a little jet of water out of his mouth at it, spitting water about five inches, *tchoo-tchoo-tchoo,* to drive the feather from one end of the pool to the other. My bucket of fish was handy so I tossed the dolphin a fish, and he did it again!

When Jimmy Kline, who was in charge of the eight new dolphins, noticed the one that was squirting a jet of water, now about six inches long, his eyes bugged out. He tossed the dolphin a fish, too, and suddenly the jet of water became nearly a foot long. The more Jimmy rewarded the dolphin, the longer the jet of water got. Finally, the dolphin was squirting a stream of water three feet long!

A dolphin that squirts water three feet is a novelty, perhaps, but not in itself an act. If Jimmy Kline had a gift, it was gnawing at an idea till it became an act of pure kitsch. Finally it came to him: fire!

Jimmy made a fire in a hibachi grill next to the pool and got the dolphin to squirt his three-foot stream of water on it and put it out. That was creative, entertaining, and potentially useful, but would it go in New York City? Jimmy had his doubts. From my vantage point at Susie's pool, I watched with fascination over the weeks as Jimmy elaborated on his gimmick, finally putting the fire in a two-story dollhouse open at the back. Then the master's touch: a skit. An announcer described the situation:

"Fire! Fire! The house is on fire! What can we do?"

Smoke is pouring out of the dollhouse.

"Hold on!" the announcer says. "Help is on the way!"

A siren wails!

Bells clang!

And now, rushing across the water, comes a dolphin to the rescue!
With—what's that on his head?
It looks like—yes, it is—*a fireman's hat!*
The dolphin screeches to a stop at the edge of the pool.
And *phrewewewew!*
A stream of water three feet long, a perfect shot, puts out the fire
and saves the house.
The crowd loved it, and so did the dolphin, for he circled the tank
to admiring applause and came back for an extra Spanish mackerel.

The Hardest Trick

When I read the script that involved Flipper's having to swim into
an underwater cave, I knew it would not be easy. The story was about
Sandy scuba diving at the Tongue of the Ocean and darting into an
underwater cave to escape from a hungry shark. But Sandy, waiting
till the shark leaves, is running out of air. Flipper discovers Sandy's
plight, kills the shark and swims into the cave to pull Sandy out to
safety, letting him hold onto her dorsal fin.

Killing the shark is simple. We did that with plastic mock-ups. And
the rescue, Flipper pulling Sandy out with her dorsal fin, is routine.
But getting Flipper to swim into the underwater cave was something
else. I wanted her to swim up to the opening, look inside and then
swim in. Two cameras would be stationed underwater, one outside
the cave entrance and one just inside, to show Flipper actually swimming in.

Usually, the only difficult part in training dolphins is to think of the
right way to communicate what you want the dolphin to do. Once
you've done that, the rest is easy. But not in this case. Kathy knew
exactly what I wanted her to do, but she didn't want to do it. She
was afraid to.

This was one of the few underwater scenes we shot at the Seaquarium. Set designers at the North Miami studio made the cave of
fiberglass. It was gray and craggy-looking with an opening about 4½
feet in diameter. They hauled it to the New York Tank on the Seaquarium grounds where the scene was to be shot. I looked it over
when they were making it. I always checked everything the dolphins
came in contact with, making sure there were no sharp edges or anything sticking out, like a nail. I ran my hand along all the surfaces.

The construction was okay. But the idea of the cave itself had lots of scary things about it—scary to Kathy.

Kathy had been in the tank with the fiberglass cave for several days so that she would get used to it, and day by day I had edged her closer to the cave entrance. Finally it was time, I thought, to get serious. We were both about eight feet underwater in the tank, I in scuba gear and with a bag of fish chunks, Kathy going up for a breath of air every thirty seconds or so and hovering near me and the fish chunks. I swam over to the cave opening, she followed and I thrust my arm into the cave, a signal for her to go in. She didn't move. I did it again. Nothing. I moved a little closer and tried the arm thrust again, very authoritatively. She wouldn't budge. Then I swam inside the cave myself to show her there was nothing to be afraid of. She still wouldn't move. I tapped on my metal air bottle with my ring, the signal for her to come. She tried but got to the entrance and stopped.

Over the years I had spent hundreds of dollars on all sorts of sophisticated electronic equipment for signaling the dolphins, but in the end I settled on the simple little "cricket." It's a small curved metal toy usually painted like a cricket, and has a stiff metal underpart that goes "click" when you press it. It used to cost about a penny. When I clicked it, it meant to come or, sometimes, that I was about to give another signal.

I had my cricket with me. I got it out and pressed it. That never failed. But it failed now. Then I tried to lure her in with fish chunks. I held them up enticingly. She held her ground, and I was beginning to wonder if this was the trick that couldn't be done.

Dolphins refuse to do tricks usually because the price isn't right. The dolphin is saying: "No thanks. Not now. I'm full."

That kind of refusal is temporary. In a few hours, the dolphin will be hungry again and jump at the chance to do the trick.

But when I tried to get Kathy to go into the cave, she was refusing in a very different way. She was saying with every fiber in her body: "Never!"

I knew that I was asking her to go against her instincts. Dolphins have an instinctive fear of underwater openings, the same as our fear of falling, of snakes, and of sudden noises. Why do dolphins have such fears? I'm not sure. Maybe when she sonars a cave, the return signals are jumbled in a scary way, possibly outlining the shape of some hideous, ancient thing in the water. Of course, she knew that there was nothing hideous or ancient in the water or I wouldn't have been there; but if you don't trust your instincts, what can you trust? Perhaps, more simply, dolphins fear being trapped underwater. For a long time, I thought it was their fear of drowning. If human beings and almost all other vertebrates (including even lizards and birds) are trapped underwater, they finally drown. They have a dive reflex that causes them to breathe involuntarily. When their sensors detect a certain level of carbon dioxide in the blood and a low level of oxygen, it's automatic. They breathe water and drown. But dolphins and other whales have their sensors at different thresholds and will die before they are forced to breathe. That means that when dolphins get trapped in tuna nets, they don't drown—which is to suck water into your lungs—they suffocate to death, holding their breath. That, not fear of drowning, was what made Kathy refuse to go into the cave.

I never questioned whether I should get dolphins to do tricks or not. I resolved this early on, deciding with my own set of instincts that if I didn't do my job somebody else would. I made sure the trick was safe and then I did everything I could to get the dolphins to go along.

I was inside the cave, so I swam back outside with Kathy. She went up for a breath of air and came back down. I put my arm around her back just above the dorsal fin. She was trembling and very nervous, going one way and the other. Scared to death.

Kathy never conquered her fear, but on the ninth day she swam into the cave with me despite it. With my arm around her tightly, I swam into the cave with her, then we turned and swam slowly back out. I let her go and she popped to the surface. So did I. And I rewarded her lavishly with fish. We did the trick again, this time Kathy all alone. I notified Ricou, the director, who had had the underwater crew on standby and ready for days. He called the camera operators, everybody eased into the water and got ready, then Kathy, still trembling, did the trick a final time for the cameras. I was happy that I never had to ask her to do that trick again.

13

Of Oyster Stew and Interspecies Communication

Imagination is more important than knowledge.
—Albert Einstein

Ricou and I didn't talk much about dolphins, certainly not as much as I would have liked to, because not much was known about dolphins and most talk tended toward speculation or mysticism, which Ricou could not abide. He didn't even take Dr. Lilly seriously. One day, for instance, Ricou said he walked into the Seaquarium and noticed Dr. Lilly gazing dreamily at the dolphins through a viewing port in the Main Tank. The dolphins, going round and round in the tank, are as interested in us as we are in them; they always notice newcomers through the ports and come over to see who they are. Then, having satisfied their curiosity, they return to their circling. Ricou said that when he walked up to Dr. Lilly, they nodded and the dolphins came over to see who the newcomer was. "I wish they would stay here awhile," Dr. Lilly said, "so that I could watch them more closely."

Ricou leaned against the tank like Dr. Lilly and a moment later every dolphin in the tank was at the port looking out at them like eager puppies.

"Lilly couldn't believe his eyes," Ricou said with a smile. "In all his years of staring at dolphins, he had never seen this before."

I asked Ricou: "How did you do it? Was it the old—"

"Yes," he said, grinning maliciously. "The old comb trick."

"That was dirty," I said.

"I know," said Ricou, "but I couldn't resist."

The old comb trick is simply to rub the teeth of a comb on the tank. This produces a peculiar sound for the dolphins, which they come over to investigate.

The closest we came to picking up on the subject of dolphin communication again was one warm morning in February when Ricou and I were jogging around Flipper's Lake. We talked about whatever came to mind: about movies, of course, about what it meant to be a native Floridian, if it meant anything at all, and about Art McKee, which reminded me of oyster stew because he always brought a gunny sack full of stone crab claws, lobster tails, key limes, and oysters up from Key Largo when he came.

"You know, there's some oysters right here in the bay," I told Ricou.

"Eating oysters from Biscayne Bay?" Ricou made a face. "The thought sickens me."

"But they've been tested. We took some over to the Marine Lab."

"And?"

"And they're okay."

Ricou wrinkled his nose. "They may have been tested, but have they been tasted?"

"Not yet. But we can do that now." We stopped jogging at the trailer. "Come on," I said. "I'll get the bucket."

Ricou and I gathered several dozen oysters, took them into the trailer and shucked them, then added cream and spices and put them on the stove.

Ricou stared down into the mixture. It was brown. "Are you sure these things are okay?"

"They're certified."

"Certified what?"

I laughed. We dished out two big bowls, sat down and began eating tentatively. I usually didn't get pushy when talking with Ricou about what he thought were my kooky dolphin ideas, but something urged me on, perhaps the oysters or a reckless sense of daring they seemed to have inspired, and I swung the talk to what had been nagging me:

"I keep thinking what it would mean if we could really communicate with dolphins."

"Hmmm," he said without encouragement.

"You know what I mean, don't you?"

He looked up with mild annoyance. "I think so, yes."

"I mean talk. Back and forth. Conversation. That's really the test, I think." I glanced at Ricou for some sign of encouragement, but there was none.

"Yes," he said. "That's what I thought it meant."

"It seems simple, but it's not," I said. "It goes like this: I say something and the dolphin says something, including something about what I just said, then I say something about that and so on." Ricou, I noticed, was looking at me in disbelief. I pressed on. "I don't mean idle chitchat, though. I mean something else, the idea being to rule out computers and conversation by rote. As I see it, Ricou, conversation is about real-life situations, life all around us at this minute, including situations that the conversation itself is a part of." I paused long enough for Ricou's two cents if he wanted to spend it here. He didn't. I wondered if something had gone wrong with *our* conversation. His expression hadn't changed in several minutes. But in the middle of a hot idea, I hate to stop.

"A lot of these so-called talking animals are really just making signs. Animal acts, like Adolph Frohn's. Well, I don't know if that's for real or not. But I know that I could find out." Again I gave him an opening. His face seemed to have been molded into a permanent expression of displeasure. But at least I was holding up my end of things. "Conversation is the key, Ricou. Done correctly, the phonies can be eliminated. I'm sure of it." I swung my right hand down like the chop of a hatchet. "Then we can get down to the real problem of communication: a common language. Not our language, not theirs. We need a *synthetic* language. Something different, something that fits their capabilities as well as ours. Just think! If we and the dolphins had the same language, we could find out what it's like to be a dolphin." Ricou was silent. Had he ever wondered what it would be like to be a dolphin? I couldn't tell. "Maybe they have a history. Maybe they are trying to communicate with us. Dr. Lilly thinks so and so do I. Who knows? Maybe we should listen to them. We listen to static that comes from the stars, why not dolphins? Maybe they could teach us things. Wouldn't that be something? What a breakthrough that would be. And you know what Cousteau says?"

"No," Ricou said, "but I have the feeling you're going to tell me."

"He says: 'We have more to learn from dolphins than they have to learn from us.' "

"I'm sure he had you in mind," Ricou said.

I chose to let that pass. I was on to something about how language works and what a perfect sort of test that makes. To use language properly, I was thinking, you have to know the world it comes from because language is based on the world, they're fused together. This is such a simple idea that we sometimes overlook it. The word "blue," for instance, is meaningless unless you know how to use words like "green," "red," and "yellow." The meaning of one depends on the meaning of the others. Looking at it through the other end of the telescope, we're all prisoners of our own perceptions, the way we view the world, and that view, whatever it may be, is itself captured in language. So we can't get outside our own language. But dolphins? I don't know about dolphins. If dolphins can read our internal states with their high-frequency sonar, why couldn't they read our minds as well? And if that's so, maybe they didn't even need a language till they met us. I was blurting all this out without pause.

Ricou had stopped eating and was gazing at me now with a look of increasing discomfort. Was it the brown oyster stew or my relentless monologue? I don't think I'd ever run off at the mouth like that before. "Sorry," I said. "I didn't mean to monopolize the conversation."

"*What* conversation?"

"But if you understand the problem—"

"Ric, I *do* understand the problem."

"Then I'll jump to the bottom line. Could we?"

He looked puzzled. "Could we *what?* Communicate with them? Of course we could. You could communicate with an oyster if you wanted to." He belched. "You see?" He put down his spoon and pushed the bowl back on the table.

"How?"

"With the right budget, Ric, we could do anything."

How pragmatic! When I said "how," I meant the method: what method would we use? He had thought immediately of money, which precedes method. One soon learns that all things begin and end with money. "Could you and I do it?" I asked.

"You and I? Of course."

"But how?"

He pretended to feel a touch of gas, got a look on his face like Chaplin, his napkin went to his lips and he passed the imaginary gas, a bubble visible only to himself, which he pretended to watch as it drifted over our heads and out the window. He pushed the chair back from the table and stood up. "Ah!" he said with relief. "Still alive!" He grinned. "Let's *not* do that again."

Exactly how Ricou would have made contact with dolphins, I don't know. He didn't tell me. But we could have done it, I'm certain, if we'd put the time and energy into it that we did into "Flipper." And it would have been a lot quicker, cheaper, and more interesting than any way devised by scientists. A lot more direct, too. It would have been something so simple that people would kick themselves and say: "Why didn't I think of that?"

Over the years I have worked with many scientists and have been struck by one thing: how blind they are to the world around them. Dr. Lilly's main contribution to understanding dolphins was to map their brains, driving electrodes through the skull and watching for electromagnetic reactions when various stimuli were applied. But who cares about what goes on in their brains? What does it matter? We don't even know what goes on in human brains when we communicate. And that doesn't matter, either. Communication is not about the sender or the receiver, it's about the sending. And that's done with language. Dr. Lilly was convinced that dolphins, masters of mimicry, were speaking English. So he tried to help them learn the language, starting with the alphabet!

And when that didn't work, he tried phonics!

To a dolphin, that must be strange indeed. A dolphin has a mouth but it's not at all like ours. Their mouths connect with their stomachs, not their lungs. The dolphin's blow-hole on top of his head is the closest thing he has to a nose; at least, it goes to his lungs. To expect dolphins to speak *our* language with *their* noses is hardly what you would expect from a "superior" species.

Beyond the physiological problem of trying to communicate with a species that must make do with a hole in the top of the head, there is perhaps the most fundamental problem of all: language is a part of culture. If we were serious about communicating with dolphins, the first thing we would need to do is to get to know their world, not just as *we* experience it, but as *they* do.

And how can we do that if we can't communicate with them?

We assume that a scientist will make the breakthrough in communicating with a nonhuman species. But maybe not. Maybe an artist will do it first. Maybe a child. Maybe a child has already talked with dolphins!

If I had a budget, I wouldn't back off from so-called oddball methods. I would try anything. Hypnosis, for instance, music, numerology, astrology, parapsychology, Esperanto. Why not?

Ivan Tors and the Jumping Turtle

For at least ten years, the movie industry in South Florida was centered in the person of one man: Ivan Tors. Besides "Flipper," he was the executive producer of such TV series as "Sea Hunt," "Malibu Run," "The Aquanauts," "Rip Cord," "Daktari," and "Gentle Ben," and such adventure films as *Lost Island* and *Clarence the Cross-Eyed Lion*. Ivan was the man with the ideas, the money, the contacts, and the influence. Ricou was his top man in South Florida. Ivan built his studios here but also had offices in Hollywood. He divided his time among Florida, Hollywood, and South Africa. Later, in 1970, when his wife Constance died, he and his three sons, Stephen, Peter, and David, moved to South Africa.

A big, friendly, vigorous Hungarian with a thick accent and a white beard, Ivan Tors believed with all his heart that life is one. And with enough empathy, he thought, we could enter the lives of others, get inside their heads and their bodies, think and feel what they think and feel, humans and animals alike. Indeed, we could all merge, as we will in death, he thought, which is the great cosmic life force from which we sprang. Ivan Tors saw no insuperable problem in communicating with dolphins and was a major contributor to the work of Dr. Lilly.

Soon after I had joined his company, Ivan Tors arrived at the Miami Seaquarium to see for himself how the dolphins were coming along. He pulled up in his chauffeur-driven limo and hopped out, dressed in khakis. He met Ricou and they went in to talk at length with Captain Gray and Burton Clark, the manager. When he and Ricou came out, I joined them. I was in my work clothes: black tank suit, Miami Seaquarium T-shirt, and barefooted.

As we walked over to Flipper's Lake and the main set, he said: "Ricou is tellink me dat you ah hafing quite a way with dolphins."

I looked at him to see what he might mean by that. He was smiling with approval at me. "Well," I drawled, "I think I might understand them at times."

"Goot!" he said explosively. "Vonderful!" He shot me a twinkling eye. "Und so to I!"

I put Susie through her paces for him, then we headed over to see Kathy. On the way we passed a new above-ground tank full of green sea turtles, hundreds of them. Every now and then the Miami Sea-quarium acquired nests of turtle eggs and hatched them out. For six or eight months, they lived there in relative safety. Then, when they were large enough to survive in the wild, they were released. If they did survive, they would grow into 400- or 500-pound monsters. Now, though, they were about the size of hamburgers, swimming in about four feet of water, climbing on top of each other, endlessly struggling. And endlessly fascinating. We stopped and stared down at them for a long moment.

In feeding the dolphins, which I did all the time, I was also training them, giving them a signal to do one thing or another before I would give them something to eat. Most of the time, I gave them the signal to jump, which was a rolling motion of the arm, like winding up a large clock. Ricou and I gave the signal so much it became a joke. It was like a delightful Mack Sennett sight gag in which a comedian, thinking that his hand itself has the power to make things jump, goes around trying it on other things. If a seagull landed nearby, we would give it a jump signal and laugh when nothing happened. We did it to dogs, fish, people—anything. Knowing that Ricou was watching, one day I found a bullfrog, elaborately put it in a chair and backed off like it was a dog-and-pony show by Adolph Frohn, then gave it the jump signal. It only sat there, and we laughed like loons.

The day with Ivan when we had stopped by the turtle tank and were all gazing down at the hypnotic labyrinth of green turtles, without thinking I gave the jump signal.

And to my amazement, one of the turtles did jump! I said: "Good boy!" and tossed him a chunk of fish, then walked off as if I had expected the turtle to jump like that.

Nobody said anything at the time but Ricou, who told the story many times after that, said that he was watching Ivan and could hardly keep from rolling around on the ground with laughter. When Ivan saw that turtle jump, Ricou said, his eyes bugged out and he looked at me as if I were some kind of a wizard.

Myris the Mentalist

At the Miami Seaquarium, we used to have a regular parade of celebrities and oddball types coming to see Flipper. It was all due to Roger Conklin's public relations stunt: a photo and a brief caption telling the world that Sonny Liston, heavyweight champion prize fighter, had been "kayoed" by the amazing Flipper. The son of Edgar Cayce, the Virginia Beach mystic, came through for a photo; Vincent Lopez, bandleader and numerologist, came through, as did Miss America, mental telepathists, and anyone else who had written a book or won a prize.

One of the most memorable was Myris the Mentalist, a white-haired gentleman of about sixty who had written a book and was on tour. When he came through, they called me to the front, we shook hands and Roger explained that they wanted the usual photo of Myris with Flipper, which Nita, Roger's wife and photographer, would take. "Maybe he'll read Flipper's mind," Roger said with a twinkling eye.

I was in the midst of training Kathy in some delicate maneuvers and I didn't want anyone to mess around with her mind. "That's fine," I said. "But we have some rugged shooting coming up. Whatever you're going to do with Kathy," I said, "do it to me first."

We were at Flipper's Lake, the four of us, and Myris nodded gravely. "I understand," he said, fixing me with his eyes. In some Eastern religions, they speak of reincarnation, souls that are born again and again and become very wise. When I looked at him I thought his soul must have been around almost forever. "Think of something," he said softly. "A name. Any name. And concentrate on it."

I chose my mother's maiden name, Mary Sammon, a name that nobody at Miami Seaquarium had ever heard.

Myris took out a piece of paper and wrote something on it, folded it over and gave it back to me. "Now, tell us: What name did you think of?"

I told them the name.

Myris the Mentalist nodded. "Now show us the name written on that paper."

I opened it up. It said "MARY SAMMON."

I went pale. Could Myris somehow have tricked me? Tricked Roger and Nita, too? They didn't know my mother's name. I hadn't written it down, even on my employment application. And if I had, how could he have known that I would choose *that* name? Had I been hypnotized? Had all of us? No. Clearly, we have something big here, I said to myself. Finally we will find out what goes on in the mind of a dolphin.

When we got to the floating dock, Myris walked out to the end and sat down on the concrete block. He leaned forward on his knees, his right hand to his face, the index finger extended along the jawline. Kathy came to the end of the dock and popped her head up, alert. Myris sat there for several minutes. He switched hands, left hand to face, for several minutes. Then he got up and came back down the dock. Halfway back, he gave us a big shrug, his arms going up in the air, his hands out. "Nothing," he said.

The Conklins and I looked at each other. "Nothing?" I said. "You didn't get anything?"

"Nothing." He shrugged again. To Nita: "Did you get all the photos you wanted?"

She nodded.

"Okay, then," Myris said. "That's it."

He was about to leave. I couldn't believe it. "You mean," I said, "you didn't get anything from Kathy?"

He looked at me as if he had just realized I might be hard of hearing. "Nothing," he said, mouthing the word clearly.

"What does it mean?"

"Nothing," he said, mouthing the word again. "Her name is Kathy? You see, I didn't even pick that up."

I laughed suddenly. "But that doesn't mean anything. That might not be her real name."

He looked at me and frowned, so did the Conklins. "Maybe Kathy— or whoever it is—wasn't concentrating," Myris said. He smiled at the others. "Maybe they don't think in images. That's what I pick up mostly. Images, pictures, impressions. I got none of that. Maybe they're in nirvana. That's a stage of meditation like heaven. I wouldn't get a picture of that, either."

I glanced at the Conklins. Roger shrugged. "That's possible?" I asked.

"Possible, yes," he said. He shrugged again. "On the other hand, maybe there's just nothing there."

"And maybe it's you," I snapped.

He smiled at me as if I were a child. "Yes, that, too, is possible."

He left with the Conklins, and when they got to the end of the lake they all turned and waved. I waved back. Kathy came up to the end of the floating dock and I sat down on the block where the mind reader had been. "Could you have made your mind blank just to fool us?" Kathy nodded her head, uttered a combination of clicks and squawks, the dolphin counterpart of laughter, and shot me a conniving look.

"You little devil," I said.

Later I tried an astrologer, Ann Forbes, who read the stars for me and Rascal, a young dolphin I wanted to train and whose exact time and place of birth I knew. Rascal and I happened to be under the same sign, Libra, and we were "compatible," she said. Unfortunately, I wasn't with Rascal enough to verify the reading, but the times we were together indicated that we would have been a good team.

Betsy the Hurricane

On September 9, 1965, Hurricane Betsy came roaring across Virginia Key.

Like the other islands in the Florida Keys, Virginia Key arose from the countless zillions of organisms that produce coral rock. Working and dying and falling in their tracks like the coolies who made the Great Wall of China, these jellylike organisms merge their skeletons to become the work site and grave of the next generation. In a sense, then, coral rock grows, and many people seem to think that it's alive; but it's actually merely the shells of all those creatures, the limestone or calcium shells left by one generation after another, going down several miles. Waves wash over the coral rock, back and forth, a slow relentless grinding that eats away the coral, forming the sand of the beaches. Gradually sand collects on the coral rock, washed there by the waves and the endless tides. The tides in Florida are not high; in most places, they rise and fall only a foot or two.

Key Biscayne is only five or six feet above sea level at its highest point. The same is true for Miami Beach, though some places are as much as ten feet high. Virginia Key, site of the Miami Seaquarium, is about three or four feet above sea level. That's "mean" sea level, or the average. And Miami itself, except for a coastal ridge that reaches a height of twenty feet at one point, is only ten feet high. As you go west into the Everglades, this drops to about five feet. All of this is changing with lightning speed in terms of geologic time. The water level off Florida is rising at a scary rate: eight or nine inches a century. What makes it scary is that for each foot the water rises, it moves inland about sixty feet. Experts at the U.S. Environmental Protection Agency say they expect the sea to rise another two feet by the year 2020, three to six feet by 2100. But nobody considers the possibility that if the coral rock grows at the same rate, it might seem as if nothing has changed.

Once a coral island gets started, it tends to grow geometrically. When the island is still underwater, mangrove trees take root. These are tough, leggy plants that can tolerate salt water. They grow fifteen feet high in places, forming a canopy of leaves above a dark and eerie world of long, thin stems and gnarled roots. Soon they become a swamp, where flotsam and jetsam collect. Birds drop things. Weeds grow, then die. Humus forms. Turtles pause there in their aimless journeys and root around. Then one day, a miracle: it's an island. No longer is the ridge of coral covered by the tides. Part of it dries in the sun. The rains wash away some of the salt. Coconuts drift in. Some take root. Maybe a sea grape grows, and sea grass. The little island has a beach now. It's a mile long and because it is so long it attracts more things from the sea, more bird droppings, more passing turtles that root more deeply. It's a harsh and elemental world, like all of South Florida, where the games are for very high stakes and without a flicker of feeling. Then one day, though it's never more than a few feet above sea level and it's still a harsh and scrubby world, a causeway is built for cars and the place swarms with tourists oiling their bodies.

The main danger of hurricanes is not the wind; it's the waves. South Florida is protected by coral reefs and a string of coral islands, so the waves are never more than ten feet high. But that ten-foot wall of water is on top of a storm surge of ten to twenty feet, a vast dome of water under the low-pressure heart of the hurricane, where the eye is.

We hadn't had a hurricane in years, not since Donna in 1960, and surely, we thought, Betsy would pass us by.

But she didn't. In midafternoon, I was at Flipper's Lake. I had tied the trailer down and pulled the shutters across the windows and locked them. The stage hands and I tied down the sets, moved submarines indoors, and secured everything else as best we could so it wouldn't be blown into the next county. There was nothing more to do. I was going to keep an eye on Betsy with the TV and radio but the electricity went off, so I came out of the trailer to look around. The wind was howling. Suddenly Ricou drove up.

"*Where is everybody?*" he yelled.

"*They left,*" I yelled back. I shrugged my shoulders and pointed along the main road toward Miami. You couldn't see the city, that's how dark it was. I yelled and mouthed the words clearly: "*Back on the mainland.*"

Ricou uttered an expletive and glared darkly at me. "*That hurricane is coming right through here.*"

I nodded.

He cupped his hands to his mouth and yelled: "*You know what could happen?*"

I nodded and shrugged helplessly. To me the hurricane was like Fate. There's not much you can do with a hurricane. No placating, no changing its course, no fighting a hurricane, either. Once you have boarded up and tied things down, you sit back and watch. That's part of the game. And that's what I was doing. Whatever would happen would happen. Simple as that. The hurricane would come. Nothing we could do. Then it would go away. The sky would clear. And the universe would roll on. It's sort of a good feeling, realizing that there are things you can't do anything about. You can prepare against a hurricane, and you should; but only up to a point. You must expect *some* losses. Part of the fun is going around afterwards and assessing damage.

"*We could lose Susie,*" he yelled.

I nodded philosophically.

"*This whole island is going underwater! Get the net!*"

Most people had run their boats up the Miami River for safety but a few had tied down their sailboats nearby and the wind shrieked through the rigging. I didn't catch what Ricou said. "*You said what?*" I yelled.

He cupped his mouth and yelled: "*Get the capture net!*"

I looked at him blankly. What could he be thinking of? "*The capture net?*"

"*Get the damn net!*"

If he was thinking about catching Susie, that would not work. *"In this?"* I grinned. He had to be joking. I made a gesture to indicate the heavens coming apart all around us. There was a crack of lightning nearby; I caught a whiff of ozone. I had never seen such fury. It was midafternoon but the sky was black! And the wind! A coconut was trundled along the ground, end over end, and fell into the lake. I heard a loud crash, like a garbage can hitting something solid. Any minute now, we could find ourselves in the middle of the bay. Was it possible, I wondered, that he hadn't noticed all this? *"You're not going to try to catch Susie in this?"* I was having trouble just standing there and I let the wind push me around to illustrate the folly of what he was suggesting.

"No choice, Ric," he yelled through the megaphone of his cupped hands. *"Get the net!"*

Ricou didn't do dumb things. He was too much the planner, though he obviously sometimes planned things very close. But I was thinking now that if this wasn't a joke, Ricou had flipped. Or was it possible that he didn't understand hurricanes? The top of a garbage can went flying through the air. The air was thick with an oily darkness, the kind that goes with tornadoes. You couldn't see the bay, but we could see Flipper's Lake. It had been beaten to a froth. *"No,"* I yelled, shaking my head gravely. *"This cannot be done."*

Ricou turned to me with a questioning look and a half-smile as if I must be joking. *"Ric,"* he yelled above the wind, *"What is this? We've got a job to do!"*

I had tried to laugh it off; that didn't work. Then I tried reason; that worked even less. What else was there? It might seem that I had a choice here, that I could walk off and declare my independence on the side of sanity, freedom, and a long life; but actually I had no choice, for I had long ago cast my lot with Ricou Browning. I braced myself against the wind and struggled to the net shed. Then I realized that I couldn't even lift the damn thing. I returned empty-handed and without a word Ricou joined me and somehow we got it down to the lake, where we faced the larger question: how could we even spread the huge, heavy, 200-foot net in this wind? It had lead weights along the bottom. Maybe when Ricou saw how impossible this was he would change his mind. I could hardly stand up. I yelled: *"Even if we do catch her, then what?"*

"Don't worry about it," Ricou yelled, flashing me a smile like Doug-

las Fairbanks, Jr. "*We'll think of something.*"

We never moved a dolphin with fewer than half a dozen guys, net handlers, divers, a golf cart and trailer, and people to lift her onto the stretcher and baby her every inch of the way. And even then it was a big job. I yelled in his ear: "*But it takes six guys to move her, Ricou. Six! What will we do if we catch her?*"

"*Four!*" he yelled, holding up four fingers. He was busy trying to straighten the net.

"*What do you mean, 'four'?*" I was next to him, yelling in his ear. Both of us were working frantically, trying to spread the net so that we could string it across the whole lake. Was he saying that four guys could do it? "*Four guys?*" I yelled.

He nodded.

I yelled at him: "*But Ricou, you and I are not four guys!*"

Both of us were bent toward the wind, squinting against the rain. Ricou dug his elbow in my ribs and grinned at me. "*Ric, it takes four ordinary guys!*"

As usual, he was right. I grinned back at him. This was not Ricou's style, doing impossible things. Usually, he would divide Susie's weight by the number of people available and decide whether they could handle her. Six people into 450 pounds, which is the weight of Susie and the stretcher, is 75 pounds each. That's easy. Even four people can do it. Four into 450 is 112 pounds. Not easy, but not really hard, either. Two people into 450 is 225. That's nearly twice what I weighed. And to carry it 100 yards—in a hurricane! That's neither easy nor hard; it's impossible. No, I decided, we could not handle Susie alone.

And Susie, excited by the hurricane, kept playing games with us. The game: "Outwit the Dummies." Time after time we caught her, or so we thought, but each time with a malicious flick of her tail she went over, under or around the net. This is my world, she was saying, and my game. Come on! Let's play! But Ricou became more determined than ever. He ran around to the other side where Susie had hidden from us. She was in the deep part. He leaped in the water, I leaped in the water on my side and we closed in on her with the net. The wind was howling at 80 or 90 miles an hour, gusts of more than 110. The rain hit like bullets. We moved forward together, Ricou and I, only our heads above water. It looked impossible, then suddenly we were three. Susie had joined us. I looked at Ricou, speechless.

"*I told you!*" he yelled in my ear. "*She wants to be rescued. Didn't*

I tell you?" He was grinning and laughing and so was I. *"I told you!
Yes! Good Susie!"* We both pet Susie and she, always laughing, frolicked with us. *"Yes,"* Ricou yelled. *"I told you so!"*

We eased her to shore and got the stretcher, then muscled her
somehow onto that and, each of us taking an end, walked her a
hundred yards through the raging wind and rain and the rising water
to the tank on higher ground. There we dumped her. And she was
safe.

It was impossible but we had done it. Two distinct thoughts flashed
on and off in my brain, one after the other: (1) I did not care if I was
swept out to sea with a tidal wave and (2) whatever Ricou and I did
after this would be—would have to be—anticlimactic.

Less than an hour after we had moved Susie, waves from Hurricane
Betsy broke over Flipper's Lake, and the lake became one with the
bay.

14

Shooting in the Bahamas

The dolphin seems to have adopted man as a friend
and welcomes our blundering invasion of his domain with
affable humor.

—Jon Lindbergh, Diver

We shot underwater scenes in the Bahamas off the west end
of New Providence island, where Nassau is located. With permission
of the Oakes family, which owns that part of the island, we put up a
big dolphin pen, a half-pie–shaped fence going out 150 feet from
shore, where the water was 25 feet deep at high tide. It was an ideal
location for filming. The water was sparkling clear, full of colorful
schools of fish, and the bottom had everything: caves, cathedral formations of coral, and, nearby, the awesome Tongue of the Ocean,
where suddenly the bottom plunges more than 6,000 feet down a sheer
wall. Bahamian waters are among the best in the world for underwater
photography. The water is beautiful, its colors rivaled only by emeralds
and aquamarines, and so clear you can see for 100 feet. It doesn't
seem that far, though; it seems like about 50 feet because the water
is like a magnifying glass.

When we finished a session of topside shooting at Miami Seaquarium, about twenty-five of us in the Second Unit flew with Ricou to
Nassau for a month or so to do the underwater shooting. The crew
included not only Ricou and his two assistant directors, but also the
camera operators and their assistants, me and my assistants to help
with the dolphins, divers who handled underwater props and wrangled
sharks, an electrician to man the generator, a wardrobe manager, a

script clerk, and the production manager and his assistant. In Nassau, Ricou hired several people, including one to handle the compressor and keep our air bottles filled, local caterers, and drivers.

The most important member of our traveling party, of course, was Flipper. Usually we took either Susie or Kathy, but sometimes, when the script required it, we took both of them. We would put the dolphin on a special stretcher with slits for the pectoral fins, then gently lift the stretcher with Flipper out of the water and place her on a three-inch-thick latex pad in a wide, eight-foot-long box made of fiberglass-covered marine plywood. Flipper was put into the box, stretcher and all, then the stretcher was removed. Later when we got to our destination, I would work the stretcher under her again so that we could lift her out easily. Except for the big red logo on the side that said FLIPPER, the box looked like a coffin. There were long detachable aluminum poles on each side so that six men, three to a side, could carry it easily. The top of the box was open, and on the bottom was a bung hole so that it could be drained.

Travel Companions

We took off from Miami International Airport aboard a Southern Air Transport C-36, a two-engine cargo plane, landing at Nassau International Airport about an hour later. I always flew with Flipper, perched on the edge of her box, my feet touching her, or leaning over the edge, my hand under the pectoral fins, or "pecs," which would be her armpit. It was like holding hands. I could tell when she was nervous. I petted her and talked to her soothingly, kept her skin wet, and rubbed her eyes lightly with Vaseline.

When moving the dolphins, I tried to look at it from their viewpoint. There was the confusion, the noise and vibrations, the sense of helplessness in being stranded, but the biggest change, I thought, was surely the pull of gravity. For dolphins, that's unnatural. Their whole lives, they're weightless, like astronauts in space. Then suddenly, in air, they feel like lead, the weight of their bodies pressing down strangely on their lungs and other internal organs. It's as if suddenly our weight increased by three or four times, from 150 pounds, say, suddenly to 500 or 600 pounds. The only other time in their lives anything like this happened was the day of their capture, the day they were taken from their families and friends, snatched up from their own world and plunked down into ours.

Handling Flipper, the most valuable animal in the world, we had to avoid panic at all costs. I've seen dolphins panic before and it's not pretty. They struggle just as they do when they're caught in a net. Their eyes get big and dart around wildly, especially aboard a very loud aircraft or one that vibrates a lot. They tense up, cry out in alarm—"*Whoop-whoop-whoop*"—and try to get away the only way they know how, by swimming, pounding their flukes up and down, working their pectoral fins, and thrashing around. When that happens, you've got to stop them because they can hurt themselves. The only thing you can do is grab their flukes and try to hold them. That's not easy; their flukes are as strong as an alligator tail. All muscle.

Aboard the plane I had a garden sprayer with a three-gallon tank of sea water, which I sprayed Flipper with, always careful, though, that her blowhole was closed when I sprayed in that area. You can see the blowhole snapping open and closed like the shutter of a camera. The dolphin's skin looks and feels like a rubber inner tube. It has no hair follicles and no sweat glands, yet it's very sensitive and easily picks up marks from the slightest of scratches. Susie and Kathy, their skins flawless, were treated like bathing beauties, which in part is what they were. Before we started on the flight to Nassau, I put a little Vaseline on my hands, rubbed them together and gently rubbed them not only over Flipper's eyes but also under her pecs to prevent chafing. Dolphins have eyelids and when I lightly rubbed Flipper's eyes with Vaseline, she would delicately close them. When I had finished she would open her eyes again, roll them at me and blink.

One big problem I watched for was overheating. The whole trip I kept touching the dolphins on the trailing edges of their fins and flukes, where they get rid of their excess heat. These areas were like a thermometer to me, and when I felt them getting hot, I cooled them down with water.

"One Whale of a Shark Here, Mon"

Each of the dolphins ate about 15 pounds of fish a day. If you figure a four-week shooting schedule, that's 420 pounds of fish, mostly blue runners but also smelt, mackerel, and herring. The dolphins ate the smelt whole; they're small. But I prepared the other fish for them. Herring, which have soft spines, I simply sliced into chunks. But I cleaned and trimmed the blue runners and mackerel. These were bigger, rougher fish. To get 15 pounds of blue runner, it took 25 pounds of fish. I cut the head only partly, then ripped it off with my hands so that it would also pull out the guts. Then I chopped off the tail. To feed a single dolphin for a month, I figured on 600 pounds of fish. Allowing for having to stay an extra week or two, I added half again that much, for a total of 900 pounds. This was packed in 200 pounds of dry ice, which became a total load of more than half a ton. When we took two dolphins, we took about 1,800 pounds of food, a total package weighing more than a ton. The fish came from the Seaquarium's big walk-in freezer. It was frozen in 25-pound cardboard cartons. If I wanted to take 1,000 pounds of it, for example, I got forty cartons, packing them in four-by-eight-foot boxes with 400 pounds of dry ice.

When we landed at Nassau, I stayed in the box with Flipper. The stress, the noise and vibrations, the people, the lights, the strange sounds and the sensation of being jerked around—landing, that's when she needed me the most. I also carried my guitar with me. That sounds romantic, but actually I simply wanted to make sure it got to Nassau in one piece. Bringing a large animal into a foreign country is in itself a herculean task, but getting through the bureaucratic tangle is equally formidable. B. J. Johnson, location manager, handled all that. Customs and immigration officials in their starched uniforms flocked around us with cargo manifests, ticking off each item and collecting special permits for Flipper and her frozen food, examining all of our special equipment and counting the motley crew. There was virtually no TV in the Bahamas and most of the officials and baggage handlers had never heard of Flipper. When they saw Flipper, most of them thought she was a big shark. And when they saw me sitting in there with her, guitar in hand, I'm sure they didn't know what to think.

Getting Flipper from the airplane to the truck was one of the critical moments. Going from one to the other, we were twenty feet in the air. If we were dropped, we would splatter like a watermelon. As the forklift operator wheeled into place, I always sat up in the box and made sure he knew I was there. It was always the same, yet different each time.

"Take it easy," I told him.

"Don't worry, mon," the forklift operator said.

"Easy does it," I said.

Gently, gently, the prongs of the forklift slipped under Flipper's box, then slowly we were lifted up—about half a foot, plenty to clear the edge of the door. I glanced at the operator and he smiled back. So far, so good. Then slowly, smoothly, we moved out of the plane, stopped, then went down slowly, inch by careful inch till we were at the level of the truck. Then in we went, and were set gently down.

"Beautiful!" I said, relieved.

"Tole you not to worry, mon." He gave a big white-toothed grin. "Hey, mon, what you doin' in dere wit a big shark like dot?"

"This is not a shark," I told him patiently. "It's a dolphin. In fact, it's Flipper."

He grinned and nodded as if he understood. A crew of baggage handlers walked by from another plane and my forklift operator called over to them: "Hey, mon! Come here! See what I got!"

"What you got, mon?"

"One whale of a shark here, mon!"

They crowded around and looked at me in the box with Flipper and laughed together in their soft, laid-back way. My forklift operator grinned and waved to me and they all went off together.

Aboard the truck, we picked up a police escort and wended our way in casual Bahamian style toward the pen. I stayed with Flipper the whole way. She always flew on an empty stomach and as soon as we got her into the water, I fed her generously by putting her through a training session. Some of the others checked her food into the hotel freezer.

Shooting with Stunt-Doubles

We did all the underwater shots for the six or seven screenplays that had already been shot topside. It was often hectic; sometimes we were underwater all day long, each of us using seven or eight bottles of air. Most of the time we wanted to be up shooting by eight o'clock in the morning, so we rolled out of bed by five-thirty. Most photographers don't like shooting when the sun is high, when it bears down harshly and creates deep shadows. But for underwater shooting, that angle is good. It lights up the water. Even in winter, when Bahamian waters are quite cold, we were in the water by 8 A.M. The only difference was that we ate huge breakfasts, wore wet suits, and ate lots of honey, using it to sweeten our tea and coffee.

Ricou was the center of it all. He stayed immediately behind the camera operator, either Lamar Boren or Jordan Kline; sometimes both. They were the best in the business, pioneers in underwater photography; Lamar shot "20 Thousand Leagues Under the Sea" and "Sea Hunt." The key spot on shore was a compressor, which was manned by a native operator who kept the bottles filled with compressed air. We always kept three or four dozen full bottles on hand, piled on sheets of plywood covered with a tarpaulin. The shore itself was studded with knife-sharp coral formations and sloped upward so steeply that we had to use a ten-foot dive ladder to get out of the water. In the middle of it all was a large tent with open sides and a table, where we ate, and down the road was a portable toilet. Six or seven of the divers worked as liaison between Ricou and the rest of us in the water and kept us in touch with land, running the air bottles back and forth, catching and wrangling sharks, and moving underwater scenery.

A lot of our shooting in the Bahamas was with stunt-doubles. We had stunt-doubles for all the regulars on the show and for guest stars who went underwater. One frequent guest star was the late character actor Andy Devine, who in one episode jumped out of a boat and was supposed to swim underwater with Flipper. He jumped out of the boat at the Miami Seaquarium set and landed in the water. But as soon as he hit the water, the shooting stopped and Andy climbed back in the boat and went ashore to put on some dry clothes. When we got to Nassau, a stunt-double took Andy's place. He had Andy's portly build and was wearing the same clothes Andy did. This time when the stunt-double jumped in, though, the cameras began to roll when he hit the water, following him on down and as he swam away. Later when the two scenes were put together in Hollywood, it seemed like one action on the screen, Andy Devine jumping out of the boat and swimming underwater.

In the deepest part of the dolphin pen were several props, which we used for various Flipper episodes, including several sunken boats and a car, which figured in the episode titled "Red Hot Car."

We also had a fifteen-foot two-man submarine, which we hauled in and out of the water. Battery operated, it looked like the real thing. It worked, too. It could go left and right, up and down. It wasn't real, though; it was a "wet sub"—full of water. The portholes had no glass. We used it to set the scene. When someone in the script was in the submarine, we showed a shot of the wet sub going through the water. In one episode, for instance, Porter Ricks, the father, and Bud are on the dock in front of their house, talking about their scientist friend, Dr. Goodwin:

> FATHER: (*Concerned*) You say that Dr. Goodwin went off in the submarine by himself?
> BUD: Not by himself, Dad. Flipper's with him.
> *Close-up of Father.*
> FATHER: (*Smiling with approval*) Then he's in good hands!
> *Close-up of Bud.*
> BUD: (*Grinning*) The best of hands, I'd say. (*Turns to stage left*) Right, Pete?
> *Close-up of Pete the Pelican.*
> PETE: (*Nodding his head vigorously*) Awwarrrk!

The scene shifts and we see the two-man sub sliding smoothly through the water, Flipper swimming effortlessly outside. As we watch, Flipper looks through the porthole, keeping tabs on his human friend. And off to one side lurks a shark.

Dr. Goodwin is not really in the sub, of course; I am. I'm steering the sub and holding my breath while the camera is rolling so that we don't show any telltale bubbles. What is Flipper really doing? I have just signaled Flipper with my cricket and she's looking for me. She wants a piece of fish.

The next scene is a close-up of Dr. Goodwin. He's in the sub, steering. The camera backs off for a wide shot and you see the interior of the sub. That shot is taken in one of the "dry" or mock-up subs at the studio north of Miami. The dry subs were really just movie sets. The actors would get into them and pretend to be driving: pulling levers, looking through the periscope, charting their course, and whatever else you do in subs. There were several sections of dry subs at the studio so that the camera could show the actors from various angles.

Though these scenes took less than a minute on the screen and seemed like virtually a single piece of action to the viewer, they were taken by three camera crews in different places and at different times.

The Sub Scene, A Closer Look

Let's look in detail at that scene of me in the sub, Flipper looking in the porthole.

We were all in scuba gear about twenty-five feet down and had been there for a while. Why the holdup? I don't know. Maybe the shark was being contrary. We wanted a shark to swim through the scene, which meant the divers had to catch him and hold him till the right moment. I was in the wet sub offstage, waiting for a signal to begin. When I got the signal, I would turn on the electric motor and hold my breath, then I'd ride the sub into frame, right to left, and signal Flipper with the cricket. Kathy was with one of my assistants offstage now, being fed chunks of Spanish mackerel to keep her occupied.

Finally, everything was ready: the sun, Flipper, the divers with their shark. Ricou and the camera operators were ready. Then suddenly my bottle of air gave out. This should never happen but it did sometimes; I had been in the water a lot longer than the others. Usually I had a couple of full bottles of air in the sub, but this time, as luck would have it, I didn't. You don't run completely out of air. But you know that you *will* run out soon, because suddenly it's like breathing through a pillow. I stuck my hand out the porthole of the sub and made a clenched fist: STOP! The last thing you want to do in the middle of shooting is to run out of air. I leaned back in the sub so that they could see me through the portholes. I raked my hand, the index finger extended, across my neck, as if it were a knife cutting my throat. That's the signal for another bottle.

Everything stopped. My signal was relayed to a diver who struck out through the water toward me. He would pick up my bottle of air, swim it to shore and pick up another one, then swim it back to me. The pressure in a fresh bottle is 2,200 psi (pounds per square inch). You can't breathe air under that much pressure, so it's damped down with a regulator and comes out of the mouthpiece at about 50 pounds above ambient pressure, the pressure of the water around you. Air pressure at sea level, incidentally, is 14.7 psi, increasing a pound for every two feet of depth. We can't feel it, but air has weight. The more you compress it, the heavier it gets. So the more air you use from your bottle, the lighter, more buoyant the bottle becomes, and the harder it is to stay underwater. I unhooked my bottle of air and dropped down through the trap door of the sub and swam out, then paddled upward to the surface. I would hang on to the fence till the diver got back.

But before the diver reached me, Kathy was there. She was always into everything. She knew more about what was going on than any of us did, including Ricou. It was her pen, after all. The bottles have backpacks with straps, and Kathy took the straps in her mouth, the same way she did in countless episodes of "Flipper," and swam quickly back to shore. There she waited till the diver caught up with her. He had seen her pick up the bottle, as she sometimes did, and had stopped midway, turned and begun swimming after her. When she reached the shallow water, the diver took the empty bottle from her mouth and walked it up the ladder to the compressor, got a new bottle and walked it back down to Kathy, who took it in her mouth and swam it back to me.

She was always doing things like that, always eager to help. Almost every underwater scene has props: a pistol, a treasure or artifact, a knife, a starfish or snorkel. Kathy and the other dolphins enjoyed bringing these things to us when we needed them. Some might think that they did it for food. But I don't think so. The dolphins never came to me afterwards for a reward and I never gave them one. It was a game to them. They were like children, the dolphins, children who want to help, happy children eager to be a part of things.

And like children, their help wasn't always that helpful. In one scene made at the Miami Seaquarium set, for instance, Sandy pulled up in his skiff and tossed out an anchor. It was a simple scene and we could have left it at that. But Ricou thought it would be more interesting if we had another angle on the anchor, if we could follow the anchor underwater as it sank. Sandy would pull up in the skiff and throw the anchor out, then from underwater we'd see the anchor splash into the water and sink to the bottom. Whether anybody really notices details like that, I don't know; but I do know that it adds something to a series: longevity. So we did it. Ricou and Lamar went underwater with the camera. Wearing the clothes that Sandy wore, I started the motor in the skiff, Ricou gave the signal for action and I took off. When I got to the right point, I killed the motor and tossed out the anchor, exactly the way Sandy had done topside. The anchor splashed into the water and was sinking, the camera was rolling, the whole thing being filmed from underwater. Perfect. Except that Flipper, always eager to help, rushed in from stage left, grabbed the anchor before it hit the bottom and brought it back to me.

Blocking the Scenes

We averaged shooting about five underwater scenes an hour, but sometimes we might work all day on a single scene; it depended on how complicated the scene was, and on the weather. A scene is any continuous shot on film and it can be almost any length. When two people are talking, for example, the camera goes from one to the other. On the screen we see one of them talking, then the other. Each of those is a scene. An underwater scene in Nassau could be as simple as swimming down and reacting to something offstage—a shark, say—or as complex as a long piece of business with Flipper and the wet sub. Whatever the scene or sequence of them, Ricou blocked them in on shore beforehand. We acted out what Ricou wanted us to do underwater or he moved us around bodily. Sometimes he sketched in the scene on a big chalkboard on shore or he just used his hands and fingers.

It was early morning on a balmy day in Nassau, with a light breeze off the water. Ricou was at the blackboard with a piece of chalk, the rest of us standing or sitting around in an open tent.

"In this first scene," Ricou said, eyeing me, "we want you swimming down into frame, surface to bottom."

Translation: The camera will be held steady and I will swim down into view.

Ricou is holding two fingers out in a "V" to represent the camera. These he holds steady. Then he holds up two more fingers on the other hand, two fingers going back and forth like a swimmer's legs. That's me. He moves me down till I am in front of the camera.

"In this scene," Ricou said, "you're Sandy in 'The Fugitive.' "

This was a story that included Burt Reynolds, an unknown actor/stuntman in those days. He played an escaped prisoner in this episode. Ricou told me who I was playing and the name of the script so that I'd know what the story was and be wearing the right clothes. This was actually the province of the wardrobe lady, but in this case I already knew that I'd be in cut-off jeans.

"Jump in the water," he says, still giving me the eye. "Wait till the bubbles clear, then swim down through the frame." He paused to let that sink in. "That's a cut." He makes a cutting motion with the back of his hand, going outward.

That's the first scene, in other words. Wearing Sandy's costume, I will jump out of the boat and into the water. Ricou is so used to talking with his hands that I am now his hand, jumping up, turning and going down into the water, a perfect jackknife. When the water clears, the camera rolls. Ricou shows the camera as two fingers shooting upward. Now the left hand swims down into frame, meaning into the camera's field of view—and out. Underwater, I can hear the camera whirring when it's on; I can also hear when it stops. So when it stops, that's a cut. The scene is over.

Ricou said: "We'll do it several times, down through the frame."

That means just what it says. I swim down through the frame several times. Ricou wants to show that Sandy is in deep water, thirty feet or so. I try to make each time I go down a little different.

"The next scene, Ric, you're swimming down, you stop and react to something on the bottom, then continue your swim on down through the frame. That's a cut."

Ricou uses his arms in a slow breaststroke and then stops suddenly, reacting to something.

"Flipper will follow you down. She'll be at your side."

That means I'll palm a piece of fish to get Flipper's interest as I swim down. If necessary, I'll even click the cricket. Getting Flipper to swim down with me is very simple.

"Third shot, Ric."

He's counting them off on his fingers and looking at me with unwavering eyes. I nod as though I'm soaking all this in like a sponge.

"You arrive at the bottom, you kneel down, look around just to make sure everything's okay, open your collecting bag and Flipper will pick up a starfish and put it in your bag."

Ricou is not an actor but he acts all this out as he speaks, "reacting" when he says I will react, kneeling down when he says that I will kneel down. My head is beginning to whirl by this time, trying to keep all this straight. We don't make notes. Notes are no good underwater. Everything must be memorized. Fortunately there are no lines to memorize. The trick with Flipper is simple. We've gone over it and she knows what to do. She knows that when she puts the starfish in the collecting bag, she gets the piece of fish that I've been palming. She knows also that she will not be fed till the camera stops whirring.

Art McKee in full diving gear,
with bar of recovered silver.
—*Dolphin Project Archives*

New York World's Fair
dolphin as fireman.—*Donn
Renn*

ABOVE: Ric O'Barry and Hugo the (so-called) Killer Whale. —*Miami Seaquarium*
RIGHT: Musical experiment with Hugo.—*Miami Seaquarium*

Luke Halpin, with arm in sling, watches O'Barry train Flipper to throw a fish into the boat.—*Donn Renn*

Keeping Flipper wet and soothed before transfer by airplane.—*Donn Renn*

Ricou Browning as the *Creature from the Black Lagoon.*—*Silver Springs*

Ricou Browning, *left,* and O'Barry with fourteen-foot tiger shark.—*Donn Renn*

O'Barry and double-jump at Miami Seaquarium.—*Miami Seaquarium*

ABOVE: Miami Seaquarium
collecting boat at Bimini.
—*Miami Seaquarium*
RIGHT: O'Barry, *left*, checking
wardrobe with Luke Halpin
before stunt doubling for
Sandy Ricks in "Flipper"
show.—*Steve Weaver, Miami
Seaquarium*

LEFT: Pete the Pelican in "Flipper" training session. —*Miami Seaquarium*
BELOW: Dolphin tailwalking in Top Deck Show, Seaquarium.—*Miami Seaquarium*

ABOVE: Carolina Snowball, world's only known albino dolphin, and companion. —*Miami Seaquarium*
RIGHT: Close-up of Carolina Snowball.—*Miami Seaquarium*

"That's a cut," Ricou says. "Next shot, Ric, is a medium shot of Flipper cruising the bottom. She locates the starfish and picks it up and swims offstage, left to right."

Flipper and I have practiced this, too. Practiced? We went over it once, which is quite enough. When the camera is aimed at the starfish about fifteen feet away, I will be off to the right, Flipper watching me. I will give Flipper the signal, pointing. It means to "fetch." It means to go, first, and if there's anything there to fetch, go get it and bring it back.

"And that's a cut," Ricou said. He turned away from me at last. "Okay, Lamar, if you have any film left, we want to shoot another close-up of Flipper, this time picking up the starfish and depositing it in the bag."

Ricou's gestures have become almost eloquent. For the close-up, he moves the V-shaped fingers, or camera, of one hand up to the palm of the other. Then when he mentions Flipper, his hand becomes Flipper, moving gracefully through the water.

Whenever Ricou finished outlining a series of scenes like this involving Flipper and me, he would turn to me and say: "Okay, Ric, now what are we going to do?"

And I would repeat it back to him, usually getting some of it wrong. Ricou patiently corrected me and had me repeat it till I got it right. Even then I sometimes messed up the scene—but we all did at one time or another. Even Flipper would mess it up sometimes, darting into a scene when she wasn't supposed to or coming in from the wrong angle. When Flipper or one of us wearing fins went near the bottom, we sometimes stirred up a cloud of sand. When Lamar saw it, he made a clenched fist—*stop!*—and then the sign for a puff of sand, the hand held out in front, fingers down like a cloud. There was nothing we could do but wait till it settled. Most of the time, waiting for sand to settle is not unpleasant. But in winter, nothing is worse. Unless it's waiting in that icy cold water wearing only tank suits. That happened when we were doing underwater scenes in the winter for the topside actors who had worn summer clothes. The one exception was Lamar Boren. Despite the cold, he always wore only a tank suit. He was just as cold as the rest of us. That was obvious. His skin got blue and he had goose bumps. But he was very macho and serious at the same time, so we never said anything about it to him. He never indulged in the underwater fun and games.

Sometimes everything was perfect till we got ready to roll, then a cloud would come over and we'd have to stop. Seaweed might drift into view. Jellyfish. A boat. Or the camera would jam. We spent a lot of time waiting because in making movies everything has to be exactly right. And waiting becomes a problem of its own. Tension builds. Attention wanders. And every minute costs money. It wasn't our money, of course; we got paid whether we worked or not. But it was worrisome all the same. During hurricanes and other bad weather when we couldn't shoot and there was nothing to do, we sometimes got on each other's nerves.

Does Flipper Ever Do Anything Wrong?

During underwater shooting, I became convinced that dolphins must have an amazing grasp of things. When I signaled with the arm-thrust, for instance, how could they know exactly what to do? It may seem simple, but it wasn't. This one signal was used to mean a number of possible things and Flipper almost invariably got it right. In fact, she often knew not only what I wanted her to do but what I *should* have wanted her to do; in other words, there were times when I told her to do something wrong because I was confused but she did the right thing anyway.

But there were other times, too. A big part of my job involved getting Flipper lined up in the right place, then I'd swim or dive out of camera range and give Flipper the signal to begin her trick.

The signal for Flipper to go to the surface and jump was a rolling movement of my hand, the index finger extended. That's also the time-honored signal for underwater camera operators to "roll 'em."

The scene we were shooting was of Flipper diving to the bottom and picking up a wrench that Sandy Ricks had dropped overboard while trying to fix an engine. The signal for that is the arm thrust again, which means "go and fetch." Flipper was ready, eagerly watching me, and so was the camera operator. When everything was ready, I dived out of range and gave the camera operator the "roll 'em" signal. Flipper saw it, shot upward and jumped out of the water, then came back for a bite of fish. And I gave it to her.

Later when we broke for lunch, one of the assistant directors sidled up to me in the sandwich line. "I don't get it," he said.

I was famished. I picked out a roast beef sandwich and a Pepsi.

"You don't get what?" I said.

He grabbed a sandwich and a Coke. I headed for a table and he trailed along. "This may be none of my business," he said, his tone oily, "but when Flipper went to the surface and jumped, you gave him a piece of fish, right?"

I nodded.

"And isn't that reinforcing what he had just done? A reward?"

I nodded again and took a big bite of the sandwich. "So?"

He smiled and said with precision: "But that was *not* what we wanted Flipper to do."

"Yeah, I know," I said, nodding agreement and chewing ravenously. My mouth was full—too full—but I said: "That was a mistake."

He pounced. "But that's what I mean. Why did you reward him for doing the wrong trick? Even I know that...."

"No, no," I said, shaking my head. I had bitten off more than I could chew and slugged down some Pepsi, then wiped my mouth with the back of my hand and made a strange gulping sound deep in my throat. "She didn't do the wrong trick," I said. "I gave the wrong signal."

He nodded. "Hmmm. I see." He unwrapped his sandwich thoughtfully. "So, he didn't make a mistake, then?"

"Nope." I shook my head. I wolfed down the rest of my sandwich and got up to go through the line again. I would get ham and cheese next. Diving gives me a tremendous appetite but I never seem to add a pound of weight.

The assistant director had narrowed eyes now. "Then let me ask you one thing more, if you don't mind."

"Shoot."

"Does Flipper *ever* do anything wrong?"

I chewed slowly for a moment, my eyes turning as if I were deep in thought, then I swallowed the sandwich down with a loud gulp and followed it with a double-slug of Pepsi. I shook my head slowly and said: "Never."

He frowned and grumbled: "That's what I thought."

15

Fun and Games

Hiii-yiii-yaaa!
—Inspector Clouseau

Filming is a team sport and if the parts don't work together right, nothing works. We all knew when things went well and when they didn't. Nobody goofed around when things went slowly. But when everything fell together right and we accomplished what we wanted to—sometimes even more than the ever-optimistic Ricou Browning planned—that was the time we loved, for it was a time of fun and games, of clowning around. Ricou started the practical jokes, and they became our style.

Diving is most dangerous when we forget how dangerous it is. And it's easy to forget. The obvious danger in diving is the simple fact that the sea, like outer space, is a hostile world. To stay underwater, we air breathers must carry our natural environment—air—with us artificially. It's easy to forget that we have created this with our technology—our tanks, hoses, gauges, and valves; that with these metal and plastic things we have sealed off the alien environment so well that we seem to have become a part of it. But this is an illusion. The better the equipment works, the better the illusion. And the better the illusion, the more dangerous it is. Thus the paradox: the better our equipment works, the more dangerous it is.

The tough part about diving is keeping alert to the thousand dangers of the sea. Ricou Browning had a typically ingenious way of keeping us divers alert. He used the Pink Panther Method.

We all know the scene, Inspector Clouseau entering his own everyday apartment in an everyday way, with a bag of everyday groceries. But wait! Something's amiss. Inspector Clouseau sniffs warily, his eyes rolling. As if in slow motion, he puts the groceries on the table, crouches, then suddenly he leaps to one side just in time to escape the "fatal" blow of his obedient servant Kato, who comes screaming at him with karate chops from the ceiling or the icebox.

What is this madness? It's the good inspector's way of keeping alert.

Ricou was like that. When things got a little dull, he would sneak up behind an unwary diver thirty feet below the surface and turn off his air. To keep us alert? There was some of that, sure. But mainly Ricou was an incorrigible practical joker.

Almost anything could be given a comic twist underwater. The shark lines, for instance. We tied some of the bigger sharks to the fence by their tails with 3/4-inch nylon lines to make it easy to find them when we needed them, so the lines were always handy. If a diver got close and turned his back, watch out! It was a comedic staple to tie the end of the shark line to his regulator. And when the diver swam off, his mouthpiece would be ripped away.

Underwater practical jokes reached their pinnacle of hilarity, perhaps, in the use of lifting bags. Lifting bags are extremely useful to divers. The bags are like little three-foot nylon or rubber parachutes, four lines coming down from the corners to a hook. Shoot some air under them and you can lift almost anything and move it. If we wanted to move part of a wrecked ship, for example, we hooked two or three of the lifting bags to it, shot some air to them from our mouthpieces and up she went. Then, two or three of us could push it through the water to where we needed it for the scene. We also moved brain coral around like that. In air, this beautiful coral formation might weigh 500 pounds; in water, it weighs about 50. With lifting bags we raised it an inch or two off the bottom, then pushed it around easily wherever we wanted it. In the hands of Ricou Browning, these lifting bags had a thousand devilish uses, the most obvious being to hook one to the back of a passing diver at fifty feet and watch his amazed expression as he floated helplessly to the surface.

Ricou and I became each other's favorite target, one trick topping the other. We had both turned off the other's air fifty feet down. That was nothing. I once hooked his regulator to a passing shark that ripped the mouthpiece out of his mouth and dragged him around the pen. And he cut my regulator hose with a knife when I was in the wet sub thirty feet down. I hooked lifting bags to his tank and yanked him to the surface. He put Tabasco sauce on the mouthpiece of my regulator. Back and forth it went, even on land. He (I'm certain it was he) put a dead seven-foot tiger shark in my bed, but I got him back with a bag of very stale mackerel in his pillow at the hotel, plus some other things I would prefer not to take credit for.

Was it dangerous for Ricou to reach into the wet sub with a knife and snip my regulator? Or for me to loop a noose at fifty feet to both of Ricou's feet attached to a pair of lifting bags and see him dragged upside-down, struggling unceremoniously, to the surface?

No, not for us. There was no way either of us could have hurt the other in the water. And unconsciously, perhaps, we realized that if you're always on the lookout for even your best friend turning off your air hose or shooting a blast of air into your wet suit, at least it keeps you in the game.

Ricou's Revenge

If you added up all the practical jokes on each side, I was ahead of Ricou—until the day of Ricou's Revenge.

It was nearly noon, a freezing winter day when the north wind howls through your very bones, and Ricou called us all together and outlined a series of scenes at the blackboard, then turned to me and, pointing with the chalk, said, "But first we want some swim-downs with you doubling as Sandy."

I nodded. That meant going to the deepest part of the pen, over by the gate. When Ricou finished briefing us, he asked me to repeat his directions; I did and got it right, then I put on my scuba gear and Sandy's summer cutoffs and headed out, swimming underwater. I was usually the first one out because I had to pick up a bag of fish and get Kathy ready. I reached the spot where the swim-downs would be, and waited. How slowly time drags by sometimes underwater, waiting for others. I was freezing. In cold water like this, the body loses heat twenty times faster than in air. All you can do about it is keep active. I checked the area and figured where Lamar would be with the camera. He would be about ten feet down, probably. My teeth were chattering.

I looked back toward the fence and could barely make it out. They wouldn't want to take that chance of having the fence show up, so I swam in another ten feet toward shore and looked back to see if I could see the fence. No, I couldn't. This was where he would probably set up. I gave Kathy a chunk of fish just to keep up her interest and waited for the others. I was turning blue, my teeth going like castanets. Gotta keep active, I said to myself, so I went through the swim-down. Where were they? I checked my watch. When you go underwater, you keep checking the time because it's easy to lose track of, and you must know how much air you've got left. I had been down thirty minutes. Thirty minutes? Could that be so? I stuck my head above water to see what the matter was. They were all on shore. They were lolling around in a sunny spot protected from the wind. They were eating, gazing out at the pen. And I knew suddenly what had happened. The moment I hit the water, Ricou told the others: "That's lunch." Everybody laughed. While I was waiting in the water for them, they ate. They enjoyed the sun and ate and waited for me either to freeze solid or to realize that the joke was on me.

Sharks

Sharks were rare in films till Ricou saw us manhandling sharks at Miami Seaquarium. Till then, sharks were in a scene only if they just happened to be there. But when Ricou saw how we got in the water with sharks and did virtually anything we wanted to with them, he took the next step: wrangling them into scenes he wanted them in.

We always needed sharks for atmosphere. Using the method I learned from Captain Gray, we caught our own. We strung a 100-foot-long shark line of ¾-inch nylon across the sea floor, a grappling anchor at each end. To that we attached twenty shark lines, one about every five feet, with swivels and a large hook, 3½ inches from barb to shank. We caught all kinds of sharks and in all kinds of condition. But catching them was only the beginning. Our sharks had to look like they do in the wild. That meant we didn't want them with hooks in their mouths, for instance, or looking dazed. So when the sharks were pulled in, the divers treated them with kid gloves. We cut off the shank of the hook with a bolt cutter, then with special long-nosed pliers we pulled the hook out backwards.

We sometimes had as many as a dozen sharks inside the pen. And how did we swim with all those sharks around us? Very cautiously. We were always looking behind us, feeling them sneaking up on us whether they were or not. It was a lot more dangerous in the pen than outside it, in the ocean. And there might have been some danger to Flipper, but not much. She knew about sharks. Most of the big ones were tied by their tails to the fence, but not always. And those that were loose, we just naturally kept an eye on. This was easy because they tend to swim in simple patterns. But we also watched the little ones. In some ways, the little ones were the worst. Little three- or four-foot sharks are feisty. They swoop in and nip you if you let them. It took several of us to manhandle even the small ones. But we got extra shark pay, which made it worthwhile, and we got to know the guys we were working next to very well.

Big sharks seem placid compared with the little ones, but you never know when the big ones will flare up, when they will suddenly get a burst of energy and go wild. That was most likely to happen when we were holding them and it suddenly dawned on them that they were not in complete control. Jimmy Riddle, one of the wranglers, and I were holding a ten-foot monster of a tiger shark, waiting about twelve feet down for the camera operator to signal us. We were on opposite sides of the shark, holding on and hoping the shark would keep dozing through the afternoon, when all of a sudden the shark surged, rearing back and knocking Jimmy's face plate off and his mouthpiece out. Jimmy couldn't breathe or see, but I could. The shark twisted his head around toward Jimmy and his big ugly mouth was snapping within inches of his face. This was it, I thought.

But Jimmy and I held on—what else could we do?—and just as unpredictably and suddenly as it began, the shark's struggling stopped. I held the shark while Jimmy let go for a moment to put his face plate back on and, with his last puff of air, blow out the water, clearing his face plate. That was a close one and I thought Jimmy must be indestructible, that we all must be; but we were not, of course: Jimmy died of exposure in a diving mishap off Cape Hatteras a few years later.

Our most common problem wrangling sharks wasn't their teeth, it was their sandpaper skin. Whenever we grabbed a shark or when they swam by, brushing up against us, they rubbed us raw. When we held them and they surged, we always seemed to land in the coral, which was as sharp as razor blades. We were always skinned up, a mass of bruises and with cuts everywhere.

We tied the larger sharks to the fence by their tails anytime we could because that was a lot simpler than having to run them down swimming free in the pen. In catching sharks that are swimming free, there are two overriding principles: (1) keep behind the part that eats, and (2) once you grab him, don't let go no matter what!

It takes three divers to catch a nine-foot tiger shark, a fourth to ride shotgun above. The one riding shotgun has the bang stick, which is a five-foot pole loaded with a twelve-gauge shotgun shell. He comes in if things go badly.

The rest of us watch the shark circle the pen and pick up on his pattern, then we take off after him as a group, moving in slowly so that he doesn't feel threatened. We're all in scuba gear and we can keep up with the shark easily unless he gets spooked. So we do things smoothly. Nothing happens for a while, all of us are swimming round the pen in the shark's pattern like we were all together. Then one of the divers gradually swims above the shark, the other two, trailing, move closer on either side. When everyone is in position, we all start coming together, the diver above grabbing the shark's dorsal fin, the other two grabbing his tail. If the divers can grab the shark at the same time and without getting him all riled up, they've got him. They can hold him and they can put a line on his tail or do anything they want. But if the shark gets mad about it, all hell breaks loose. Then the diver riding shotgun has got to come in fast and blast the shark. I remember thinking the first few times we did this that what we were doing with those sharks was a lot more interesting than what we were taking pictures of.

The first few years of the "Flipper" series, we killed most of the sharks we used in the film. The Bahamian Tourist Bureau wanted us to do that. Government officials said that if a shark were to attack a human in the Bahamas, it might be claimed that the shark had been "trained" by us. That was silly, of course. But killing them was a simple way to avoid the charge. It's easy to kill even the largest shark. You simply shoot him between the eyes with the bang stick. That takes out his brain. Shark brains are relatively small and primitive, shaped like the wishbone of a chicken or turkey. Later in the "Flipper" series, we stopped killing the sharks. We let them go or filmed them outside the pen where it was easy for them to escape.

Most scenes with sharks were outside the pen anyway, where the camera wouldn't show the fence in the background by mistake.

If we had just caught a frisky shark and wanted him in the scene, some of the divers would walk him off to the side. At the right moment, they would "throw" the shark in front of the camera to another group of divers who "caught" him and walked him on the other side till they needed him again.

The Ten-Foot Hammerhead

We were always on the lookout for something new, something we had never filmed before. Good film footage is valuable. One day I was stunt-doubling for Sandy, free-swimming with a snorkel outside the pen and near the Tongue of the Ocean. Ricou and Lamar were back about fifteen feet or so with the camera. Riding safety with a twelve-gauge bang stick in a launch above was Jimmy Riddle. The scene was for me to free-dive left to right into frame, but I noticed Ricou signaling "shark," his hand like the head of a shark, the thumb and fingers snapping like a shark's mouth. Lamar was pointing the camera to the right of me and I heard the camera whirring.

Ricou was not one to flout the rules of safety unless it was important, so I knew that we had lucked into some very prime potential footage when he signaled me to attack the shark. I looked in the direction he was pointing. It was a hammerhead about ten feet long. Of all the creatures in the sea, I like hammerhead sharks the least. Ricou knew that. Hammerheads (*Sphyrna mokarran*), with their big, round eyes on the ends of those primitive meat-ax heads, are one of the scariest-looking creatures in the world.

A few weekends earlier I had been rummaging around for artifacts at the bottom of Nassau Harbour. You can find bottles, silverware, coins—all kinds of things. It was a beautiful bright sunny day and I was forty feet down when suddenly everything got dark. I glanced up and the "Harbour Master," a fifteen-foot hammerhead, was cruising about an arm's length above my head. That monstrous fish is legendary in Nassau. They talk about him on the fish boats when the sun goes down, I once heard a native song about him, and he's been the subject of native tales going way back. Whether this is a single hammerhead shark they're talking about or a race of them, I don't know. But as he passed above me, I heard an incredible pounding in my ears. It was my own heart. I couldn't catch my breath. I thought I had run out of air. Everything stopped for a long, black moment as that monster took forever to go by. I felt sick and wanted to throw up. I was weak. When he was finally gone, I drifted upward slowly, hauled myself into the dinghy and returned to my hotel room to lie down. I felt cold and clammy and for a long time I couldn't seem to get a good deep breath of air.

And now, Ricou was holding an imaginary bang stick and jabbing with it. This meant for me to get the one Jimmy Riddle had, come down and blast this ten-foot monster in front of the camera.

"What a great idea," I thought. "Wonderful film!"

I went up to the launch and spat my snorkel mouthpiece out. "Bang stick," I gasped to Jimmy. With most dinghies, you can reach in and grab things because they have a standard distance from the water to the gunwale, the upper edge of a boat's side. But this launch's freeboard was nearly four feet. I couldn't reach in.

"What's up?" Jimmy asked, leaning over.

I shook my head. "I'll tell ya later, Jimmy." I was still out of breath and excited. I gasped: "Gimme the bang stick."

"Want me in the water?" He started to get up.

"Damn it, Jimmy! The bang stick!"

He handed me the bang stick.

"Now a shell! Quick!"

Jimmy, his mouth open in amazement, handed me the shell. I loaded the bang stick. "See ya later," I said. I hyperventilated, taking three or four deep breaths to get plenty of oxygen in my lungs, then just before I went down, I took about half a breath. That's the secret of holding your breath a long time, that half breath. Down I went, bang stick at the ready, holding my breath. I could hear the camera whirring. Ricou and Lamar were now back to back, which is a good way to fight off sharks. Ricou was pointing downward. I looked. The ten-footer was moving ponderously out of frame. "Damn," I thought, wishing I had scuba gear on. But what made this sequence so great was that it was practically hand to hand, me with a bang stick, yes, but quickly running out of air. Since I was still in Sandy's clothes, the writers could build a good story around this one spectacular scene.

Down I went after the hammerhead shark. I had dispatched many sharks with a bang stick, but none like this one. To be most effective, you've got to hit the shark solidly between the eyes where the brain is, and to do that you must be in position, which is above and slightly ahead of him. I pulled up behind him. I couldn't hold my breath much longer. Though the hammerhead seemed not to notice me, I thought he had picked up speed. If you were drawing a graph of this, one line (my air) would be curving down rather sharply. I would be running out of air. The other line, which would be going up, would be the speed of the shark. I had to be in position before the lines met.

My lungs aching and with a throbbing pain in my temples, I made one final surge, kicking my feet as hard as I could, and got to the right spot. What luck, I thought, he still hasn't spotted me. Then with all my might, indeed, the very last of it, I rammed the bang stick home: *Thunk!*

Nothing happened!

The shotgun shell was a dud!

The ten-foot hammerhead shark had been aware of me before, but dimly. Now his big round slate-gray eyes on the ends of that misbegotten head rolled my way in anger.

And that is all I saw.

But Lamar got it on film. It shows me ramming home the bang stick and when it didn't go off—this is what everybody laughs about—when it didn't go off, there I was *apologizing* to the shark, me flashing a big grin like Chaplin tipping his hat, and then suddenly I'm gone. I wish Lamar had been able to film my retreat because it would be an incredible training aid for the Olympic swim team. I shot to the surface like a Polaris missile and landed right in the middle of Jimmy Riddle's launch. That's the same launch I couldn't reach over the gunwale of when I went up to get the bang stick.

Flipper Swimming Free

The last year of shooting in Nassau was in a way the best—at least for me—perhaps because I was a little looser than I had been. We all knew that this was the last year. We weren't cancelled. Ivan Tors just decided to drop the series. Anyway, I had a good idea. Or, to be exact, a good idea had me. A lot of times, ideas have lives of their own. They're just floating around. As everybody knew, for instance, it would be a good idea to get a shot of Flipper jumping as a free dolphin. Up till then, we had jumping shots of Flipper by the hundreds, by the thousands or by the hundreds of thousands, Flipper jumping in every imaginable way but one. As we were all intensely aware, the other shots didn't show that he was not really free. Usually he was shot jumping from a high elevation, the camera shooting down so you couldn't see the horizon or so that the background was out of focus. But storywise, Flipper was a free dolphin. He lived in the ocean but he came to the Ricks' home on the lagoon because he wanted to. To establish that, we needed Flipper jumping in the open ocean, nothing in the background but water and sky. I knew it, Ricou knew it, we all knew it.

And here we were, in the last year of the series, the last of the Flipper stories, a time for tying up loose ends. I got into the limousine with Ricou as usual, the others piled into another limo behind us or into the truck we had leased, and all of us headed for the dolphin pens. I looked around sadly, thinking that this was perhaps one of the last times we would ever do this. I said to Ricou: "Why don't we get Flipper in the ocean today?"

Ricou was thinking about something else. He turned to me. "Flipper doing what?"

"Jumping. Free. You know, a shot of Flipper outside of the pen."

Ricou gave me a long, steady look and ground his teeth for a moment. "What do you mean?"

"Don't you think we need a shot of Flipper against the horizon?"

He considered it for a moment, frowning, his head cocked slightly. "You mean let Flipper outside the pen?"

"For the shot, yes. Why not?"

I knew what he was thinking. He was thinking about what would happen if a dolphin escaped. He was balancing the prospects of a great shot on the one hand, a shot we needed and wouldn't often have the chance to get anymore, against the prospect of Flipper's escaping and all the heat that would come down on him. "What if she escapes?"

"Don't worry about it," I said glibly. "I'll take the blame." I was actually as responsible for the dolphins as Ricou was, because I was still with Miami Seaquarium; I was on the Miami Seaquarium payroll as well as that of MGM. So I represented the Miami Seaquarium. But Ricou was responsible in a more basic way than that; he was responsible because he was Ricou, a responsible kind of guy. Me? I was responsible, too, but it was different. Over the years I had developed an image of responsible irresponsibility, which means that my sense of responsibility increased in direct proportion to the degree of wonderful craziness of the plan we were following.

In the cool yellow-gray of first light, even before the hordes of bicyclists had hit the roads, the limo was tooling along Bay Street. It was a glorious day, the sky so unbearably beautiful that anything might happen. "She won't escape, Ricou. I'll be right there."

He smiled at the prospect, nodding. His hands came together and the index fingers met like the steeple of a church. He bounced the fingers together thoughtfully. "Are you talking about Kathy or Susie?"

I shrugged. "Either one. Both. Why not?" I glanced at him. He was smiling. I couldn't tell whether he was going along with it or suffering from gas. "Okay, then," I threw in as a clincher, "Kathy. She's got fewer hangups."

"Um-hmm."

The limo had gathered speed and was racing along the two-lane blacktop toward the west-end location. A few native Bahamians on their bicycles were on the road. Soon the streets would be packed, bikers three and four abreast, all ringing their bells at the slightest provocation. "What if I guaranteed that we wouldn't lose them?"

He looked at me quizzically. "How can you do that?"

"I'm serious, Ricou."

"And so am I. You know what I think? I think you want to let those dolphins go. Free them. Don't you?" He was giving me a look with one raised eyebrow, as if he had found me out. "If they escape, Ric, it's my neck."

I shrugged. "I'm prepared to face that."

He shot me a hot look. "I said *my* neck." He settled back in his seat, frowning.

"Better your neck than mine," I muttered.

"Yeah? Well, it's *your* neck, too!"

This is where I could have got up on my soapbox about the dolphins. Perhaps I should have come right out and said that yes, I did want to let them go. Now that the series was ending, a little honesty had crept into my life and I now realized that we had used them enough, that we owed them something. Their freedom. The simple right to live their own lives, their lives uncomplicated by ours.

But of course I didn't. You don't preach to your best friend, someone who already knows everything you might say. Still, I wish I had. The limos and the truck pulled up to the pen area and stopped. Men in the crew piled out and formed little groups, looking with approval out over the beautiful waters, the heavy metal-green now touched with rich currents of gold. I glanced across the beach to the water and held up my hands at arm's length to form a square as photographers sometimes do. "There she goes," I said, like an announcer, "Flipper, free at last, against a real horizon!"

Ricou got out of the car. "Oh, hell," he said. "If you guarantee—"

"Yes, I do!" It was meaningless, my guarantee, but I gave it anyway and he accepted it.

"Then go ahead, Ric." He nodded, his lips pressed tightly together. "Actually, it's a damn good idea."

To my surprise, getting Kathy out of the pen was harder than I thought it would be. I thought—we all assumed—that they would both dart out the moment we opened the gate. We had always taken such precautions to keep that from happening, and now this. We thought the difficult part would be to get them back. Susie and Kathy knew the gate was open. They swam excitedly back and forth in front of it, scanning it. Wearing scuba gear, I was in the water with them and could feel the scanning. I could hear it, too. It's a pinging sound. Susie and Kathy had stopped near me and were shooting sonar at the opening where the gate was. Since their capture, when both of them were just babies, they had lived in tanks or relatively small bodies of water and their sonar always came ringing back at them. They must have thought that was normal. But when the sound waves didn't come back, when the sound went through the gate and kept on going—the way it's supposed to for a dolphin—it scared them to death. Go through that gate? Into the unknown? Never! Swimming just under the surface, I got outside the gate and clicked my cricket, which meant to come. Ricou and everybody else were standing around waiting, but I couldn't get Kathy out. Susie refused totally. No way was she going through that gate.

"What's the matter?" Ricou yelled at me.

I took the regulator out of my mouth. "She's scared," I yelled back. And she was. She was as tight as a drum. I put my arm around her. "Come on, Kathy," I said. "This is for you."

Ricou looked at his watch. My time was running out. Ricou always planned for the unexpected, but this wasn't his plan; it was mine. And I wasn't pulling it off.

It took me nearly an hour of patient luring to get Kathy to swim out. Kathy swam by and I grabbed her around the body. She didn't bolt. She knew what I was doing. Still tense, she huddled under my arm and we swam out together slowly through the gate and into the ocean. I let her go. I hoped with all my heart that she would take off. But she didn't. She hung around close to me at first, then later when she got used to it, she loosened up and enjoyed it.

As it turned out, taking Kathy out of the pen for the jumping shots was a great idea. There, in the early morning light, camera operators shot her jumping against an open horizon. They shot the jump from various distances and with various lenses most of the morning, then we went back into the pen. Late that afternoon we went out again— the same way, she under my arm, but with less trouble this time— and shot her jumping again in silhouette.

These shots proved to be important. Though we were almost finished shooting the Flipper series, it was going into syndication and these shots of a free Flipper jumping in the ocean were spliced into earlier scripts.

16

The Trouble with Susie

The dolphin is swifter than a bird and he hurls himself forward in the water faster than an arrow launched from a powerful machine.

—Pliny the Elder, Greek naturalist

As the television series wore on, the dolphins tended to get rougher with the actors and others in the water. It was like play, but scarier. The dolphins came up under anyone in the water, divers and crew members alike, unexpectedly brushing past them without warning or slapping their tails on the water threateningly. Tail-slapping, the dolphin's style of assertiveness, has the same effect as someone pounding his fist on the table. It doesn't hurt—the dolphins never hurt anybody—but it gets your attention. Unmistakably a threat, tail-slapping kept the actors and crew on their toes, yes, but it also interfered with their work, especially in the case of the actors, who obviously couldn't show their fear.

Toward the end of the first year's series of TV shows, the problem became serious with Susie. We got the feeling she was testing us, going a little further all the time, like a spoiled kid looking for limits. And she was spoiled. All of the Flipper dolphins were spoiled. From the beginning they realized how important they were to us and knew as if by instinct how to bargain and manipulate us down to the penny's worth. But it was more than that, especially later on. It was frustration, I thought, the frustration of being at odds with one's true nature.

One day we were about to shoot a scene of Flipper bringing a starfish to Tommy. He would take the starfish, pat Flipper on the head and say:

"Thanks, Flipper. That will do just right!"

When Tommy started to climb down into the water, he stopped halfway. I was there with my bucket of fish, as always, and Tommy asked me apprehensively: "How does he feel today?"

He wanted to know if he was safe with Susie.

If we had thought that it was dangerous for Tommy to go into the water, we wouldn't have let him go in. Safety came first. But right on the heels of safety was our concern that Tommy might *show* his fear of Flipper. Susie in fact had been feisty all morning, but I couldn't tell that to Tommy.

"She's okay," I said, smiling with confidence. Then I did my best to mollify her, tossing her lots of fish.

Susie's bad attitude was not her fault. She had been trained to expect a reward immediately after doing a trick. But in scenes where that was impossible, Susie got angry. Then the tail-slap: *Whamp!* Or she would rush up to you and splash you with water or hit your forearm with her snout or push you around and cut you off from shore as if in an excess of play. The rush and splash is the way dolphins off the coast of Georgia herd mullet and other fish into the shallows so that they can be picked off. Susie never hurt anybody in her whole life, but she could scare the hell out of you. When she didn't get fed after doing a trick, she thought she was being teased. Ricou and I knew what was going on, but there was nothing we could do about it. Gradually I phased her out, replacing her with Kathy. When Luke or Tommy climbed into the water, they asked:

"Which one is it today? Susie or Kathy?"

When I told them that it was Kathy, they breathed a sigh of relief.

Learning from the mistake I had made with Susie, I taught Kathy not to expect an immediate reward for doing a trick.

Before I switched to Kathy, I tried Patty. That was a mistake. She was even more aggressive than Susie. We were in the middle of shooting a scene and it wasn't going right because Patty kept slapping her tail. The director called me aside:

"Can't you *do* something about that?" He had a round face, pink from the sun, and a fringe of thin, blond hair. He ran a hand over his scalp and squinted at me. "That too much to ask?"

"I'm not sure, sir," I said, shaking my head helplessly.

"Aren't you the dolphin trainer?"

He knew that I was. "Yes, sir," I said.

"Then why haven't you trained him? We can't have this." He frowned. "Is there a problem I don't know about?"

"What do you mean, sir?"

"Look at us!" He threw his arms out wide. "We're stopped! Your dolphin has stopped everything! Am I getting *through* to you?"

"Yes, sir."

"Excellent." He nodded his head. "Now I really don't care about how you solve this problem, so don't tell me about it, please, but— have you ever heard the expression 'on with the show'?"

"Yes, sir."

"You know what it means, don't you?"

When people in authority resort to condescension or sarcasm, that means they're losing control and I tend to go military, head and eyes straight ahead. "Yes, sir," I said.

"Good. Then I want to know when we can go on with the show."

I told him it would take me a couple of hours, that I would have to switch Kathy for Patty.

"Two hours, then." He checked his wristwatch. It was 10 A.M. "You'll be ready by noon?"

"Yes, sir."

His head was bobbing. "One more thing. You say that's Patty in there now?"

I nodded.

"I don't want to work with Patty—*ever again*. Understood?"

"Yes, sir."

Even Ricou asked me what was wrong with Patty. "She's got the boys scared to death of her."

"What do you want me to do about it?"

He looked at me from afar. "You *are* the dolphin trainer."

But I couldn't do a thing with Patty except retire her from swimming with people. She alone of all the dolphins loved to travel, though, and so she became the mascot of the Miami Dolphins football team during the early days at the Orange Bowl.

Prodding Patty

You can't really punish a dolphin. Except for one time, which I painfully regretted, I never even tried. I looked on my job as teaching, the main part of which is gaining the learner's cooperation. Learning is something you've got to *want* to do. And that means sweetening the pot. If you don't want to jump through a hoop, maybe you'll want to for a fish. That's true whether you're a dolphin, a student, or a middle-level manager. It's called operant conditioning and in subtle hands it can steal your very soul.

Since food is so important to dolphins, it might seem that you could withhold their food and force them to follow orders. But that doesn't work. Mistreated, the dolphin becomes a titan of individuality. He might even kill himself. Dr. Lilly reports that a number of his experimental dolphins once dived to the bottom of their tank and wouldn't come up. He suggests that dolphins may consider suicide an acceptable solution to an unacceptable life. In that same report, incidentally, Dr. Lilly suggests, or allows the reader to infer, that this incident occurred when the dolphins *read his mind* and realized that he was about to cancel his experiments with them.

Although I was their trainer, their friend, and special envoy to the world of human beings, the dolphins who played Flipper nevertheless pushed me around about as much as anyone else. But I always thought I understood the reason for it and didn't take exception. Except once. Patty had gone too far and frankly I was glad it finally happened, because it gave me an excuse to do something about it. I went to Jordan Kline, underwater engineer and photographer who owned a dive shop in Miami. He made amazing underwater devices of all sorts. "Could you make a dolphin prod?" I asked him.

"You mean like a cattle prod?"

"Exactly."

"I don't see why not," he said. "Give me a week. I'll get back to you."

A week later he called and said he had something. I went out to his shop. He handed me a tube about two feet long, like a policeman's billy club. On the business end were two silver knobs, at the other end a red button. I held the prod in one hand and bounced it in the other. "Have you tested it?"

"I looked for volunteers but there were none," he said, "so I tried it out on myself."

"And?"

"It works."

"What's it like?"

"Like sticking your finger in a light socket."

I smiled. "I'll take it."

"When the two silver knobs make contact," he said, "you push the button."

I took it into the water with Patty several times but couldn't get it to work. I probably didn't want it to. I was about to take it back to the shop and get it worked on again when I walked by some of the divers at the reef tank.

"That the shock stick?" Dave asked. He was intrigued by anything that might keep the dolphins in line. "I heard about it. How does it work?"

"It doesn't," I said.

"Let me see it," Doug Bonham said. "You probably just don't know how." Doug had gone through the same diving school I had, the Divers Training Academy, and had taken my place in the Underwater Show and the Top Deck Show when I went with "Flipper."

"I know how it's supposed to work," I said. "All you have to do is push this red button right here, and you see these metal contacts down there?" Everyone was leaning in to see. "All I've got to do is make contact with these silver points—" and at that moment I touched the contacts to Doug's knee. He shot up like a rocket about four feet and came down in the reef tank with a big splash.

"I've got news for you," Doug yelled. "It works!"

Years later I came back to the Miami Seaquarium—I needed to borrow a dolphin (Sharkey) for a movie called *Danny and the Mermaid*—and the dolphin trainers, all of them attractive young women now, asked me about the shock stick.

"The what?" I had forgotten about it.

"The shock stick," Joan Caron said. She was the head trainer. "We found it in the storeroom." She glanced at Sally Roth, her fellow dolphin trainer, then back at me. "Did you use it when you trained Flipper?"

By now I knew what they were talking about. "Oh, that," I said. "No. I never used it. I tried it once or twice, but couldn't get it to work. It was a bad idea. In fact, the only time I ever used it was on Doug Bonham. He jumped about four feet in the air. When he came down, they wanted him to jump with the dolphins four shows a day. He would be a star and get a raise in pay—all the fish he could eat. But you know Doug. He wouldn't go along with it."

Punishment

Though I was never able to get the shock stick to work on Patty, I'll never forget the one time I did punish her. She was always more belligerent than the other dolphins, rushing at the actors and others in the water, slapping her tail and giving us the clear signal that she expected more out of life than this.

I had heard about the way she acted but I was never there when it happened. Then one day, I was there. It happened to me. It was around noon and I was at one end of Flipper's Lake, everybody else at the other end shooting a scene. I had waded in with my yellow Flipper bucket to put Patty through a training session, which is the way I fed the dolphins. I was about waist deep when she came over with an unnecessary splash, then dived down and flicked me on the head with her tail. It was quite deliberate.

"Good," I said. "I've waited for this moment."

The dolphin's tail is pure muscle. All his life it pumps up and down, never stopping. Even when he's still in the water, the tail is moving. Patty had turned and headed back. I made a fist and when she got to me, bang! I hit her on her back, next to the dorsal fin, as hard as I could. No, it didn't hurt her. But it gave her a message. "This is *me* you're messing around with," I was saying, "and if this is the way you want to talk about it, that's fine with me!"

As Patty swam past me, she glanced at me in a new way. Good, I thought. I was tired of being the good guy all the time. And if this worked, well, I hated to admit it, but maybe Dave was right. Why hadn't I thought of this sooner? Patty went out to midlake. I watched her dorsal fin cut through the water. She turned briskly. She was heading back. Is she swimming faster than usual? I asked myself. The dorsal fin sliced through the water like a knife. I made another fist. "Come and get it, Patty," I said. "This will be a lesson you will never forget."

She cut through the water, a torpedo now, then a blur from about three o'clock in the sky, and the next thing I knew I was in Mercy Hospital, a knot on my head. Ricou was there with Jack Cowden.

"What happened?" Jack asked.

I shook my head, confused. "The last thing I remember, I was disciplining Patty." I looked around. "How did I get here?"

"Concussion," Ricou said. "Jack saw you up on the shore. We brought you here."

"I was up on shore? Don't kid me, now. The last thing I remember, I was waist-deep."

Ricou shrugged.

"You know what that could mean?" I said.

"It means you probably staggered up there yourself," Ricou said.

"Unless Patty *pushed* me up there?"

Ricou made a disapproving face.

"It's possible," I said.

"Nobody saw it, Ric."

I glanced shrewdly at Ricou. "I think I remember being pushed up there by a dolphin."

Ricou and Jack exchanged looks; nobody spoke for a long moment.

"I saw you first," Jack said, "but I didn't see that."

"Nobody saw it," Ricou said flatly.

"You don't think—"

They were shaking their heads no and I dropped it. I was kept in the hospital for three days, and during that time I tried to remember if I had staggered up on the beach myself or if Patty, perhaps overcome with remorse at having tail-slapped me, had pushed me there. I decided finally that it could go either way and that, alas, because there were no witnesses, I would never know.

Exceptions

Flipper was one of the friendliest creatures on earth. He was always laughing, smiling through any adversity or pain. He never complained, either. He was intelligent, helpful, enterprising, and lovable—and sometimes positively psychic.

It might seem, therefore, that all dolphins have an inviolable love affair with human beings. But that's an overstatement.

If I was a good trainer, it was because of one talent I may have had in more than average amounts: empathy. I thought I could understand the feelings behind the dolphin's smile. I could tell when they were cooperative, and when they wanted to be left alone.

After the "Flipper" series, I was the head dolphin trainer in *Key Tortuga,* an ABC-Paramount Movie of the Week that was shot at the Britannia Beach Hotel & Casino at Nassau's Paradise Beach. The scene we wanted was simple, a dolphin pulling an actor through the water. The hotel had two dolphins available in its lagoon, Abaco, a female, and her mate, who was called The Big Male. They had been there for years. I chose Abaco to work with because she was obviously more cooperative. In fact when I first saw The Big Male, I realized that he was suffering from "burn out." He was mad as hell and wasn't going to take it any more. Nevertheless, we had a job to do. We blocked him off into a small portion of the lagoon so that we could work with Abaco. And he went off the deep end. The gate to the lagoon was actually a heavy double-plywood door held in place with two by fours. The Big Male battered desperately at it with his head.

I had never seen anything like that in my life. I told all the movie people and everybody I saw that The Big Male should be left alone, that he was dangerous. I couldn't explain it but I knew that The Big Male had suffered enough and despite himself he would hurt someone if they went even a little too far.

I told the hotel manager. He was a young native Bahamian with gleaming black slicked-back hair who wore an expensive silk suit. "What do you want me to do? Can't just turn him loose. He's been here longer than I have." He shook his head and turned the corners of his mouth down. "He'd never make it in the wild."

"That's true," I said. "But he's not making it now either. Keeping him in that little lagoon is cruel and inhuman."

The manager looked puzzled, then smiled. "Inhuman?" He gave an explosive laugh. "But dolphins *are* inhuman."

"No," I corrected him, "*you* are inhuman, dolphins are *non*human."

The manager shrugged. "Whatever. Don't look at me. I don't have the answer."

I left. I didn't have the answer, either. What we needed was a way to ease dolphins back into their own world again. A kind of repatriation. It's merely romantic to think that dolphins always hear a clarion call of the wild, that they can go home again anytime they want to. Dolphins who are full of human impressions are virtually cripples. Dolphins who live in human society very long need deprogramming. They are alienated from their true selves. They get used to being pets and having people swim around with them. As they adapt to being hand-fed dead fish, they put aside the skills of survival like catching live fish in the sea and staying clear of sharks. They need time to readapt, to learn how to live with natural dolphins. They need to brush up on their signals and sounds. They need to forget swimming round and round in a tiny tank because in the sea they will swim mile after mile in a straight line. To make a successful transition from life in the human world to their own, dolphins need a halfway house.

One of the associate producers of the movie seemed to feel a special relationship with The Big Male. On his free time, he used to lie on the edge of the dolphin's pen and pet him on the head and, strangely enough, reach into his mouth and fondle his tongue. I walked by one day as he was doing this and told him as I told everybody that he was tempting fate.

"Really? But we're friends," he said.

Then one day shortly after that, it happened. I wasn't there, but I heard about it. The Big Male simply closed his mouth on the movie maker's arm and ripped off most of the skin. It was not an accident; it was quite deliberate.

Happily, nobody suggested that The Big Male be punished. After all, I had told them something dreadful like that was sure to happen.

17

When the Wheels Fall Off

Don't worry about everything. Nothing is going to
be all right.

—Richard O'Barry

We knew all along that the TV series would come to an
end one day. Nothing lasts forever. Nevertheless, we felt that it would
never end. When the series did end, everyone scattered to the winds.
Everyone but me. They wanted me to keep the dolphins ready in case
they were needed in another film. For more than a year I tended them—
Kathy, Patty and Squirt, Susie and Scottie—feeding, training, and
living with them as it seemed I always had. Then one day it ended for
me too. I was stunned. I took it rather hard. It was like a death in the
family. They had treated us shabbily, I thought, as if were were props,
the dolphins and I, to be used and then put back on the shelf. Nothing
made sense.

It was not just losing the job, though it was a terrific job. I received
offers all the time: stunt jobs in the movies, promotional tours, training
dolphins in various aquariums around the world. But I couldn't see
myself doing any of that.

What happened next is hard to talk about and impossible to explain
so I won't even try, except to say that for an endless time I replayed
everything that had happened to me as if it were a movie, running it
over and over, making little changes here and there to see what would
have happened if I had done things differently. I seized on certain
scenes and kept coming back to them, scenes like Ricou warning me,

"Don't get attached to them," Jimmy shaking his head and saying, "Do it like I told you," and Dave protesting, "You have no idea what's going on here, do you?"

I became a recluse. I stuck to my room. No radio, no TV, no phone. I got rid of everything I owned, my expensive car and all my other toys, everything but a bicycle. I became a vegetarian. And I read a lot, and meditated, and tried to figure out what had happened. Then all at once, everything became clear. I realized that we are all drops of water, and that all of us, having been splashed into the air, are now falling back into the sea.

One day as I gazed through my back window at the pattern of shadows the sun was making as it fell through the palm fronds, my landlady knocked on the door and left a message for me from Ricou— how he found me I can't imagine. I was to contact Burton Clark, Seaquarium manager, about helping them with Hugo, the Killer Whale they had just acquired.

I knew nothing about Killer Whales then. Few people had ever worked with one. I got my *U.S. Navy Diving Manual* down and looked them up:

> The Killer Whale has a reputation of being a ruthless and ferocious beast. They are fast swimmers, will attack anything that swims, and have been known to come up under ice floes and knock seals and people into the water. If a Killer Whale is seen in the area, the diver should get out of the water immediately.

Intrigued, I called Mr. Clark, who said that Jimmy Kline didn't want to work with Hugo. "Okay," I said, "I'll come back and give it a try."

Burton Clark was a student of marine biology and loved the animals in his care. He spent an hour every day strolling around the Seaquarium grounds. But as a middle manager, he had little real power, serving only as a buffer for those above him who, it seemed to me, must have had as much conscience as a vending machine.

When Mr. Clark showed me Hugo, I shook my head in disbelief. "But this tank is much too small," I said. "It's impossible. Look!" I pointed at the end of his tail flukes. "He's longer than the tank is deep." It was true. Hugo was thirteen feet long, the tank only twelve feet deep.

"I know. But it's the best we can do at the moment."

"He's just a baby. He'll grow twice this big. Leave him in here, Mr. Clark, and you'll have the Humane Society down on your ears."

"I know. I know," Mr. Clark said, nodding his head. "But we're doing something about that. Come with me." He walked me over to where there was a big hole in the ground.

I looked at it in dismay. "This is it?"

"They're working on it."

"But in the meantime. . . ."

"In the meantime, Ric, we want you to keep him happy."

And I did. I had been thinking about getting into serious marine mammal research anyway, and Hugo, the only captive Killer Whale east of the Mississippi, could be an ideal project. So I set myself up with Hugo and decided to get acquainted. I got a big bucket of fish for him. I had heard lurid stories about Killer Whales, how they roamed the ocean in angry herds, attacking ships at sea, eating dolphins and sharks and anything else they could fit into their mouths. I studied Hugo's mouth. It looked like it would hold a small house. If Hugo can do that, I reasoned, he can certainly rip off an unwary arm. I held out one of the blue runners by the tail very gingerly for him. He opened his huge mouth and strained upward, then with the utmost gentleness, took the proffered fish. I realized that they were wrong about him, that I was in the presence of the most sensitive creature I had ever known.

"Hugo!" I said with a grin. "You're nothing but a big, wonderful dolphin!"

That's the way I treated him. Jimmy came by and told me never to get into the water with him, but I did. I used to get into the water and feed him. You cannot trust him, Jimmy told me. But I did. And Hugo trusted me. He allowed me to ride on his great back and, to amuse the tourists, I rode around on his back playing the flute and guitar. Hugo loved music. His tank, which was kept at sixty-eight degrees, was elevated slightly, steps leading up on one side, down the other. I set myself up in a director's chair next to the tank and answered the tourists' questions. The Seaquarium had sought to capitalize on Hugo by splashing an artist's conception of him on billboards along the highway leading south: Hugo the Killer Whale thrashing through the frothy water, with an angry countenance and huge, bloody teeth. Most of the questions people asked were about how dangerous he was, and my answer was a variation on the theme that he was the gentlest creature in the world.

Then they would ask why such a placid and gentle creature was called a Killer Whale.

I told them that Hugo is called a Killer Whale because that's his name. Scientifically he's an *Orcinus orca,* I said, the "orca" from the Latin "orcus," which means "lower world," his name thus perhaps more purely translating as the Demon Dolphin.

Early on I noticed one regular visitor to the tank in particular. He had a crewcut and was built like a fireplug. He wore a white, short-sleeved shirt with a bow tie, smiled a lot and watched everything I did with Hugo very closely. One day he introduced himself as Dr. Henry Truby, professor of linguistics at the University of Miami. "But call me Hank," he said.

"Okay, Hank. And you can call me Ric."

He laughed easily and I liked him at once. He was intense but loose at the same time.

One day I caught him staring at my head, which was a jungle of curls. "Anything the matter?" I asked.

He smiled. "Oh, no. But I was wondering. Were you ever in the service?"

"Yes," I said. "Navy."

His face brightened. "So was I. Army intelligence."

I looked at him a long moment. "I was in Naval *un*-intelligence."

He roared with laughter. "*Un*intelligence!" He slapped his knee. "Ric, that's funny! Do you mind if I write that down?"

"Not at all," I said. "But what for?"

"You never know," he said, taking out an old pad and a stubby pencil. He wrote it down with a flourish, read it over, nodded with pleasure and put the pad and pencil back in his pocket. Dr. Truby liked rubbing elbows with real people, but lusted for intellectual recognition, once boasting that he had written a book that only six other people in the world could understand. Technically, he was tops in his field, which was linguistics and most especially the spectrographic analysis of voice prints.

Dr. Truby's expertise had attracted Dr. Lilly, and for more than three years the two had worked shoulder-to-shoulder at the Communication Research Institute in Coconut Grove. When Dr. Truby asked if I would mind his bringing some equipment down to analyze

Hugo's sounds, I leaped at the chance. Also, I was flattered by the way he questioned me in such minute detail about dolphins and so meticulously wrote down everything I said.

Dr. Truby and I realized that we were on the leading edge of one of the most significant scientific investigations of all time. If we could establish that dolphins do have a language and then have meaningful conversations with them, it would be as important as any other discovery ever made. The interspecies connection would open up new fields of knowledge and revolutionize everything that had gone before. We were aiming high, Dr. Truby and I, and we had every reason to think we might hit the mark. Never before had anyone worked as closely as I had with dolphins and the Killer Whale, never before had anyone applied so much technological expertise and equipment to breaking the dolphin code as Dr. Truby. Together we were one hell of a team.

He was as fascinated by Hugo as I was, and of all the people I ever knew, Hank and I spoke most nearly the same language—but not quite. "I've always been interested in intraspecies communications," I said when we first met.

"*Intra*species?" he asked. "You mean *inter*species, don't you?"

I didn't know there was a big difference. But I said, "Yeah, I guess so."

"Intraspecies communication means communication *within* the species. One human being to another; one dolphin to another. What we're interested in is interspecies communication, communication *between* the species, human to dolphin and dolphin to human."

"Oh, sure," I said. "I must have slipped."

He smiled patiently. "And you don't mean *communications*, either."

"Did I say communications?"

"Yes, you did. And that's wrong. You meant to say *communication*, without the 's'." He grinned. "You don't mind if I correct you from time to time, do you? As a teacher—"

"Not at all. I appreciate it. To me it's like taking a graduate course."

He smiled. "If we're going to work together, it would help if we spoke the same language."

"Actually, I appreciate your correcting me. You don't mind correcting me, do you?"

"Not at all." He shrugged his hefty shoulders. "It's what I do."

"Thank you, Dr. Truby."

"Call me Hank." He beamed at me.

"Thanks, Hank."

Dr. Truby arrived the next morning with an old reel-to-reel tape recorder. The white short-sleeved shirt with the bow tie was his uniform, I realized, just as blue jeans or a tank suit with T-shirt and Topsiders were mine. He had all the latest electronic equipment and spoke a jargon I didn't always understand. I attended some of his lectures at the university and he referred to me as "Mr. Dolphin," telling his students that I knew more about dolphins than anyone else in the world.

I don't know what he did with all the notes he took of our conversations, whether he ever used them or not. He saved them, though. Of that I'm sure. Dr. Truby saved everything. One time he returned from a conference in Sweden and said he wanted to show me something. He reached into a folder and carefully removed a piece of tin foil that had covered some chocolates he had bought there. "Isn't that something?" he said with wonder. I agreed with him, and he lovingly folded it up again and put it away.

All that summer Dr. Truby recorded Hugo and made voice prints. He showed up sometimes with a couple of his students, explaining to them what we were doing. I once caught myself listening because I wasn't sure of it myself. But that's how it's supposed to be, I think, when you're on the leading edge of research as we were. We were especially interested in the effects of music on Hugo and the Flipper dolphins. A steady stream of musician friends of mine came through and played at the edge of Hugo's tank, Hugo responding in his own fashion, Dr. Truby recording everything, especially Fred Neil and his twelve-string guitar.

Though my research with Dr. Truby and the musicians seemed to justify my working at the Seaquarium, I had moments of doubt. One morning, for instance, Colonel Mitchell Wolfson, who owned Wometco, appeared at the tank. He was a middle-aged man with soft features and thin sandy hair who wore rimless glasses and an inoffensive beige business suit. I had been riding Hugo and had just stepped off with a splash of water when I looked up and saw the colonel.

He smiled pleasantly. "How's it going?"

We all knew who he was. "Doin' okay," I said.

"That's really some fish you've got there. What's his name?"

I hated it when people referred to marine mammals as fish. I looked at the round, happy face of Colonel Wolfson, my face a blank, thinking that this man owned Hugo and Flipper and all the rest of it here, including me, yet he didn't know anything at all about it. "His name is Hugo," I said simply.

He nodded. That seemed to please him and he left.

Another moment of doubt occurred when Dr. Jess White, a large, burly man, first signed on as Seaquarium vet. He came around one night and discovered us playing music with Hugo and putting speakers into the water. "Hey, what's going on here?" he demanded.

"These are music experiments," I told him.

He shook his shaggy head and frowned. "I'm responsible for the well-being of all the marine mammals. And doing this—whatever it is you're doing—with the Orca is not doing him any good."

"It's not hurting him either. We've been doing it for years," I said.

"Just what are you doing?"

"I don't even know myself," I said.

He looked at me strangely. He grumbled and walked off. "We'll see about this."

Dr. White marched off in a huff and I didn't hear anything more about it. We continued our musical experiments. And later Dr. White and I became the best of friends.

Sometimes when I wondered if I was on the right track, I ambled over to Flipper's Lake, where they kept Kathy. I tried to cheer her up but it wasn't the same. I checked in with Susie, who was now with Adolph Frohn under the Golden Dome. He hadn't really wanted her. She had been put in a tank by herself. People said that divers couldn't get into the water with her anymore. But I went over one day and got in and it was like old times. She knew all the old signals perfectly. Later she was sold to a traveling circus in Europe as the original Flipper. I heard that she died of pneumonia.

Hugo was eating 100 pounds of fish a day, and the bigger he got, the smaller his little whale bowl seemed. Nobody was more conscious of this than I, but every tourist who came through, thousands of them every day, pointed it out to me as if it were a great discovery. When Mr. Clark came by on his afternoon rounds, I told him what people were saying.

He shrugged helplessly. "We're doing everything we can about it."

He meant the new tank they were building for Hugo. I walked over to it every day. Some days I could see a little progress, other days none. It was taking forever. I stopped complaining to Mr. Clark about it—what could he do? But I couldn't control the strained silences between us, which became more and more tense. Then I noticed that he wasn't coming around to see us anymore. I couldn't blame him. And I was tired of taking the heat myself, but the tourists relentlessly poured it on:

—Did you know that he's too big for the tank?
—This is cruel and inhuman.
—You ought to be reported!
—What do you think he is, a sardine?

I've always liked people and wanted them to like me. That was the fun of working at the Seaquarium. Now this! So why am I doing this? I asked myself. For the research, I replied. And the answer came like a moment of truth: *What* research?

I left, this time for good. I went to India, where for a time I contemplated my navel.

Hugo survived till the summer of 1975, seven years after his capture. Killer Whales usually live from three to seven years in captivity, according to some whale researchers, eleven to fourteen according to others. But all researchers agree that Killer Whales live a lot longer in the wild, at least forty-eight years, some say, and as long as a hundred years for females.

When I returned to my apartment from India, I thought at first that nothing had changed. I looked out of the back window at the palm trees. They seemed the same. That was good, I thought. I looked for that familiar shadow of palm fronds in my back yard that once intrigued me. But it was gone! And suddenly I felt very sad. For the shadow? No. That was nothing. But it was also everything, because I realized with an intensity I had never felt before that everything— *everything!*—is passing.

The next day or a week later or whenever it was, there came a knock on the door; my landlady, with a message from Bob Baldwin, supervisor at the Seaquarium. I should call him immediately. "He said it was urgent," the landlady yelled through the door. I got to a phone and called Bob. It's Kathy, he said. She's not doing well at all. They put her in one of the tanks, he said.

"What did they do that for?" I asked.

"You should come at once," he said.

I got on my bike and pedaled over the causeway. Kathy was okay when I left. What could be wrong? Bob Baldwin was not one to panic. If he had known what was wrong, he would have told me. If it's just that she won't eat, maybe I could do something. But why did they move her? If I had been there, I wouldn't have allowed that. I pedaled furiously and, dripping with sweat, reached the Seaquarium and rode right through the gate without stopping. Somebody new at the gate yelled after me but I kept going. I rode over to the tank where Bob Baldwin said she had been put. I went up to the tank and looked in. I was stunned! It was Kathy, yes, but not the Kathy I had known. Her back and head were black with blisters. Horrible! Big ugly black blisters covered almost her whole body and she lay there on the surface of the water, barely moving.

"My God! My God!" I cried. "What have I done?"

I leaped in the water with her, clothes and all. She came over and into my arms, I held her a moment and felt the life go out of her. Her tail flukes stopped and she was dead. A foul white foam had formed on her blowhole. Without thinking I washed it away. I carefully forced the blowhole open with my thumb, very careful not to let any water in. I cradled her in my arm and held on to the edge of the pool so that I could apply pressure with my knees to Kathy's ribcage. But Kathy was dead. I pressed her ribs in and out, keeping up a breathing rhythm. But I knew that she was dead. How long I did that, I don't know. But she was dead and nothing could be done about it. I let her go and she sank to the bottom and all of a sudden I felt very dirty. I got my bike and pushed it to Bob Baldwin's office, tears streaming down my face. When I saw him, I tried to speak but couldn't.

"You don't have to say anything," he said.

I kept trying to speak but I was sobbing too much, then for just a moment I cleared up and blurted out at him: "Why are we *doing* this!"

He shook his head, lips compressed. I turned and got on my bicycle and pedaled slowly back to my apartment. I was thinking only one thing: that something had to be done. Within a week I was in Bimini, trying to free Charlie Brown.

18

Working Without a Net

The time will come when they will sell you even your rain.
At the moment, it is still free and I am in it. I celebrate its
gratuity and its meaninglessness.

—Thomas Merton, *Raids on the Unspeakable*

When the Bimini trial ended and I returned home to Coconut
Grove, I had no idea what I would do except now that "Flipper" was
finally over, I could devote all of my time to dolphins. My long-range
goal had not changed. I still wanted to free captive dolphins. But not
with impulsive gestures. What good had that done? I wanted to do
dolphin research. When I could prove to the world what dolphins are
really like, nobody would dare keep a dolphin against his will. But I
was trapped in Lilly's Paradox: to prove that dolphins should be free,
you've got to capture a few for study and research. It's a tough position
but not an impossible one.

I was mulling these things over when there was a knock on the
door. It was Fred Neil and a friend of his. Fred lived like a recluse a
few blocks away and used to drop by from time to time. People used
to say we looked like brothers, both of us about the same build and
with curly brown hair; except that he was freckled like a spotted
dolphin. He was actually a little taller than I and heavier. He always
wore dark glasses, too, like a disguise. He was very shy, spoke slowly
and in a deep voice. "You know Stephen Stills here?"

"No, but I know *of* him," I said.

We shook hands. I had followed Stills's career with the band Buffalo
Springfield and loved his music. Fred had told me about his houses in

Colorado and just outside of London, but I hadn't expected Fred to bring him to my door.

"He likes dolphins, too," Fred said.

I asked them in but they said it was such a beautiful day—it was winter and chilly but the sun was out and the wind was light—they'd rather go sailing. Fred wore a windbreaker but Stephen, a stocky blond and athletic looking, was in a T-shirt. "Aren't you cold?" I asked him. "You can use one of my windbreakers if you want to."

"Me? Cold? No, thanks. To me this is just right."

We went down to the marina and rented a day-sailer, then drifted around in the bay, talking about music but mainly of dolphins. Some modern musicians are as fascinated by the relationship between dolphins and music as musicians in antiquity were. Fred, at the tiller, was telling Stephen about his musical experiments with Hugo and Kathy. "It's not necessarily the music," Fred said, "it's the tone and sound of sustained chords. When Kathy heard a chord on the twelve-string guitar, she had the gentlest way of putting her snout on the vibrating strings themselves and on the wooden box, feeling it like it was something very special. And it is to them. I've worked with them a lot and they seem to like the D-chord best."

"That's not surprising," Stephen said. "The earth itself is in D."

We all nodded and looked at one another. I was in the bow of the boat and we all felt that we were in the beautiful presence of something very rare, a fundamental truth about the world itself, when suddenly a pod of dolphins appeared off the port bow, heading out. "Look!" Stephen cried.

Half a dozen dolphins swam past us and off toward the channel. We watched in silence. Then Stephen said: "This project of yours, Ric, the musical research with the dolphins, swimming with them in the wild and the readaption programs, all this sounds good to me. I'd like to help. The only problem I have is that business of yours in Bimini." He shook his head with disapproval. "If I'm in it, it's got to be totally within the law. If not. . . ."

"Bimini happened," I said, "because it had to happen. But it won't happen again."

"And what about the dolphins we use in experiments?"

"That's already settled," I said. "They are always treated humanely. With respect. Always."

"And when the experiments are done?"

"We turn them loose again," I said. "We make sure that they will survive, but then we turn them loose. I think there's something obscene about a dolphin dying in captivity."

Stephen smiled. "If that's so," he said, turning to Fred, "then count me in."

When we got back to the dock, he gave me his phone numbers in England and Colorado. "Keep in touch," he said.

Now that we had support, we needed a dolphin. I headed for Grassy Key, just north of the Seven-Mile Bridge that leads to Key West. That seemed appropriate somehow because Grassy Key is where *Flipper,* the original movie, had been shot and where Mitzi, the original Flipper, was still held captive. She was the star attraction in the dolphin show staged by Milton Santini and his wife, Virginia. They operated a spread of a few acres with wooden, pastel pink docks running fifty yards into the Gulf and a number of pens, one like a small lake where the show itself was held, the others in rows for about twenty dolphins. It was called "Santini's Porpoise School," then "Flipper's Sea School." Later it was renamed the "Dolphin Research Center."

When I showed up that late-spring morning on their dock, they knew who I was. The newspapers had depicted me as "The Dolphin Avenger" or something, and the word had spread. Milton Santini and Virginia were a perfect team; he the muscle, a big, powerful man, she the brain, a genius of bottom-line thinking. Milton was a one-man collecting team. He caught dolphins in the Gulf by himself. At the Miami Seaquarium, we had heard Santini stories for years. In his work boat, he would spot a pod of dolphins, pick out the one he wanted— usually a young female—then run her into the flats and keep running her till she was exhausted. At that point, he would jump out and grab her like cowboy bulldogging a calf, then heave her into his boat. I liked him, though, and we got along because he liked dolphins too.

When they came down to the dock, I probably looked a little scruffy, needing a shave and my hair a tangle. I had been up all night, thinking. At this moment, I was hovering on the edge of at least two plans, one to free every last one of these dolphins, the other to try to talk the Santinis into letting me use one of their dolphins for research. I didn't get to first base with Virginia.

"On the way down," I said, as if making small talk, "I noticed the billboards." The Santinis had half a dozen small billboards along U.S.

Highway 1 advertising the dolphin school. It was touted as the "Home of Mitzi, the Original Flipper, and DeeDee, the dolphin owned by TV Personality Hugh Downs."

Virginia gave me a matter-of-fact look.

"We may have a mutual friend," I said carelessly. I glanced at Virginia to see if she cared. She didn't. "Hugh Downs," I said. Art McKee and I had been on his "Today Show" some years before. Hugh Downs, a sailor and diver, had gone out with Art diving for treasure once and decided that he would make an interesting interview. I was invited along with my scuba gear to show the difference between the old hard-hat diving school, which Art had been a part of, and scuba diving.

"You're a friend of his?" she said.

"I know him," I said. "And I think he might let me use his dolphin for research."

She looked at me skeptically. "What kind of research?"

"I want to work with dolphins in the wild."

She gave a small, tight smile, then snickered. I had the feeling that I was applying for a loan and had already been turned down but hadn't been told yet. "We usually see dolphins in tanks," I said. "We see them swimming round and round. But in nature—the ocean— they swim in straight lines."

Her small smile had frozen.

"If you ever saw a dolphin swimming in the ocean the way they swim in aquariums, you would say to yourself, 'That dolphin must be crazy.' So it's my thought," I said, "to study them in their natural environment, the way they are in nature. That's the only way we can find out who they really are."

Virginia had fixed her gaze on the pens in front of us. She glanced at me quickly, then looked back without saying anything.

"We'll never know them in aquariums," I said. "Not the conventional kind, anyway, where specimens are on exhibit in little bowls. Know what I mean?"

She shot me another quick look. Milton wagged his head understandingly.

"If I had the money, I'd set up an underwater viewing platform. I call it an inverted zoo. That's where the animals are not behind bars, we are." I glanced at them. I wondered if they had ever heard of such an idea before. Both of them kept staring out at their pens. "If we wanted to see them," I said, "we would go in boats out to the platform. We would tie up, then go down to the viewing level. It would be round. Several levels. Maybe a restaurant. Lots of glass. Wouldn't it cost a lot of money? I get asked that all the time. Sure. Lots of money. But it would pay for itself. Probably make money. Who knows? And it's the only way we could see the dolphins and other forms of marine life as they really are, you know, free."

"No," Virginia said, shaking her head. "Dolphins are not free. Dolphins are expensive. Know how much DeeDee is worth?"

She had misunderstood me. I let it go. "How much?"

"Fourteen thousand dollars."

"You get that much for them?"

"For DeeDee? Yes. He's a trained dolphin."

Milton chimed in, "DeeDee is a star of the show."

"Hugh Downs paid that much for DeeDee?"

"No. We gave him DeeDee," Virginia said. "He likes dolphins. He likes us. And it's good for business when he comes down."

"That way you figure you can use his name in advertising?"

"He doesn't mind."

I looked at her for a long stony moment. "He'll let me use DeeDee if I ask him," I said.

"It's his dolphin. If he says it's okay with him, it's okay with us. Right, Milton?"

Milton shrugged indifferently. "Sure."

"But without his okay—" I said.

"Without his okay," she said, "you get nothin'."

I returned to Coconut Grove to think this thing through. If I was involved in a cause, I decided I would at least need a bunch of T-shirts. I went to a place on Southwest 8th Street, in Little Havana, and ordered a gross of them, all sizes.

The shop owner asked, "What kind of logo do you want?"

"I don't know," I said. "I hadn't thought about it."

"It's a project of some sort?"

I nodded.

"What kind of a project?"

"A dolphin project."

"Then why don't you call it the Dolphin Project?"

I rolled it around in my head for a moment and said it aloud:

"Dolphin Project. Yes! That's good! Can you do me a sample one?"

He went into the back, set up a form and ran one of them off. When he showed it to me, something clicked. It was perfect. Already my campaign to free the dolphins was rolling. It had a name, a logo and T-shirts. I took off the Miami Seaquarium T-shirt I was wearing and threw it away, then put on the new one. I looked at myself in the wall mirror. Yes, I decided, it was me. I called the airport, got a ticket and the next morning I was in New York. Wearing my Dolphin Project T-shirt, my usual blue jeans and Topsiders, I went directly to the NBC building, walked into the lobby and checked the directory. Hugh Downs's "Today Show" was near the top of the building. I went to the phone in the lobby and called his office. A secretary answered. Hugh Downs was very busy, she said. He was in a meeting. I told her I had just flown in from Miami, that I was in the lobby downstairs, that I had been on his show some time before and he might remember me, that I would like to talk to him about using his dolphin, DeeDee, for my dolphin research, that the only good his dolphin was doing anyone now was advertising on the Santinis' billboards, that the dolphin was bored to death in his pen and that Hugh Downs would benefit dolphins all over the world if he would donate DeeDee to the Dolphin Project.

"To the what?"

"The Dolphin Project. You've heard of it, haven't you?"

"Hmm, I think so," she said. "Hold on a minute, please."

I waited in the phone booth for several minutes. Then she came back on: "The answer is yes," she said. "You're in the lobby?"

I said that I was.

"Take the elevator," she said. "I'll have a letter for you by the time you get up here."

And she did. Hugh Downs had already signed the letter donating DeeDee to me and the Dolphin Project. DeeDee was mine.

When I flew into Miami with the letter, I called Martha from the airport. Soon she arrived in her big green Pontiac convertible. She was a model, tall and slim with long, dark-brown hair. She had the "natural look," and even with no makeup at all, she looked great. We drove directly to Sears and bought a cabin-tent, then headed down to Grassy Key. I showed the Santinis the letter from Hugh Downs, then I set up the tent next to DeeDee's pen, where I began taking care of him, feeding him, swimming with him and walking with him in the flats outside the pen while he swam at my side. The idea was to see if he would come back if I let him go. The step after that was the important one, to free him—let him return to the ocean—yet maintain contact with me. From there, who knew? Perhaps my dolphin would contact other dolphins in the sea and tell them about me, becoming my ambassador, so to speak. For several months I worked on that, then one night a thunderstorm flattened the tent. Lightning shattered the aluminum tent pole. Martha and I looked at each other. "That's it," I said. We took it as a message from on high and moved back to civilization. Funds were low, so some of my musician friends and I staged a series of music benefits for the Dolphin Project. Alphabetically, they included Eric Andersen, Jimmy Buffett, David Crosby, Rick Danko, Dion, Phil Everly, Richie Havens, Bob Ingram, Vince Martin, Joni Mitchell, Fred Neil, John Sebastian, Stephen Stills and Jerry Jeff Walker. Some money came in, most of it in the form of memberships. We had about a thousand members at $15 each. Everyone received a decal for his car and a newsletter. The Dolphin Project was rolling.

One of the members was Captain Joe Maggio, who at this time owned an old fifty-foot Greek sponge-diving boat. He had been a Green Beret gunboat captain in Vietnam and wrote a book, *Company Man,* about his experiences with the CIA. One sunny day with a twelve-knot breeze from the south and a light chop on the bay, Captain Maggio and his family and a whole boatload of Dolphin Project volunteers sailed out to the Gulf Stream, where, amid stacks of flowers, Captain Maggio married Martha and me.

A few months later, funds were low again. This was becoming a chronic problem. I was on radio talk shows a lot, newspapers picked up on it, and the Dolphin Project became a continuing story in the press. But it seemed to me like it was all talk. I drove back down to Grassy Key to work with DeeDee but he wasn't in his pen. Virginia came down to the dock. "Where's DeeDee?" I asked.

"He's gone," Virginia said simply.

"I can see that," I said. "But where is he?"

"He's gone as in 'dead.'"

"Dead!" I stared with disbelief. "He was okay when I saw him last. Are you sure?"

"You think I don't know a dead dolphin when I see one?"

"Dead, huh? You didn't sell him, did you?"

She shook her head, the corners of her mouth turned down. "Gone." She sighed. "But don't worry about it. We've got another dolphin you can have."

I didn't know whether I was getting a fast shuffle or not. But it didn't matter. DeeDee was a very valuable animal—but not to me. He was valuable to the Santinis; they had trained him for fourteen years. For the Dolphin Project, a young dolphin might be better anyway.

So I went along with it and they gave me another one. I named her Opo in honor of the dolphin of that name celebrated in Opononi, a little tourist resort north of Aukland, New Zealand. Townspeople memorialized the dolphin with a life-sized statue in the 1950s. She was credited with having brought the town back together. People in the town had been quarreling for years about something nobody could remember anymore. Then one day Opo showed up at the beach and began playing with a ten-year-old girl, Jill Baker. She ran home and told people what happened, that she was playing with a dolphin. Word spread. This was so unusual, everybody in town went down to the beach to see for themselves. When they saw the friendly dolphin, they all went swimming together, laughing and playing and forgetting their quarrel. It's a beautiful story and it really happened, beautiful in that it sums up the way dolphins affect people. The original Opo was the prototype of Flipper.

I spent a lot of time with Opo, commuting back and forth from Coconut Grove to Grassy Key. Meanwhile the Dolphin Project continued to catch the public's eye. Rock star David Crosby sent a $1,000 check from his home in Mill Valley, California. We bought a freezer with it and a lot of Spanish mackerel. Memberships poured in, including some people who could help us in other ways. One of those was James A. Ryder, of the truck rental company. One of the Dolphin Project members told me that Ryder owned several acres that could be used for the dolphins. They were at Mashta Point, the southwest tip of Key Biscayne. I drove out and looked it over one day. It was perfect, a beautiful site with a skyline view of Miami and a 200-foot man-made lagoon on the bay. In the old days the lagoon had been a yacht basin. Originally it belonged to Dr. William J. Matheson, who built a Moorish mansion there in Miami's boom days. But the unhappy combination of hurricanes and neglect, together with the fact, some historians said, that the contractor had used salt water in the cement, caused it to fall, first into disrepair and then into rubble. Motorcyclists and drifters lived amid the squalor. I went to see Mr. Ryder at his office in the penthouse of the Coconut Grove Bank Building. He was a big guy in a big office with lots of sailing photos on the wall. A secretary said something on the intercom. "No," he said to her, "hold my calls." We talked about environmental things. He stood up suddenly—I got the feeling he did that a lot—and gazed out of the big picture window. From there he could see the property across the bay. I told him we needed the lagoon for the dolphins. "If you need it," he said, "you've got it."

We cleaned up the site, erected a fence with a large gate across the mouth of the lagoon and got all the permits necessary for moving Opo. Then, using one of Ryder's trucks, we got Opo into a box like the one I used in moving Flipper, I crawled up on the box with her, just like in the old days, and we took off, a caravan. Bob Marchetti, one of the few in the Dolphin Project to be paid a salary, drove the truck, followed by Dr. Truby and several of his students, all of them taking copious notes. Martha was driving in our car, a couple of officers from the Department of Natural Resources followed in their official gray car, and behind them was a pair of uninvited guests, square-jawed men wearing suits, wingtip shoes and dark glasses. On the trunk of their car was a telltale antenna. They were Secret Service agents. They watched everything we did because next door lived President Richard Nixon and his family at the Little White House. From our site, we could sometimes see him and Pat, Trisha, Julie, and David Eisenhower on their dock, or flying in on a helicopter from the Strategic Air Command Base at Homestead, or chugging by on B. B. Reboza's forty-two-foot blue Chris Craft houseboat. We waved back and forth, they without encouragement. But our main connection with the Nixons was the Secret Service. Anything we wanted them to know, we said on the phone.

Once, when our funds had gone dry again, I called Dr. Truby. We had just formed the World Dolphin Foundation and made him president of it. His credentials would help raise funds, I thought. On the phone I told him I was going to ask President Nixon for a research grant.

"Excellent idea," Dr. Truby said. "Do you want me to provide you with the scientific parameters, a resume, background data, anything like that?"

"Thanks anyway, Hank. This is more informal than that. I thought that since we're neighbors, after all, I would send him a neighborly little letter. Maybe set up a dialogue. What do you think?"

"Excellent plan, Ric. Later, if you want me to, I'll outline the implications of interspecies communication. As you know, Ric, the implications are mind-boggling. Mind-boggling! At this point, though, yes, a personal note is perhaps more appropriate."

"I think so, too. Then later if he seems to be interested—"

"We can update him about our ongoing projects, the spectrograph voice prints and so on." Dr. Truby's voice darkened with import. "As you are aware, Ric, the president's support of worthy scientific research is well known in academic circles."

I knew that Dr. Truby was talking for the benefit of the Secret Service, and probably they did, too. "Yes," I said. "He's got to wonder what we're up to over here. I'll hand-deliver the letter. What do you think, Hank?"

"Hmm, I'm not sure. But why not? Yes, another excellent idea!" Dr. Truby said. "But of course you can't just walk up to his house and slip it under the door."

I laughed lightly. "Right. I'll just give it to one of the Secret Service men out front. By the way," I said, "how do you address a letter to the president, anyway?"

"Hold on. I've got something here on the proper protocol." Dr. Truby looked it up and read it to me over the phone. I fixed up the letter and signed it, then walked over to the barricade. About twenty people with signs were demonstrating against the war. They were always there. The Secret Service agent saw me and waved. I went over. He smiled and said: "Hi, Ric. Got the letter?"

"Yes, here it is," I said, and handed it to him. "He'll get it okay?"

"He'll get the letter, all right."

"Thanks." Then I left.

But we never received an answer. I suppose he was busy with other things at that point in time.

Mr. Williams and His Roadside Attraction

When anyone saw a dolphin with a problem, they called me about it. This was the part I didn't like. I was not a policeman. But who else would do anything? In the summer of 1973 I received several calls from David Kent, Everglades photographer, about a couple of dolphins on display in the Everglades. I hopped in my car and took off down the Tamiami Trail (U.S. 41) to the little truckstop. On the wall, a crude hand-lettered sign said:

SEE THE DOLFINS
$1.00
KIDS—50 CENTS

I pulled in at the gas station and parked to one side. It was early afternoon. Hot. Big, yellow grasshoppers were mating in a seasonal orgy all over the ground. In a series of wire cages off to the right were several dozing pit bulldogs, and tied with a chain to a scraggly tree out by the bushes lay another one, black and white, a heavy-featured brute with a deep scar cutting across the nose, his big tongue hanging out the side of his mouth. I walked in and paid my dollar to an assistant, a thin, leggy young man with lank blond hair that he kept in place with a sporadic snap of his head. He took me out back to a rock pit. We were standing on a rickety wooden scaffold above it. The assistant pointed a bony finger downward. And there they were: two dolphins lethargically treading water.

"Here you go," the assistant said. He grinned at me. He had a bucketful of very strong-smelling gar, a primitive fresh-water species of fish native to the Everglades. "Watch this!" He took a small gar and, with a conspiratorial glance at me, tossed it out. The two dolphins wheeled and raced for the rotten morsel.

"Ain't that somethin' now?" the assistant said. He grinned and snapped his hair into place.

I had seen enough. "I'm with the World Dolphin Foundation," I told him. I produced a card showing that in fact I was the field director of the foundation. "I want to see this degrading spectacle closed down immediately."

The assistant's mouth gaped open. "You what?"

"I want to see—oh, forget it," I said. "I want to speak to whoever is in charge here."

His head was bobbing assent. But he said: "Oh, I wouldn't do that if I was you." He shook his head, then he snapped it negatively and his hair fell into place. "No," he said, "you don't want to do that."

Words sometimes fail me, but I almost always know the right thing to do. I flared my nostrils and breathed heavily at him.

He looked at me with amazement, then, shrugging, he said: "Oh, all right. But he's not going to like it."

When the assistant left, I made my way down to the water and checked out the dolphins at close range. They were pale and sick and very thin, even their eyes were almost white. I had brought a small bottle with me and filled it with water from the rock pit. I thought it was brackish, a dirty mixture of fresh and salty water, but the University of Miami Marine Lab tested the water for me and discovered that it was fresh, which is even worse for a dolphin than brackish water. Mr. Williams arrived and I climbed back up to the landing. He was a big man with sloping shoulders, thick forearms, and narrowed eyes who clomped around heavily in cowboy boots. He came up to me wiping his hands on an oily rag, turned to his assistant and said: "He the one?" The assistant nodded and Mr. Williams cocked his head to one side, squinting warily at me. "What's the problem?"

"These dolphins here," I said, shaking my head.

"My dolphins are a problem for you?" He grinned. He had big yellow teeth. "Who are you, anyway?"

"O'Barry," I said. "Richard O'Barry." Then I told him my connection with the World Dolphin Foundation, which he acknowledged with a careful nod. "It's my unpleasant duty," I lied, "to inform you that you must return these dolphins to the sea at once. They cannot survive in this place."

He nodded again, his eyes squinting almost closed. "Let me get this straight," he said. "You're telling me you want me to let my dolphins go?"

"Free them, yes. And it's not what I want, Mr. Williams, it's the law."

"This a joke?" He turned to his assistant, wringing the neck of the rag he had in his hands. The assistant flipped his hair into place with a sudden convulsion that snapped his head first to the left and then to the right.

"No, this is not a joke, Mr. Williams," I said. "I assure you of that."

"Yeah? And I'll assure you of something, Mr. Dolphin Foundation." Mr. Williams had perfected the technique of grinding his teeth and speaking at the same time, which he did now. "I pay taxes here. This is my station, my general store, my land, my home, my everything, including my dolphins. Follow me? I paid good money for those two dolphins. And until I make my money back on 'em, my money and a little more, the only way you'll get your hands on 'em is to buy 'em." He turned suddenly and flashed a grin at his assistant, who grinned back. "Or steal 'em." Then Mr. Williams pushed his face into mine and I became aware that he had a gum problem of enormous proportions.

But I love it when it's easy to tell who the bad guys are. I said, "Mr. Williams, you shouldn't take this personally, but I am the field director of an international organization that has complete and total authority over all dolphins. You say you bought a dolphin?" I shook my head sadly. "No. You only think you bought a dolphin. Buying a dolphin is like buying. . . ." I stopped, searching for a simile that would compare dolphins with something as independent as himself. ". . . like buying you, Mr. Williams."

He looked confused for a moment, his face a turmoil of revulsion, and he squinched up his eyes in a sly smile. He had his hands on his hips and suddenly his shoulders went forward aggressively, but mixed, I thought, with weariness. The man was dog tired. "For the right price, Mr. Dolphin Foundation, you can buy anything I own, including the dolphins, all this," he lifted his hands slowly, palms upward, like Moses, "and even me."

"I'm serious, Mr. Williams."

He dropped his head to one side, his squinty eyes following me like a snake's. "And you think I'm not? Everything I've got is for sale. Everything. But I'm not givin' it away, and you're not takin' it from me, either."

"For the last time, Mr. Williams, you have got to set those dolphins free. Without salt water, they'll die."

For a long moment we breathed hard at each other.

"And if I don't?"

Unaccountably, a wave of sympathy swept through me. I could remember when I too would have seen nothing wrong with having a few dolphins in a rock pit. His dolphins, his rock pit. I would have laughed at anyone who said there was anything wrong with that. But now I knew it was wrong and when I looked at Mr. Williams it was like looking at myself as I once had been—and not liking it. I spoke to him with a directness I usually reserved for myself. "You're either going to close this stinking show down, Mr. Williams, or I'm going to close it down for you. And if you think you've lost money buying these two dolphins, you don't know what it is to lose money."

He flashed me a corn-cob grin. A pair of big yellow copulating grasshoppers fell onto the platform between us and tumbled over one another several times. We all watched a moment, transfixed. Then without a word Mr. Williams stepped on them with his cowboy boots. That was me if I got funny with him.

When I got back, I called state officials in Tallahassee, told them what I had seen and that the World Dolphin Foundation was very interested in this matter. A week later I drove back to Mr. Williams's truck stop. The sign was gone, and so were the dolphins. I didn't see Mr. Williams but the assistant was there. He saw me and looked away. Later, following up on the case, I discovered that the Florida Department of Natural Resources had ordered Mr. Williams to return the dolphins to the sea. And he did.

19

25.05° North, 76.40° West

Freedom: ... [the] state of being at liberty rather than in
confinement or under physical restraint.

—*American College Dictionary*

Meanwhile, Opo languished in the Mashta lagoon and the
Dolphin Project continued to go public. Dr. Truby handled the civic
club circuit, explaining scientific aspects of our research to local movers
and shakers; I talked through the media to the little people. I was on
radio talk shows a lot, television and newspaper feature interviews,
and I spoke to school children who came by the busload to see the
dolphin and to hear how Flipper had been trained. They always asked
me why I named the dolphin Opo and I told them the story about the
village in New Zealand and the original Opo.

They asked physical questions about the size of dolphins like Flipper,
(seven or eight feet, 300 to 400 pounds), how long they could hold
their breath (five minutes), how deep they could dive (more than 1,000
feet), how fast they could swim (25 miles an hour after two seconds),
and how big their brains were compared with those of humans (dolphins average 1,600 cubic centimeters, humans, 1,400).

The underlying fascination with dolphins always involved their intelligence, which invariably was reduced to the problem of criteria or
how things are proved. Most Westerners, I pointed out, tend to rate
life forms in terms of how they control the environment. The history
of the world as we know it is written from that viewpoint. But perhaps
a relationship more indicative of intelligence, I said, was how well one

adapted to the world and became a part of it.

The thrust of my message, however, was that we must stop the three dolphin collectors on Biscayne Bay: Milton Santini, Jerry Mitchell of Key Largo, and the Miami Seaquarium.

"I can remember when the bay was full of dolphins," I said. "Now, because of these collectors, you seldom see a dolphin anymore."

This was true and it touched a nerve. But my position was undermined by a contradiction, and one woman listener shrewdly noticed it. She called in to the talk show and said, "That's all very well, Mr. O'Barry, but don't you also have a captive dolphin?"

She was right. I told her that we were planning to release Opo. It was part of our plan all along, I said, and if it would serve to close down the professional hunters in Biscayne Bay, we would release Opo immediately. The Marine Mammal Protection Act (MMPA) had not been passed but it was in the air. The public was incensed that tuna fishermen alone were killing half a million dolphins every year. But the MMPA was flawed. Not only did it give professional hunters like Santini and the Miami Seaquarium a loophole to keep collecting dolphins, it provided a penalty only for the "willful" killing of them, a word that would simply turn the killers free again. When the law doesn't work, the people must resort to public gestures.

Though I didn't say so publicly, we would soon have to release Opo anyway. We were running out of funds again. Martha had given birth to our son, Lincoln, and a sudden sense of responsibility overwhelmed me one day at the grocery store. I went there to buy Spanish mackerel for Opo and milk for Lincoln. When I got to the checkout counter, I went to pay the clerk and discovered that I had money for one of them but not both. I left the fish.

Bob Marchetti, the Dolphin Project's paid employee, lived with his wife Alice and their new baby on the houseboat at Mashta. Bob served as watchman and tended Opo. He and Alice knew as well as I that the money had seeped away, not just for Bob's meager salary and mine but also for Opo's food, the electric bill, the phone bill, and the portable john. We talked about it all the time. Despite everything, the Dolphin Project was dying. But I thought perhaps it was meant to be. I had been having moral doubts about keeping a dolphin captive when the objective was to free them all. I asked Bob: "Have you seen Dr. Truby lately?" Bob shook his head.

*   *   *

Dr. Truby had been named president of the World Dolphin Foundation not just because of his academic background; we thought that he would be able to attract some grant money. We needed a juicy grant, enough money to pay the bills and keep going for several years. I had talked to Dr. Truby about it but he said that grant money had too many strings.

"Money is money, Hank," I said, trying to be reasonable.

Dr. Truby shook his head slowly. "Not really. I've done it that way before and it's not what I want to do. I want to do *my* research." He gave me a big open-eyed look. "*Our* research, Ric. When you use *their* money, you have to do what *they* want. I want to do what I think is important without having to spend all my time accounting for each penny we get. That's why the Dolphin Project is so perfect, Ric. Don't you see? The money is without strings."

"The money is without strings? *What* money? We're out of money, Hank. That's what I've been telling you. We can't afford to stick up our noses at grant money anymore. Let's take it. We need it. Even if it has strings."

Dr. Truby's research had resulted in a number of papers with titles like "Voice Recognition by Man, Animal, and Machine," and, with John Lilly, "Psychoacoustic Implications of Interspecies Communication." That was fine for his reputation, but it didn't help the rest of us.

Sadly I told Bob: "We'll have to free Opo."

We had not let Opo become bonded to any of us. She was still wild. A pod of dolphins had been coming to her gate. Bob and I both had seen them. "We'll leave the gate open," I said.

I thought that Opo would rush out to join them. But she didn't. She hovered near the open gate and probed it with her sonar, but she didn't go through it. Not at first. But about a week later, she was gone. We never saw her again.

When Dr. Truby heard that we'd freed Opo, he came by to see me. "I didn't know things were that tough," he said. "If you had said something about it...."

"You were busy."

He shook his head as if it was a joke on him. "I wasn't that busy."

"You were always busy, Hank. I did everything I could. We spent our last dime on Spanish mackerel."

"You should have said something."

I turned on him hotly. "Maybe *you* should have said something."

He nodded, his lips compressed. "Yeah. Maybe I should have said something."

"I've got a family, Hank." I stood up and would have paced back and forth but the living room was too small for that and Martha was in the other room trying to get Lincoln to sleep, so I sat back down on the couch, slumped and put my feet up on the coffee table.

"Responsibilities. I've got to have money coming in all the time, something to equal the damn bills. Know what I mean?" I looked at Dr. Truby for some sign of sympathy but he showed nothing. "This is the first time in my life I ever really worried about money, Hank. But I'm making up for it. Not that I always had money, because I didn't. But I seemed not to need it, either. I always got by somehow. If I needed money, there it was. But not now. You think having a child is just one more little mouth to feed but all of a sudden your whole life revolves around it. Eating, sleeping, planning things—the whole future, twenty years of worry opens up and it's scary." I put my hands together at the heels and opened them up like the jaws of a whale. "There's no end to it. I had no idea it would be like this. But you know what I mean, don't you! Hell, you've got five kids! How do you manage?"

Softly, like a ghost moaning, he said: "One day at a time."

I felt like a fool, me talking about my problems when Hank had five kids! There was nothing more to say about freeing Opo now. It was over. It didn't work out. I hate to say that it was a misunderstanding between Dr. Truby and me, because that's too simple. It was more like we were on different but parallel paths all along and finally they just diverged. Most people have the idea that scientific research is devoid of emotion. But it's not. Science is full of all the deepest human feelings, the feelings that musicians merely sing about, the hopes and the lonely struggle, the sacrifice and love—yes, the purest love there is—and then, inevitably, the heartbreak and the dry heaves when tears won't come. It's glorious because it's really living, but what good is dwelling on it? I wanted to end it. "I feel really bad about it, too, Hank. It's been a dream of mine, doing dolphin research. You know how much that meant to me. But I guess we just ran out of gas. It happens."

He jammed his hands down into his pockets, looked at the ground and shook his head. "Okay, Ric. Nothing I can do about it now, I guess." He swallowed hard. "But down the road if things work out right...."

"We'll be in touch."

I got on the phone and called half a dozen musicians, including Stephen Stills, and told them that the Dolphin Project was about to go under for lack of funds. They dropped what they were doing and came in to help. We had several musical benefits and made a pile, $15,000 overnight one time, which was more than we'd ever made before.

Martha, secretary-treasurer of the Dolphin Project, was counting the money. Wearing shorts and a Project T-shirt, she sat at the kitchen table, her long legs crossed at the knees. There were piles of money all over the table, and when she finished, she pushed her hair back and smiled at me, her green eyes shining. "What are we going to do with all this money?"

"Didn't I tell you? That's all settled. We start up the Dolphin Project again."

Her mouth fell open. "Like that? I thought at least we'd talk about it."

"Talk? What's there to talk about?"

"Ric...a Dolphin Project without a dolphin?"

"Not for long," I said. "We're going to have lots of dolphins. We'll start with a pair of them. Then we'll raise our own. We'll buy some, let them breed, do research. See how all this works together? This is a long-term project, Martha. And it fills a need. Who knows what will happen with dolphins when that new law comes in. Think about it! No, first, get Hank on the phone for me, will you? Tell him we're back in business." Martha dialed Hank's number and handed me the phone. I told him we were riding high again and he came over, wearing his white short-sleeved shirt and the bow tie, all smiles. He rubbed his hands together. "This is fabulous," he said, his face beaming, "and I mean that literally." He had several projects in mind. He said that he and his students would bring their gear to the lagoon tomorrow and set it up. I called the Santinis on the phone. Virginia answered. "We're back in business," I said. "We need a couple of dolphins."

"We've got 'em," she said.

"We want a mated pair."

"You going to breed 'em?"

"I imagine they'll handle that on their own."

Virginia snickered. "Well, come on down. We've got 'em."

"I'll be down in the morning!"

Stephen Stills went down to the Santinis' place with me the next morning and wrote the check for the dolphins himself. The Santinis charged him $3,500.

That was a lot higher than it used to be, probably anticipating the effect of the new marine mammal law. I asked Virginia about it. "The price has gone up that much already?"

"When the law takes effect," she said, "this might be cheap."

"But it's not in effect right now."

"Sure it is," she said. "We just charged you $3,500 for two dolphins because of it."

Virginia and I never seemed to understand each other.

"If that's the charge," Stephen said, "I'll pay it. Money well spent."

I looked at the dolphins closely. They seemed to like each other. I named them Florida, the female, and Liberty, the male. I saw not just a pair of dolphins but the beginnings of a dynasty.

We had the same caravan as before for moving the dolphins: the truck with me and the two dolphins in back; the cars; Martha and Lincoln in one, the gray one with two State Natural Resources officials; the Secret Service; and Dr. Truby with his students, taking note of everything. Dr. Truby, his old ebullient self, moved his equipment in and the tests began. Equipment was set up around the lagoon. Students monitored it day and night, voice prints taken and frequency ranges compared. Each dolphin is said to have its own sound signature, a certain frequency it utters when it joins a group or comes into a new area. It's like they're saying, "Hi! I'm Liberty! Liberty! Liberty!" Except it wouldn't be that name, it would be the individual sound he makes, which is his real name.

I didn't know how Dr. Truby's experiments were going, but I knew how the money was going. It was going fast. And after a few months, once again the money was gone. Money is a sometime thing with me. When it comes, it comes in big chunks; and when it goes, I miss the hell out of it and try rather frantically to find out how to make it come in big again.

I was almost at my wits end when, from out of the past, Ricou called. He was doing another film, *Salty, the Sea Lion,* and he wanted me to be the head trainer.

"Talk about answering prayers!" I exclaimed. "Ricou! When do we start?"

"I'm heading over to Nassau now," he said. "Look, I'm in the neighborhood and I've got Salty with me."

"You've got Salty? Where are you anyway?"

"Just down the road apiece. Salty's in the car with me. He's like a dog. Comes when I whistle. We go everywhere together. Look, Ric, you've got a couple of dolphins there, right?"

"Right."

"Wonder if I could drop by and let Salty play with them?"

"Sure. Come on by," I said.

He arrived with the sea lion. It was like old times, the good ole days. Salty scampered out of the car and into the lagoon. We watched them play around. "What are you doing here?" Ricou asked.

We were standing on the seawall at the lagoon. A gentle south wind was blowing, puffy cumulus clouds dotted the sky, and sailboats skimmed over the lightest of all possible chops. I made a simple hands-up gesture to include it all, including the magnificent skyline of Miami.

"It's beautiful, yes," he said. "but what are you really doing here?"

I explained about the Dolphin Project, the goal of releasing dolphins and maintaining contact with them.

"You haven't changed, have you." He grinned. "Any money in it?"

I shook my head.

He laughed. "No, you haven't changed a bit."

"You want to hear the really long-range goal?"

Ricou was idly watching Salty and the dolphins. "Sure."

"We've already got a spot in the Caribbean. One of our members, Mrs. George L. Dyer, says we can move to her plantation there. It's called "Rust op Twist" on St. Croix, U.S. Virgin Islands. How does that sound?"

"Sounds wonderful to me."

"To me, too, Ricou. We could train them and let them go free and maintain contact with them, my reverse zoo where the animals are free and we're behind bars—it's like a dream come true."

Ricou was grinning. To him it was not a dream, it was a total fantasy. We let Salty out of the lagoon and she swam free in Biscayne Bay for a while. I asked Ricou if he was sure Salty would come back.

"Simple," he said. He put his fingers to his mouth and whistled. Salty was having the time of her life. She loved these balmy waters. She poked her sleek head up, Ricou whistled again and Salty came swimming home, hit the beach and scampered up to be petted by Ricou.

"Clean up your business here," Ricou said, "and I'll meet you in Nassau in about a week."

I left the Dolphin Project with Dr. Truby and the others, but maintained almost daily contact by phone. Then, one day a few months later, Bob Marchetti and Dr. Alan Cohen, one or our most devoted Dolphin Project regulars, flew in and we talked all night. Bob said that they were having big problems at the lagoon, that I would have to go back and straighten things out.

"I can't do that," I said. "My job is here. I've got a family. Responsibilities. I've got to think of them."

"You can't just turn your back," Bob said. "The problem is that nobody is in charge. Florida and Liberty, they're being spoiled. People are swimming in the lagoon with them, posing as dolphin experts for the media. Nobody's in charge and it's a mess." He shook his head miserably.

Dr. Cohen said, "You're the only one who can do anything, Ric. The permit is in your name."

"And that's not all," Bob said. "You know when you told us to free them like Opo...."

I had told them earlier when funds were down to nothing that the only thing we could do was open the gate and let them go. Liberty did go out but he was found a few days later on the flats just off the Little White House. A shark had bitten him. They took him to the Seaquarium, where Dr. White patched him up, then he was returned to the lagoon with Florida, none the worse except for the scar on his back, and nightmares, probably.

"The problem," Dr. Cohen said, "is that Dr. Truby wants to turn them over to a hotel in Hawaii."

I shook my head. I knew about the hotel. "That's out," I said. "That doesn't work." I was wishing I could put off deciding this, but there was no way. "I can't run things from here," I said simply. "Even if I could, I don't have time for it."

"Then there's only one thing we can do," Dr. Cohen said. "We've got to let the dolphins go."

He was right. For a long time I was silent. We were out on the porch, sitting on the stoop in the soft Bahamian breeze. It was late at night, when beautiful ideas seem most possible. But all I could do now was clean up the mess I'd left. This would hurt Hank. It would hurt me, too. He was my friend. He had always wanted his own dolphins, his own project, his own research lab. Both of us wanted that. But it wasn't to be. I stood up suddenly and laughed. "This is like a soap opera! Either I go back to the lagoon and leave Ricou in the lurch or I let the dolphins go and hurt Hank. But the choice is obvious."

"You'll let them go?" Dr. Cohen said.

"I have to. I'll be back in a few days."

"Want us to tell Dr. Truby?"

"No," I said. "I'll tell him."

I took a couple of weeks off, flew back to Miami and took over the Dolphin Project again. If the dolphins were going back into the wild, they had to learn how to catch their own live fish again. Almost miraculously, the lagoon was full of schooling mullet, all sizes. I watched Liberty and Florida to see what would happen. I had already cut down on feeding them by hand. And when the mullet came through the fence in waves, the dolphins started catching them. It was a beautiful sight. When they began catching live fish and throwing them in the air, playing with them, I knew they were full and now I was sure they would make it in the wild.

Dr. Truby argued vehemently. "We have important research going on here," he said. "We could be on the brink of an important breakthrough. Think about it!" he exclaimed, his eyes aglow. "Ric. This is what we've always wanted! You and I! The interspecies breakthrough!"

I would give anything—*anything*—for that. But at this point I saw only a pair of dolphins who would be better off in the wild.

When I told him that we must free Liberty and Florida, Dr. Truby was stunned. "Free the dolphins? That's not fair to them. We don't know what would happen to them if we let them go."

"We let Opo go," I said.

"And what happened to her?"

I shrugged. "I don't know."

"And that's what I'm telling you. We don't know. That's the problem, Ric. We don't know about dolphins. We have our fantasies about them, but we don't really know." He had made a fist with on hand and slammed it into the other.

"Are you saying that I want to let them go because of a fantasy?"

"Did I say that?"

I looked at him askance. "I thought you might be thinking that."

"What does it matter what I think?" Dr. Truby said. "We're dealing with realities here, or at least we're trying to. And the reality is that we cannot lose these very valuable animals."

"No, Hank. The reality is that we must free them."

"You know what happened to Liberty when he got out? He was bitten by a shark. Nearly killed. Listen to me, Ric, it's a jungle out there."

"Sure it's a jungle out there. But they can make it if they go out together, one helping the other."

Dr. Truby shook his head stolidly. "Even if they could make it in the wild, it makes no sense, Ric. It's illogical! It goes counter to every instinct in my being. These dolphins are our door to the future. Not just yours and mine, Ric. More than that, much more. I hope it doesn't sound pompous—I don't mean it that way—but these dolphins and the plans we have for them are a step toward the future of the human species and that of dolphins and of the two together. Can you throw all that away?" He made a despairing gesture with his hands and glanced up at the ceiling of the room. "For God's sake, Ric, let's keep it going."

"It's settled, Hank. I'm making arrangements with Chalk Airlines in the morning."

"But if we've got to let the dolphins go, then at least let them go so that we can get them back again."

I perked up my ears. That was the Dolphin Project's goal all along. "What do you mean?"

"I mean—look, Ric." He was sitting on the edge of a chair, eagerly leaning toward me. "There's a hotel in Hawaii. It's a nice place. I've been there. They want the dolphins. They have some dolphins already. They'll take the dolphins off our hands. When we get the Dolphin Project going again, we'll get them back. These are valuable animals. Valuable! With the new Marine Mammal Protection Act, we might never get another pair of dolphins like them. And to lose the work we've already done in interspecies communication, Ric, it's irresponsible to let these dolphins go."

"Irresponsible to let them go!" I stood up suddenly and threw my hands into the air. "Ha! That's the best I've heard all day! It's irresponsible to let them go? No, Hank, it's irresponsible to keep them. What right have we to pen them up like that? We have no such right. And the hotel in Hawaii? Forget it!" I yelled. "Those dolphins will not spend their lives in a damn swimming pool!"

"It's a lagoon. I've seen it. For them it's a wonderful life."

"It's not a lagoon. They call it a lagoon but it's a damn swimming pool."

"Ric, it wouldn't be forever."

"I'm sorry, Hank"

"To lose these precious dolphins, to virtually throw them away is a terrible mistake. Terrible!" His hand went sensitively to his temple. "It gives me a throbbing headache. To flush everything down the drain, everything we've worked so hard and so long on—Ric, you're not listening to me."

"I'm listening, Hank, but I've already heard all this."

"I don't want you to make a mistake. Let's start over again."

"We made a commitment to free them when it was over, and Hank, it's over."

Moving dolphins by air is a big, expensive job but by now we were experts. I called Chalks and chartered a twin-engine seaplane. With scores of people watching, about a dozen Dolphin Project workers caught the dolphins and put them in their boxes, Bob Ingram got the Ryder truck and we were almost ready.

Dr. White, Seaquarium vet, arrived in his jeep.

"Come on over," I yelled. "Glad you could make it. Ready to brand them?" We had already planned this, using a brass branding iron in a mixture of dry ice and alcohol. It's painless and we would always be able to identify them as ours if they were ever captured again.

"I've got everything I need," he said. He came over to the boxes and studied the dolphins. "They look good," he said.

"Think they'll make it?"

"I don't see why not."

He poured about six bottles of the alcohol into a stainless steel bucket, then added a couple of pounds of dry ice. It bubbled and spewed white smoke. Then he put in the brass branding iron. He left it in for seven minutes, timing it with his wristwatch, then I wiped both of the dolphins clean with a towel just below the dorsal fin on each side. Dr. White took the iron out of the bubbling mixture and carefully placed it on the spot for twenty-two seconds. The dolphins quivered a little and that was it.

Six of us flew with the dolphins. Drs. Cohen and White and I, Bob Marchetti and Bob Ingram and, to my surprise, Dr. Truby.

En route, I got into the box with each of the dolphins in turn, feeling their fins to see that they were not too hot, spraying them with salt water as I had so many times before with Flipper, and keeping them calm. We flew across the Gulf Stream and deep into the Bahamas to the waters just west of Eleuthera, a long island just east of Nassau. From the air the sea was a brilliant turquoise, with small palm-covered islands scattered here and there fringed with golden beaches. Way off in the distance, we could see a squall moving slowly like a shroud with its rain beating on the water. Below us we had noticed a large pod of dolphins and a number of pairs. We circled and landed on the water, the pilot turned off the engines, and we were surrounded suddenly by the deep, soothing peace of quiet. The copilot tossed over a Danforth anchor and we drifted out to the end of the anchor line.

"This is it," I said. "Where is it, exactly?" I asked the pilot.

He checked the instruments and told me: 25.05° North, 76.40° West. I pointed to the island. "And that's Eleuthera?"

"That's it."

We were all grinning at one another, everybody but Dr. Truby, who had said nothing the whole trip. He looked glumly at what he viewed as our romantic, perhaps even our antiscientific, gesture. I didn't know it at the time, but later I discovered that "eleuthera" is the Greek word for freedom. Greeks were among the first settlers of the Bahamas.

I stripped off my pants; I wore my black tank suit underneath. I sat down at the edge of the open door and slipped on my flippers, put on my face plate and adjusted the snorkel. I caught a glimpse of the silent pleading in Dr. Truby's face, then I eased into the water. It was clear and pure, warm and invigorating, and I felt very good. "Okay," I said. We had already talked about how we would do it, first releasing Liberty, the male, then Florida. It took everybody except me—I was in the water—to lift them out of the box on their stretchers and carry them to the doorway. Dr. White was in front. He nodded at me to make sure it was okay. I nodded back. Then, they gently tilted the stretcher on its side and Liberty splashed into the water next to me and was gone. Then Florida. Both of them disappeared.

I had hoped to swim with them a little before they left, but it all happened too fast. I came up and took my snorkel out. "Which way did they go? Can you see them? Are they together?"

Bob Ingram and Dr. Cohen were both standing on tiptoe. Then Bob, his face beaming, pointed. "I see them! Here they come!" They both laughed and were pointing. "They're together! Here they come, Ric!"

I adjusted my face plate and dove, and that moment Liberty and Florida came flashing past me—I felt the wash of their tail flukes as they went by. Then they were gone, merging with the Bahamian blue. I had seen them only a few seconds. I came up and took my snorkel out of my mouth and pushed the face plate up. I slipped off my fins, crawled up the ladder into the flying boat. It happened so fast I didn't have time to reflect on it. But I felt wonderful. We all did. All of us were grinning, shaking hands, and clapping one another on the back, all but Dr. Truby, who sat alone and silent. I wanted to tell him that I was sorry our plans hadn't worked out, that I understood his position and that if things had been only a little different—but why go into it? I put my hand on his shoulder and tried to say something about the way I felt, but couldn't. I said only: "Sorry, Hank. I had to do it." He looked out the porthole, away from me.

We lost sight of the dolphins and the seaplane took off, a big ponderous gathering of speed, a shudder as we broke free from the water, then climbing powerfully up, circling. All of us went to the windows and looked out, spotted the two dolphins and watched in breathless silence, grinning. If there had been the least of doubts about what to do with them, that was gone now and I felt good about it. The plane circled once and we watched them swim together, Liberty and Florida, in a straight line, mile after beautiful mile. Free.

EPILOGUE

The Journey Home

> I feel at ease and, in an indefinable way, *at home,* when dol-
> phins are around. I now know when they are nearby before
> they appear. I dream after they leave.
>
> —Virginia Coyle

Seven years later, in 1980, two young Atlantic bottlenose
dolphins swimming in the Gulf of Mexico off Mississippi were captured to become the subjects of an ambitious experiment in communication.

Using a sophisticated program of computer-aided sonar analysis,
investigators of the Human Dolphin Foundation (HDF) working at
MarineWorld/Africa USA in Redwood City, California, sought to create or find a language common to dolphins and humans. When both
dolphins and humans understood the language and could use it back
and forth, the dolphins would be returned to the sea as ambassadors
to the world's population of wild dolphins.

If this sounds like something that Dr. John C. Lilly might have
dreamed, that's exactly right. Except that the real force behind it was
his wife Antonietta (Toni), president of HDF and a cetacean researcher
in her own right.

The two dolphins, Joe and Rosie, were named in honor of two
principal backers of HDF, Joseph E. Levine, producer of the 1973 film
Day of the Dolphin, and his wife Rosalie. Leslie Baer-Frohoff described
HDF's research in the November, 1984, issue of *Hardcopy,* a computer
magazine. Though the experiments lasted several years, the results
were only partially successful, ending at a point not much beyond the

basics of animal training. Investigators succeeded in Phase I, teaching
Joe and Rosie a vocabulary of forty word-whistles. But they did not
get into Phase II, where the dolphins were supposed to use the word-
whistles in talking to the investigators. Before that phase began, investigators became disenchanted, and the research fizzled out.

At about the same time, MarineWorld/Africa USA folded, and someone had to decide what to do with Joe and Rosie. It would seem
simple. Why not return them to the sea as promised? But to do that,
a permit was required. And though many dolphin experts had often
tried to get permits for the release of dolphins, none had succeeded.
In fact it was easier for professional dolphin hunters to get permits to
capture a dolphin than it was to get a permit to release one. Once a
captive dolphin, always a captive dolphin.

For lack of a real alternative, Joe and Rosie were first shipped to
the Dolphin Research Center on Grassy Key, Santini's old "Porpoise
School." Alan B. Slifka of New York, chairman of the board of the
Big Apple Circus and one of the main backers in the dolphins' capture,
came down to see how they were doing. By this time, they had been
transferred to Dolphins Plus, a dolphin attraction in Key Largo.

He was appalled that they were still in captivity. He vowed, there
and then, to return them to the sea.

Soon after that, Alan Slifka and three others, including Virginia
(Gigi) Coyle and James L. Hickman, formed the Oceanic Research
Communication Alliance (ORCA) to handle the problem. Gigi was
the director of the ORCA Project, Jim the project manager. When I
heard what they were doing, returning captive dolphins to the wild,
I had to be involved. I contacted them and was hired as consultant
and research coordinator, responsible for the everyday care and feeding
of the dolphins.

Gigi Coyle is a bright, sensitive woman, somewhat mystical and full
of ancient symbols, but tough, too, with an iron grip on her main
goal: peace. Peace as in tranquillity, yes, peace for the world, peace
for the soul and peace forever, a peace so profound that she and peace
are one.

Why dolphins? Gigi is a dreamer, working now to help awaken the
dream of interspecies communication. Gigi says that when she first
got in the water with Joe and Rosie, she felt a sense of harmony most

wonderful, not just with the dolphins but with the universe at large.

"I felt greater clarity, strength, and instantaneous unprotected love during my first swim with Joe and Rosie," she says, "than I had ever experienced before."

Gigi is a teacher with a strong sense of the flow of things. It's as if she were keeping the flow of events straight in her head so that later on she could write about it. "So here we all are," she would say to us of the ORCA team, "near the end of an important phase in this most significant of projects, the return of Joe and Rosie to their home in the sea, the end of their journey home." By this time everybody knew what was coming and would form a circle, holding hands. Gigi would look around with a cool smile and nod. We all closed our eyes, still holding hands in a circle, whether we were alone in the vastness of the Georgian marshlands or in a busy Miami restaurant, and meditated.

She and Jim Hickman, psychologist, have for some years spent about a month during the summer living with the killer whales in the waters off British Columbia. Jim, whose home is a houseboat in Sausalito, California, looks like a banker—a stocky, balding banker with piercing blue eyes—but he's actually an extremely innovative "citizen-diplomat" with a wide variety of connections in the Soviet Union. His expertise is working behind the scenes to get seemingly impossible projects under way, like the John Denver Musical Ambassador Tour of 1985 and Billy Joel's Bridge Tour of 1987.

He's a former director of the Esalen Institute Soviet American Exchange Program of San Francisco, California, and before that was director of the institute's transformation archive. The Esalen Institute of Big Sur, California, is a center for offbeat studies with mystical overtones: auras, mental telepathy, dreams, meditation, clairvoyance, yoga, telekinesis (mind over matter), water birth, and even soul travel. The serious study of such things is part of the "New Age" movement in this country; in Russia it's called the "human potential" movement. From the viewpoint of mainstream science, New Age thinking is an outrageous opposition to conventional wisdom, and the mainstream media of both countries consider it bizarre—which some of it probably is. But some of it is surely also the frontier of tomorrow's establishment science.

Abigail Alling, president of Ocean's Expeditions Inc., and I made up the rest of the principals of the ORCA team. Like myself, Abigail has spent much of her life with sea mammals, and we have a similar understanding of dolphins.

A graduate of Yale, she was the ORCA project coordinator, responsible for the design and implementation of research. She also suggested her family's island property in Georgia for the release site. As a marine mammal scientist, she had previously sailed the Indian Ocean, tracking and researching both small cetaceans and the great whales. She had participated in research with dolphins and porpoises off Labrador, Canada, with humpback whales off Greenland, and with small cetaceans in the Atlantic Ocean.

Abigail's home is the R/V *Heraclitus,* a unique, three-masted, eighty-four-foot, ferrocement Chinese junk. The ship and its youthful crew are devoted to the study of the ocean, marshes, and coral reefs for the Space Biosphere II in Oracle, Arizona. The expedition leader, Abigail interrupted the ship's schedule to sail to the offshore Georgia island where the ORCA Project was to culminate. Her family once owned the entire island, but had sold most of it to the federal government to protect its pristine beauty as a national wildlife refuge. To protect the family's privacy, ORCA promised that the name of the island and its exact location would not be made public.

It was a childhood dream come true for Abigail to work with dolphins on the island. She started by recording the underwater ambient sounds of the creek near the new pen area in Georgia before Joe and Rosie were moved to the site. Then she played back the new sounds for them at their holding pen on Grassy Key. This would reduce the stress of the transition and make Joe and Rosie feel more at home once we moved them.

Operating under a National Marine Fisheries Service Permit for Scientific Research, the ORCA Project was funded not just to return the two dolphins to the sea but also as a pilot program to find out how captive dolphins in general should be readapted and returned to the wild. We know from the number of permits that there are about 450 captive dolphins in the world today, and there is no doubt what happens to them all. For lack of any alternative, they languish in their tanks.

During the years that Joe and Rosie lived in captivity among human beings, for the most part they had been treated as well as possible by our standards, but poorly indeed by theirs. They were entirely dependent on human beings, swimming with them, playing with them, and receiving endless signals, human imprints overriding nature. And in all that time they hadn't chased a single live fish and gulped it down. Living in tanks they could never get up to full speed for very long in a straight line, they could never dive down and down and feel the pressure building just for the hell of it, nor did they dare let loose a real blast of sonar. Living in isolation for years, their natural dolphin ways were corrupted and distorted, their native memories blurred and forgotten. They had missed the simple but important things like tides and currents, the eerie open sound of an endless sea with breakers plashing on a golden beach, the wild sea tastes, and the electric fright of big sharks with jaws snapping.

We had made them live in such a phony world that they had lost many of their skills to defend themselves, not only from predators but also from diseases. And socially they were misfits. They had lost their place in the hierarchy of a pod and had no idea where to go for food, safety, love. Indeed, because the pod is where a dolphin discovers its own identity, Joe and Rosie were nobody any more. For all those years their lives revolved about the wishes of their human counterparts, their own lives becoming a humanized mess.

And in the case of Joe and Rosie, the confinement was especially unfortunate. As we discovered early on, they were less than compatible. Before they swam to freedom, I expressed my doubts that they would go off together in storybook fashion. "I think they'll go their separate ways," I said. From time to time I mentioned this, but nobody seemed to hear it. And when we finally did release them, I thought with a sinking feeling that I understood, that though Rosie had become pregnant by Joe—he was always trying to push himself on her—in a horrible mismatch of chance, Joe and Rosie must have been brother and sister. In the wild, they never would have mated.

When I mentioned my doubts to Abigail, she gave me a big blue-eyed look of utter skepticism. It was Thanksgiving Day on the Georgia island, and we were in her family's big wooden house, their vacation home. It was cold and beginning to rain, and we had all just come in from an inspection of the site where we would build the halfway house holding pen for Joe and Rosie. Gigi and Jim had gone into the kitchen to fix the turkey, I made a fire in the big fireplace, and Abigail, dressed in a black wool sweater and black slacks, had drawn her chair up to the fire and was rubbing her hands together. I stood with my back to the fire and we were silent a long time, but then she spoke. "I've been giving this project lots of thought, Ric, and the whole thing hinges on de-programming Joe and Rosie, doesn't it?"

"That's exactly right," I said. I turned to the fire and held my hands out to get them warm. "That's the key."

"But how?"

"No problem," I said with assurance. "There's a method for that."

"A method?" She cocked her head to one side. "Should I take notes?"

"No need. It's simple. I learned it from a friend of mine."

"What method are you talking about?"

"It's called Common Sense."

Abigail has a wonderful full laugh, it just comes out all of a sudden, and that's what happened now.

I said, "We've got to train them exactly the reverse of what they've been taught in the past seven years. Reverse training."

"Hmm, I see. That's interesting, Ric. If you train them the reverse of what they've been trained, you will become the world's first dolphin untrainer."

We laughed together and she was very beautiful. Then she got serious. "One more question."

"Shoot."

"How will you do it?"

"Trust me," I said. "I know what I'm doing."

Later that spring when the project was under way and I was un-training Joe and Rosie at Grassy Key, I noticed Abigail coming down the pier with her camera—she was also ORCA's official photogra-pher—and I knew that she was documenting my untraining methods. In fact at that moment I was sneaking up on Joe and Rosie as part of the untraining process. I had half a bucket of water with several live fish in it and I was sneaking from one piling to the next like a cartoon figure. Joe and Rosie were at the far end of the pen and hadn't seen me. That was crucial to the method. Usually they were given fish to eat when they had done a trick. The fish were a reward. What I wanted to do was to toss the fish into the pen when they had done nothing.

That's the common sense key to my untraining method. Begging for food wasn't going to work anymore.

It seemed simple enough to me, but some of the people at the Dolphin Research Center couldn't seem to grasp the concept. I kept having run-ins with them. Looking back, perhaps that's how it will always be between trainers and untrainers. In a sense I was undoing their work. But more basically than that, they objected to the very idea of freeing dolphins. In turn, I objected to their training whistles at DRC. Joe and Rosie would hear the whistles and associate them with their earlier training. This hurt Joe especially, because he loved to perform. He would have been a wonderful show dolphin. When a whistle blew, I had to make sure that Joe and Rosie were not being fed at the same time, otherwise they would tend to associate the whistle with the reward. An important part of untraining was to steer people away from the dolphins. I didn't want anyone even walking near Joe and Rosie or gawking at them. And especially did I not want them petted and babied as most people seem compelled to do. Untraining can't be done overnight. It should be done in the same gradual way as training. By this time my son Lincoln had grown into a fine young man, and was my assistant during the untraining process.

In undoing what had been done to the two dolphins, I realized that since some trainers tend to be trained by the dolphins, I was at the same time trying to undo what had been done to me. I mean that nobody can be sure who is really being trained, and if any trainer had ever been trained by a dolphin, I had. If Joe and Rosie sought my attention, I looked the other way. If they wanted me to swim with them, I refused. If they leaped up and flipped, I turned my back. When they begged for food, I ignored them. When I seemed to be merely sitting in a deck chair on the floating platform in the dolphin's pen while they cavorted around, actually I was hard at work, ignoring them, doing a negative something that's like a positive nothing.

There were two exceptions to this. Every day I taught them a signal, the sound of two hardwood sticks clapped together a certain number of times in a certain rhythm. The sound signature recall signal was to call them back in case of emergency, if, for example, the readaptation experiment wasn't working and we wanted them back. When amplified and played through underwater speakers, the signal could be heard three-quarters of a mile away. I never had occasion to use the signal in earnest, though. Also, because we didn't want to literally have to push Joe and Rosie out of their holding pen in Georgia, I gave them "gate training" at Grassy Key to overcome their instinctive fear of going through an opening. At Grassy Key, gates opened from one pen to another, and I simply opened the gate and got the two dolphins over to it, then I enticed them into the other pen by tossing fish in.

Weaning them off dead fish was also a slow, gradual process. I kept a couple of fishing lines in the water to catch snapper, yellow tail, sailor's choice, and grunts. I had constructed two wire cages, three feet on a side, that floated in the water just below the platform. When I caught a fish, I dropped it into the cage till it was time to feed the dolphins. When I first started giving them live fish to eat, Joe and Rosie looked at me as if I had lost my mind. When I tossed the first live fish in the pen with them, the fish scooted off and away to freedom. Joe and Rosie were much too slow. To give them an advantage, I trimmed the fish's tails with scissors.

I remember the first time Joe caught a fish. I reached in the bucket and got a little mangrove snapper, trimmed its tail with scissors, and tossed it into the pen. It splashed and the little snapper went off frantically at a rakish angle. Joe, responding to the moment, whirled and caught the little fish in his sonar, gave a powerful pump of his broad flukes and spun with him, the water turning to froth. Then suddenly Joe broke to the surface with the little fish in his mouth and brought him over for me to see. Joe bobbed his head, tossing the fish around so that it was positioned right, then gulped it down. After that it was simple. Rosie caught on and they both spent a lot of time at the live-fish cage, watching their next meal, entranced.

We freeze-branded Joe and Rosie on both sides of their dorsals, Joe's mark an arrow and Rosie's a circle, so that they could be easily spotted after their release. We studied every angle of the move to the Georgia island. The water, though dark as coffee, was of excellent quality and teemed with fish. The temperature was like that of Grassy Key. The main difference was the tide. At Grassy Key the tide was never much more than a foot or two. But on the Georgia island the tides were always six to eight feet and sometimes, at spring tides, as much as ten. When the water was high, small fish and shrimp scattered into the marshlands, looking for food. When the tide turned, it ran out through the marshes to the creeks and down to the sea, the small fishes and other creatures going with it, and the large fish and dolphins came in to eat the little fish.

Wire fencing works well in the holding pens at Grassy Key where the tide is not a factor. But in Georgia we needed something that would fold up like an accordion when the water dropped so the dolphins wouldn't get tangled up in it. David Jessup, land manager of the project, designed an ingenious holding pen of PVC piping. Eighty feet long and forty wide, it floated, going up and down on the tide like venetian blinds. One of the side sections of piping, the gate, was constructed so that when we untied it, it would sink quickly to the bottom without endangering the dolphins. At each end of the halfway house pen was a triangular section of two by sixes, on one of which was the tent I lived in.

I fell in love with the Georgia island the first time I saw it. Abigail and I walked barefooted for miles along the beach without saying a word, without having to say anything, and I knew that this was the place to do it because of the clean beaches and water, the pristine purity of it all. The land could have been like this, I thought, a million years ago. The clincher, though, was the great abundance of fish.

For all the problems we had because of the strong tides, the water's current was a blessing, too. It acted like a treadmill for Joe and Rosie. When the tides turned, they spent several hours each day getting into shape by having to swim against the tide. Another unexpected payoff was that fish were drawn to the pen as they are to wrecks and reefs, and the dolphins feasted on them night and day. I know, because I was sleeping—or trying to sleep—right above them. I could hear them sometimes all night chasing the schools of fish that came through. One night as I listened to Joe and Rosie breathing, I heard another dolphin come to the holding pen, a much bigger dolphin than Joe and Rosie, with a darker, deeper sound that mixed with theirs, and I could feel an immense intelligence sweeping over me. Lying motionless in my tent, I tensed, waiting. But then the third dolphin snorted and suddenly was gone. Joe and Rosie got very excited and all that night they swam back and forth like someone pacing. We were visited many nights after that by wild dolphins, especially at low tide.

Around noon of the day Joe and Rosie were to be released, Gigi got us all in a circle, about fifteen of us including Alan Slifka and his wife, their eight-year-old son David, Jim Hickman, Abigail and me and several crewmen from the R/V *Heraclitus*. A National Geographic Society crew filmed the event. We held hands and meditated. Then we got in the water and untied the gate. It fell and Joe and Rosie zoomed out and up the creek toward the interior of the island. We waited, all of us, watching as for the first time in years Joe and Rosie swam without constraint for twenty minutes. They meandered around, then came back to the pen, swam in one last time and left again, this time in the other direction toward the sea. Abigail and Gigi followed at a distance in a fourteen-foot inflatable with a thirty horsepower kicker, tracking them into a small side-creek, where they waited apparently for the tide to come back in.

Everybody left except me. I stayed at my tent, thinking perhaps they would return. But they didn't. I thought that I should feel happy about it. But I didn't. I was up all night, waiting.

A little before dawn, I was watching, bleary-eyed, down the creek when the orange inflatable came chugging around the bend. It was Abigail, coming in from the *Heraclitus*. She pulled up and killed the motor, drifted up to the holding pen, and I got the bow line and tied up her boat. She glanced into the pen. "They didn't come back?"

I shook my head. I was wearing a straw hat with a wide brim and I took it off and wiped my brow with the bottom of my shirt. Then I put the hat back on and kept gazing down the creek for them.

"That's good," she said, glancing sharply at me. She was wearing shorts and a black sleeveless T-shirt with an ancient Greek dolphin coin printed on it. She handed me a thermos of coffee. "Last I saw of them, they were in that little creek up ahead," she said, nodding back the way she had come. "I suppose when the tide came in, they worked their way to the ocean."

I nodded and said, "Yeah."

"Think they'll make it?"

I shrugged at the question, watching the turn of the creek for some sign of Joe and Rosie coming back. "I think so. We know they can hunt again. And they're a lot smarter than even we give them credit for."

"But now it's for real," she said. "They're on their own."

"I know. I know."

Wild dolphins were dying in the ocean that summer, their bodies washing up on the northeastern seaboard by the hundreds. We followed the reports with horror and not without realizing the irony of our efforts to return Joe and Rosie possibly to the same fate. The deaths were almost certainly related to pollution, we thought; we watched for news every day.

We were looking down the creek now for Joe and Rosie because as the sun came up, each moment was different, the gold of the dawn on the marshes fading into reality. We wanted to see them coming back and yet we didn't want to see them.

"Do you think they'll make it?" Abigail asked.

"They've already made it," I said. "Their journey home *is* successful because success is the journey. Success is not some destination one finally arrives at."

Shrimpers and other seamen in the ORCA sighting and tracking network reported seeing Joe and Rosie several times after that. They were in different pods.

THE DOLPHIN PROJECT INC.

BOX 224

COCONUT GROVE, FL 33133